John Timon Reily

Conewago

A Collection of Catholic Local History

John Timon Reily

Conewago
A Collection of Catholic Local History

ISBN/EAN: 9783337337254

Printed in Europe, USA, Canada, Australia, Japan

Cover: Foto ©Lupo / pixelio.de

More available books at **www.hansebooks.com**

CONEWAGO.

A COLLECTION OF

CATHOLIC LOCAL HISTORY.

GATHERED FROM THE FIELDS OF CATHOLIC MISSIONARY LABOR

WITHIN OUR REACH.

An Humble Effort to Preserve Some Remembrance of Those Who Have Gone Before, and by Their Lives, Their Labors and Their Sacrifices, Secured for Succeeding Generations the Enjoyment of Happy Homes, and All the Blessings of Our Holy Catholic Religion.

By JOHN T. REILY.

HERALD PRINT,
MARTINSBURG, W. VA.,
1885.

DEDICATORY.

To the Reverend Fathers,
JOSEPH ENDERS and FRAN. XAV. DENECKERE,
Noble Gentlemen, Devoted Priests and Kind
Teachers, Untiring Laborers in Every Cause of
Religion, True Missionary Representatives, Faithful Disciples of Their Divine Master, and Worthy
Sons of Ignatius de Loyola, these Pages are
Gratefully Dedicated, in all Consciousness
of their Imperfection and Incompleteness,

BY AN HUMBLE PUPIL.

BY WAY OF INTRODUCTION.

The Church has reason to rejoice, that Catholics are awakening to the justice and importance of reclaiming and preserving the early history and records of the religion of their fathers. Want, intolerance and persecution drove them from their native land. They came into a strange and unsettled country,—cast adrift in the Indian wilds of America, without homes, without a church or a government, and without anything necessary to life and happiness.

This generation, with all the grandeur and perfection of its civilization, can never fully understand nor in the least appreciate the sufferings and struggles of those who cleared our fields and built our homes. The enjoyments and comforts we now possess, are ours only by inheritance as the fruits of their labors.

By the sweat of their brow and the valor of their arm, grew this mighty religious and social fabric,—the Church to teach, to bless and to save,—the State to guard and protect.

Before a settlement had been formed or a law enacted, the Church was here. Before a Calvert or a Penn had been granted a charter, the Jesuits watered the forests primeval with their blood. They planted the Cross and offered up the Holy Sacrifice, that soon there might be labor in the desert wastes before them. Others came, and in many a lowly wigwam and humble "Mass-house" were heard the praises of God, in the celebration of the divine mysteries of the altar. Follow the names in history or geography,—from the St. Lawrence to the Pacific, from the Lakes to the Gulf, from Maine to Florida,—at every step there is some living evidence of the Catholic Church. Time and its changes can never obliterate them. Their impress is indelibly blended on every monument of greatness, on every work of genius; in the laws and institutions of the country, in the lives of millions of its inhabitants, in the memory of millions more.

BY WAY OF INTRODUCTION.

How fit and proper that the children of the Church should remember all she has done for them. From Rome herself sprang this desire, when Pius IX. of saintly memory opened to the world the treasures of her lore. Men took up the good work in this country; historical societies were organized, researches made, and Catholics have every reason to be proud of the history of their Church.

The East has a grand but unwritten history. The Church wept over the graves of the founders of that "Happie Marieland." She in turn rejoiced over the cradle of her hierarchy in America. Every hill and valley and sub-division of country, bear names derived from the Catholic Church.— Every foot of ground is to her a land-mark. Will her great and gifted men never respond to the inspiration of the memory of all that is Catholic in Maryland?

Conewago is one of the oldest of the Maryland missions. Though in Pennsylvania, it was founded under the impression, and no doubt rightly so, that it belonged to the Maryland province. To write its history is an undertaking far beyond our ability. "Under other circumstances," we had once hoped to do it justice. Alas! they will never come.— Partly educated and living with the Jesuits, misfortune turned our course, and Remembrance alone remains.

The only motive that now prompts us, is the desire to add an humble mite to one of the grandest histories America will ever have,—that of the Catholic Church. It is intended simply as a collection of scraps gathered by the wayside of early life. Time and means and ability are wanting to put them properly together. The critic will say, better to have left it alone. Far better, for others much more capable have passed along and gone their way. Conewago's history was not written. This is a poor attempt at writing it, but at least the fragments we have gathered shall be preserved. By confining ourselves within the limits of our knowledge and purpose, we hope to avoid the more serious faults of rashness and error. One great desire is to write in a Catholic spirit, and in accordance with the teachings of the Catholic Church. That done, we hope the want of polish and learning may be the more readily overlooked.

MARTINSBURG, W. VA.,
Feast of Corpus Christi, June 4th, 1885.

THE CHURCH AND ITS HEROES.

How wonderfully dependent upon each other, are men and their actions? Great or small, near together or widely separated, there is a bearing in all things, for good or for evil. It may not be felt, nor seen, nor thought of, but it exists; and openly or silently, the tendency is carried out in time and beyond.

Who could have discovered a common end between the child born in the Chateau of Loyola at Biscay in Spain, 1491, and the hardy sailor planning and explaining to the learned men and before the Courts of Europe, in that very same year! But there was. Conewago is an atom in the sea of results flowing from the lives and labors of Christopher Columbus and Ignatius Loyola. So all through life, from the humblest details that are passed by unnoticed, to the mighty events that mark the centuries in distinction.

Then let us for a moment skim over the main of discovery and settlement, and take a few flowers here and there from the beautiful treasure-gardens of American heroism, in which the fairest in bud or bloom is a Catholic virtue and a Catholic deed;—happy enough if we may call our own the ravel-string that binds them.

"In the foreground of American history there stand these three figures,—a lady, a sailor and a monk. Might they not be thought to typify Faith, Hope, and Charity."—D'Arcy McGee.

Columbus is the grand central figure. The lady, Isabella the Catholic, "one of the purest and most beautiful characters in history." The monk, Juan Perez, who brought Columbus back to confidence and success, when in despair he was about to quit Spain forever.

Columbus! so much like St. Ignatius. Devoutly Catholic, pure and holy, he lived and labored only for the greater honor and glory of God. His devotion to the Blessed Virgin is the corner-stone of America's consecration to her honor and to the service of her Divine Son. In her honor he named his vessel and his discoveries; and sailing under her patronage, he sang her praises over all the broad ocean. He remembered his religion in all things,—himself in nothing.

Columbus is the type and model of his successors in the Catholic voyages of discovery,—Alonzo de Ojeda, Vasco Nunez de Balboa, Hernando Cortes, Cabral, Orellana, Magellan, and others. Wherever they went, these navigators and explorers planted the cross, and their memory shall perish, NEVER. Sebastian Cabot gave England a continent, but "no one knows his burial-place."

In the far north, the names of towns and rivers to this day give evidence of the religion of Cartier, Champlain and La Salle. In 1679, the latter built the first sailing vessel on Lake Erie. With his name goes that of the explorer of the Mississippi, Ferdinand de Soto,—the associate of Pizzaro and a worthy companion of Columbus. He slept in the bosom of the Mississippi in 1542. "The priests chanted over his body the first requiems that were ever heard on the waters of the Mississippi."

With such characters of nobility we may place the brave and generous Montcalm. What a difference between the early heroes Catholic Europe gave to America, and many of those who came from there in a more infidel age?

It is impossible in this short space to follow the progress of discovery or the missionary labors. This broad land is marked by such foot-steps from one end to the other.

"Amid the West India isles, through Mexico, Peru, Brazil and the southern continent, the cross was borne by the missionaries of Spain and Portugal: the Norwegian, Irish, and later the French and English, bore it through our own more northern climes."

The Franciscan, Dominican and Jesuit achieved the greater part of the toil, and reaped the greatest harvests.

The Irish discovered Iceland and established christianity

there, then planted a colony on the southern coast of North America. A pagan Icelander, driven there in 983, was baptized in the colony.

The first American See was founded by Erc, consecrated by the Archbishop Adzer at Lund, in Denmark, 1121.

"The ancient *tholus* in Newport, the erection of which appears to be coeval with the time of Bishop Erc, belonged to a Scandinavian church or monastery, where, in alternation with Latin Masses, the old Danish tongue was heard seven hundred years ago."—*Royal Society of Antiquarians.*

The Italian friar, Mark, 1539, traveled from Mexico through the deep forests to the Pacific, and named that vast realm San Francisco.

"In 1625, just a year after the Jesuits had reached the sources of the Ganges and Thibet, the banks of the St. Lawrence received priests of the order, which was destined to carry the cross to Lake Superior and the West."—BANCROFT.

Montreal, (the town of Mary,) founded in 1640, was the starting point of the Jesuit missionaries. From 1634 to 1649, sixty missionaries visited the wilderness of the Hurons, carrying the glad tidings of the Gospel to the surrounding tribes. Father Allouez, in 1665, on a voyage of discovery, heard for the first time from the Indians of the great river, "Mesipi." The first colony of French settlers in the Mississippi Valley was established by the Jesuit missionaries. In 1637, Marquette explored the Mississippi.

The Jesuit missions in America are the grandest monuments in the history of the Society. Sublime are the lives of its members. The Catholic Church has no more glorious record. Their labors, sufferings and deaths are as inspiring as the Lives of the Saints or the Trials of the Early Martyrs.

"Here a missionary is frozen to death, there another sinks beneath the heat of the western prairie; here Brebeuf is killed by the enemies of his flock, and Segura by an apostate—Dennis and Menard die in the wilderness, Dolbean is blown up at sea, Noyrot wrecked on the shore; but these dangers never deterred the missionary. In the language of the great American historian, 'the Jesuit never receded one foot.'"—SHEA.

"Why be at war with history? The Jesuits are there, in the outer gate of all our chronicles. Speak them civilly as you pass on. For us, cold compliments are not enough.—Our blood warms at witnessing their heroic virtue, and we are compelled to raise our voices in evidence of our homage. They were the first to put the forest brambles by; they were the first to cross the thresholds of the wigwams of every native tribe; they first planted the cross in the wilderness, and shed their blood cheerfully at its base. Shall we not study their lives and recall their words? Shall we not figure them on canvas and carve them in marble? Shall we not sing the song of their triumph, and teach it to our children's children, until the remotest generation? We have never had cause to be ashamed of them; and God grant they may have none to be ashamed of us. I ask again of those not with us, Why be at war with history? The Jesuit is in the gate, and you can no more enter the first chapter of your own chronicles without meeting him there than you can enter Quebec in time of war without giving the sentry the countersign."—McGEE.

The priests who came with Columbus on his second voyage, consecrated a chapel in Isabella, in Hayti, on the feast of Epiphany, 1494. The early Dominican and Jesuit missionaries in Florida were murdered by the Indians, one after another. One grand deed of theirs was the liberation of all the natives of Florida, held as slaves in the islands. It stands out in bold contrast with the inhuman traffic afterwards carried on from that direction. Besides the wail of the dusky slave, that land is cursed by the groan of the exile and the lamentation of the flower of Ireland for its home and kindred.

In 1570, a band of Jesuit missionaries from Florida, with a converted Indian for a guide, found themselves on the lonely banks of the Chesapeake. They hurried into the unexplored forests, eager to bring to the Red Man the light of christianity. Deserted by their guide, they perished by his ungrateful hand, at the foot of a rude altar on which the Holy Sacrifice was being offered.

This country has been redeemed by such acts of heroism. Who can recount them? Many of them are not recorded, for the fairest flowers always bloom unseen. Catholics may well be proud of American history. It is their own; theirs in discovery, exploration and settlement; theirs in religion, purchased by their blood; theirs in peace and in war, in science and in progress, in its laws and government,—theirs in the peaceful possession of life, happiness and prosperity. Grandly their own, but not selfishly. There is not a blot of Catholic intolerance on its pages. It is the common country of a free and independent people.

May we not take the beautiful words of Fenelon, and with them exclaim: Oh Land of America! Oh sacred Land! Oh dear and common country of all true christians! And then we listen in rapt admiration to the end that so beautifully crowns the work of the scholarly MacLeod:—

Who then has the true claim to the ownership of North America? The red Indian steps noiselessly forward and says, "It is I! For ages immemorial my fathers fished these waters, or struck down the game in these yet undesecrated forests." "I claim the land," saith the Spaniard, "I, who redeemed those Southern pampas, and first taught the Gulf and the lagoon the sounds of Christian praise." "It is mine," says the fiery Gaul. "The snow-wastes of Canada were crimsoned with French blood: it was a French sword which tamed the fierce Iroquois, and tribes of every tongue, the roaming Algonquin, from the mighty ocean to the mysterious great lakes."

"The land is mine," says the English Puritan from Berks or Huntingdon; or the English Cavalier from Derbyshire, York, and Cumberland. The Highlander, in gutturals deep as those with which he turned away from the red, red field of Culloden, demands at least the mountains of the Carolinas and Georgia, the cold coasts of Nova Scotia, and part of the shores of Saint Lawrence.

But we cannot grant to any one of these the fulness of his claim. Wherever they are found as agents acting subserviently to the fulness of our own claim; wherever they shall seem to have advanced and aided that, we will give them the praise of worthy servants.

Reverence then for the silent Indian; reverence, deep as justice, mute as himself, for the olden lord of this land! Honor to the swarth Iberian who planted the yellow standard of Castile on the shores of the Mexican Gulf; honor to the chivalric Frank who swung the lilies out to the icy air of Canada: honor to the broad-chested Briton, for he named his first town Saint Mary's: honor to the sinewy son of the green old Island of Eire: honor to the patient toiler who came, singing harmonious choruses, from the arrowy rush of the Rhine—but glory supreme to the Lord of Hosts, from whom all blessings are! For whom and for His Mother, we claim as theirs, by right of first discovery and seizure, this North American continent. Glory to God, the Eternal, and honor perpetual to Immaculate Mary.

PENN AND CALVERT COME.

The history of Europe for two hundred years before the colonization of America, is one of warfare and persecution. The terrible tragedies that were enacted in the name of religion and patriotism, are recalled with horror in this more peaceful age and country. Humanity is the strangest study of creation. Habit and custom are so strong in man that they cling to generations. To these add human prejudice, through which a ruling point is transmitted from father to son, carried from one country to another, and kept alive from century to century. The greatest blemishes on the history of America can be traced to their source, thousands of miles away and hundreds of years ago. The purely American record is fair in comparison with the fruits of an inherited prejudice, felt to this day in many ways and seen in many things.

It is not our purpose to review points of history ; but one thing leads to another, until we come to that humble part which is dearest to us as the object of our labor. For all the rest of the vast and ever-changing sea around us, it is sufficient to know that the Catholic Church has survived the ever-flowing and never-returning tide of the world ; and that this humble part of history we are about to record, came through the church and in all things belongs to her. We know the past. Faith steps in at the present, and beyond the twilight of the future into the growing shadows of its night, we see from the broken arches of London bridge the sad ruins before us ; and at the tinkling of a little bell adown where the chapel cross glitters in the sunlight stealing over the dark waters, every knee is bowed and every heart is hushed as of old, in the solemn silence of the Sanctus ! Sanctus ! Sanctus ! the last Hosanna of which will resound through eternity.

The revolutions in Europe drove the colonists to this country and settled America. Freedom of thought and freedom of action were denied them in the land of their fathers, and they looked to the New World for happier and more peaceful homes. Persecution followed them, led by many an evil genius of mother-land intolerance. Every change of tyrant-ruler in Europe was severely felt in the colonies, until the glorious patriots with their taste of freedom could stand no more, and Independence was proclaimed in the land of the free and the home of the brave. Would that we could recount the struggles of the heroes of Independence, but you have the history of your country before you; study it well and let your children drink it in from their youth, that this great Union of States and Union of Hearts may be preserved and perpetuated forever.

The first Pennsylvania settlement was made by the Dutch, in 1609. The Swedes and Fins settled along the Delaware in 1627. Penn's charter was dated Westminster, March 4th, 1681. In December of that year, the first vessel arrived at Chester. Philadelphia was founded in 1682.— Penn followed an honest and peaceful policy in all his dealings with his people. Catholics should hold the Friends in respectful remembrance. Like Washington, Penn had a kindly feeling for Catholics, especially after passing through many trials himself. The laws of the mother-country and many of our own early enactments, must be taken into consideration when passing judgment upon the course of Penn. The influence of prejudice established by English law was great, and in the end overcame Penn himself. In the other States Catholics fared worse. For the cause of the severe penal laws in the Provinces, look to "the glorious revolution of 1688." Then arose the "No Popery" cry in New York, and "Down with the Jesuits." Massachusetts and Virginia were thereby aroused against the Catholics. Under William and Mary liberty of conscience was allowed to all christians, "except Papists." Then it was that the "pious Acadian" suffered. In 1692, the Episcopal church was established by law in Maryland. Acts were passed "to prevent the growth of Popery." Priests could not say Mass, nor teach, nor perform any religious rite, under a severe penalty of the law.— Rewards were offered and imprisonment inflicted. One hundred pounds for sending a child abroad to be educated in the Catholic religion. The Catholic youth who upon attaining his majority refused to take the oaths prescribed, forfeited his lands by descent, and the next of kin being a Protestant succeeded. Catholic worship was prohibited in Pennsylvania in 1734 and 1736. The Acts of 1757, regulating the militia, did not allow Catholics to enter military duty or to have any ammunition or weapons in their houses or possession. Brighter days came. The Catholic, tried by persecution, was found true and loyal to his country and his God. He knew how to live, how to suffer and how to die. He sat in the Councils of the nation, and signed her great Declaration of Independence. He did not cease, though, to be persecuted by prejudice, and never will. His religion stands over and against him in this world. It ever did and ever will. This old-time hatred crops out here and there to this day.— But Catholics are respected and honored by the mass of American co-religionists. Their religion is recognized as a power for good. Let them guard it well, and keep aloof from all political entanglements, exercising their rights as American citizens according to the dictates of their conscience—supporting men and measures and not party. This persecution and opposition to Catholics was not born in America; it has its origin farther back than Smithfield or Tyburn, farther still than Nero or Diocletian; it is coeval with christianity itself, and is one of the strongest proofs of the true church, foretold by its founder, Jesus Christ.

Wm. Penn was born in London, Oct. 16th, 1644. He was expelled from Christ Church, Oxford, and disowned by his father, for being a Quaker. He was twice imprisoned for preaching in public. His possessions in the New World were taken from him, on suspicion of his being in league with King James in exile. These suspicions were declared unfounded in 1694, and he became a friend of King William. Burdened with debts, he closed his life in gloom and obscurity, 1718. The last claims of the Penns were purchased by the Legislature of Pennsylvania, in 1779, for one hundred and thirty thousand pounds.

Sir George Calvert, Baron of Baltimore, was born in Yorkshire, England, 1582, and died April 15th, 1632. He was a man of wealth and position, and was in attendance at the French Court of King Henri IV., of Navarre, whose daughter, Henrietta Maria, wife of Charles I., gave to Maryland her name.

"In an age when religious controversy still continued to be active, and when the increasing divisions among Protestants were spreading a general alarm, his mind sought relief from controversy in the bosom of the Roman Catholic Church." He resigned his political honors, retired to Ireland, and after visiting his settlement in New Foundland, he took up a grant of land in 1629, lying to the south of James River in Virginia. This grant he afterwards surrendered for the large and beautiful territory lying to the north of the Potomac. His charter was from Charles I., and descended to his son, Cecil, who was succeeded in 1675 by Charles Calvert.—The Calverts were deprived of their rights for a time, but were restored under Queen Anne as proprietors of Maryland and held their possessions up to the American Revolution.

Leonard Calvert, brother of Cecil, and about two hundred people, set sail in the Ark and Dove from Cowes in the Isle of Wight, on St. Cecilia's day, Nov. 22, 1633. They placed themselves and their ships under the protection of God, and invoked the intercession of the Blessed Virgin and St. Ignatius. They sailed safely up St. Mary's River, and on the 27th of March, 1634, took quiet possession of the Indian town of Yoacomoco; "and religious liberty obtained a home, its only home in the wide world, at the humble village which bore the name of St. Mary's." * * * "The Roman Catholics, who were oppressed by the laws of England, were sure to find a peaceful asylum in the quiet harbors of the Chesapeake; and there, too, Protestants were sheltered against Protestant intolerance."—BANCROFT.

After nearly two hundred years a selfish prejudice questions the motives which led to religious toleration in Maryland. Had the persecuted colonists in the other provinces been granted this priceless favor, they never would have asked from what motives it proceeded, but embraced it as the choicest blessing from Heaven.

"'I will not.'—such was the oath of the Governor of Maryland,—'I will not, by myself or any other, directly or indirectly, molest any person professing to believe in Jesus Christ, for or in respect of religion.'"—CHALMERS, 235; McMAHON, 226.

"An apprehension of some remote danger of persecution seems even then to have hovered over the minds of the Roman Catholics."—Third Assembly of Maryland, 1639.

It came, indeed, only too soon, and gave in exchange for Catholic toleration and a prosperous colonial government, all the evils of religious persecution in a reign of disorder and misrule.

Catholic Maryland is the brightest gem in the crown of States. Religion lent not her charms in vain. In the dark days of her trials in America, the church looked to Maryland for hope and encouragement. Whatever fault may now be found with the policy of the great lights of the church in Maryland, let it be said they acted well their parts, and laid the foundations of their building on solid rock. Now when the building is up in all its massive strength, and able to withstand the beating rain and the fury of the storm, it is easy for little and petulant minds to pick flaws here and there in its rugged gray foundation stones; but it requires the height of genius to accurately measure the labor and material that entered into its erection, and the depth of learning to outline the circumstances upon which the plan of structure was laid.

Catholic Maryland! I might never tire to wander in thy broad and beautiful fields of religious culture. Every plant and shrub and tree is so familiar and home-like, and reminds me of the gardens of my mother, the church. Every name is dear to a thousand memories in the household of faith. Thy laborers, I know them full well; they have worked in the Father's vineyard in the heat of the day and bore the burden of the toil;—they are Jesuits! You meet them everywhere cultivating the barren wastes and the broad fields of waving grain; they never rest nor weary, and murmur not at their scanty pay. Happy Maryland! I should like to count your treasures over, but it may not be. Time calls me away.

On Annunciation Day, 1634, the Pilgrims celebrated their first Mass at St. Clement's on Heron's Island. That sacred place is now a sand-washed waste.

In 1636, there were four priests in the Maryland mission. The Indians were for the most part friendly to the Catholic missionaries, until excited and misled by the enemies of the church, when they turned upon their best friends in the world. Fathers White and Altham obtained a hut from the Indians and used it for a chapel. They converted the great Indian King, Tayac, and his wife, called Mary in baptism. At their marriage, Gov. Calvert and many distinguished men came far distances through the wild country, to be present at the ceremony, which was made as impressive as the scanty facilities of a new settlement would permit. A cross was erected and the Litany of the Blessed Virgin chanted.

The first printing press in any British colony was set up by these Jesuit Fathers, and a Catechism printed for the Indians. A copy is preserved in the archives at Rome. An Indian grammar and dictionary were also printed.

During Clayborne's rebellion, Father White was sent in chains to England. After many trials and sufferings, he was banished, but returned and died in London, Jan. 6th, 1657, in his 78th year.

The Maryland historians have allowed the missionaries the credit of their labors, but not as they deserved. The part they took in the settlement of the country was the leading one, and great was the influence of their labors, and lasting. Davis in his *Day-Star* pleads for justice to their memory: Let not the Protestant historian of America give grudgingly. Let him testify, with a warm heart; and pay, with gladness, the tribute so richly due to the memory of our early forefathers. Let their deeds be enshrined in our hearts;

and their names repeated in our households. Let them be canonized, in the grateful regards of the American; and handed down, through the lips of a living tradition, to his most remote posterity. In an age of cruelty, like true men, with heroic hearts, they fought the first great battle of religious liberty. And their fame, without reference to their faith, is now the inheritance, not only of Maryland, but also of America.

BOUNDARY DIFFICULTIES.

When we look over the broad and fertile fields of the Conewago Valley, we see in the great natural wealth around us the reason why every foot of its ground was so bitterly and persistently contested. The hard-working German farmer was eager to push across the Susquehanna's legal barrier, and take up the rich bottom lands along the Codorus and the Conewago. The English gentry from the ranks of the Calverts, with their baronial ideas of grand estates, knew full well the value and advantages of these forest hills and valleys bordering the tributaries which drained the land from the mountains to the rivers. The poor Irish peasant looked over the half-cleared patches with envy, and remembered the marshy wastes and barren hills of his own green isle with sadness. The restless, self-willed "squatter" comes along, despising metes and bounds as he does law and order, and cares only to go where he pleases and do whatever he wishes.

Baltimore County, in the Province of Maryland, was formed in 1659. Many of the oldest deeds to property in the Conewago Valley, are from the Proprietaries of Maryland, when the land was claimed to be within the bounds of Baltimore County. For this reason, we do not agree with those who accuse the Maryland settlers of coming into the Province of Pennsylvania without leave or license. Chester County, to which the land originally belonged under the claims of Penn, was not formed until 1682, twenty-three years later than the formation of Baltimore County. Carroll County, now part of the border-line between the two States; was formed from parts of Baltimore and Frederick Counties, 1836. Tracing the land down on the Pennsylvania side, we find it was included in Chester County from 1682 to May 15th, 1729, when Lancaster County was formed; in Lancaster until Aug. 9th, 1749, the date of the formation of York County; and in York until Jan. 22d, 1800, when Adams, the present County, was cut off from York. Conewago Township was formed May 25th, 1800, out of parts of Heidelberg and Manheim Townships, York County. Baltimore was laid out in 1729, on lands of Charles Carroll. Frederick was laid out in 1745; Georgetown in 1751; Hagerstown 1762; York in 1741; Hanover in 1764; Gettysburg in 1780; Littlestown in 1765; Abbottstown in 1753; New Oxford in 1792.

From various causes, the boundary claims and title difficulties through this border country, from the Susquehanna to what is now Mason & Dixon's line, were the longest in dispute and the most conflicting of any in the history of the Provinces. The poor settler might feel reasonably secure after having his tract entered in the Land Book for the County of Baltimore and that of the Philadelphia Land-Office, with a release from the Carrolls, but great is his surprise when along comes Dudley Digges, claiming to have an order from the Council to make him give up his lands! No wonder the settlers determined to defend their homes with their lives.

As soon as Penn's grant was announced, a difficulty arose between himself and Lord Baltimore about the dividing line. They met together several times, but never came to any satisfactory understanding. First they agreed to adopt the border fixed by the decree of 1685, but royal decrees did not satisfy the increasing dissensions among the settlers. Quarrels arose, in which the laws of both Proprietaries were invoked, or taken advantage of and misconstrued. Many acts of violence were committed, and great evil and lawlessness existed. The courts of justice were far away, and there being no real or recognized authority, designing men used this state of affairs to their advantage. Petitions were sent to the Governor and the State Council, and royal orders were attempted to be enforced, but the difficulties continued. The section of country became a refuge for evil-doers, as the laws of either Province could be resisted and protection claimed under the other. In the same way, taxes were refused to be paid by men who enjoyed all the privileges of government with those who contributed to its support, for the majority of the settlers were honest and well-meaning, ready to submit to lawful authority wherever established. A Temporary Line was run by commissioners from both Provinces, but the difficulties continued. In 1757, the Grand Jury of the County made all conform to the royal order, that titles were good no matter on which side of the Temporary Line located, and designated as far as possible to which Province they belonged. The final settlement of the troubles was made in 1766-67, when by order of the English Court of Chancery, Charles Mason and Jeremiah Dixon, noted astronomers in England, run the present line, placing at every mile a stone with the letter P. and arms of Penn on one side, and the letter M. and escutcheon of Lord Baltimore on the other. Some of these mile-stones are standing to this day.

By the grant of Charles II. to Wm. Penn, the southern boundary of the Province of Pennsylvania was made "a circle drawn at twelve miles distant from New Castle, northward, and westward to the 40th degree of northern latitude, then by a straight line westward." Lord Baltimore's northern boundary, by his grant, was also the 40th parallel, but the circle twelve miles distant from New Castle would not intersect the 40th parallel, the distance being more than the twelve miles prescribed by the charter. "Each party consequently claimed the intervening strip, and the adherents of each, ignorant of real or assumed lines, claimed much more than their lords and masters."—SMITH'S *Annals of Hanover and History of York County.*

Lord Baltimore's grant included all the present State of Delaware, and a portion of Pennsylvania, including the Counties of Chester, Delaware, Lancaster, York, Adams, Franklin, Fulton, Bedford and Somerset. In their attempts at settlement of the grant troubles, it was urged by the Penns that the Swedes and Dutch had settlements before the charter of Lord Baltimore was obtained.

The charter of Maryland defined the western boundary by the meridian passing through the first fountain of the Potomac. Whether it meant the North or South branch is an open question to this day, and commissions were recently appointed by the Legislatures of several States now divided by this line, to determine questions coming from boundary uncertainties.

Penn's policy always was, to issue no warrants for lands unless first obtaining titles from the Indians. The Indians west of the Susquehanna were subject to the Five Nations.— Penn empowered Thomas Dougan, Governor of New York, to purchase of the Five Nations their right and interest in the lands west of the river. The purchase was made about 1688. Jan. 12th, 1696, Dougan leased for 1000 years all his right and title west of the river to Wm. Penn for 100 pounds sterling and a yearly rent of a "pepper corn." Jan. 13th, 1696, Thos. Dougan sold to Penn all lands from the mountains or head of said river, and running as far as the Chesapeake.— Penn was not satisfied but obtained a deed from the Susquehannas, the originial, though defeated, owners of the soil.— The Connestoga Indians denied the right of the Susquehannas to sell the lands west of the river. Penn, always ready to settle any claims against lands he held, purchased a deed from the Connestoga Indians. The Five Nations still asserted a right to said land, and they sent their chiefs to a great Council held in the country of the Onondagoes, in the summer of 1736. A deed was signed Oct. 11th, 1736, by eight Onondagoes, six Senekaes, four Oneidas, two Tuscaroras, and three Cayugas, conveying said lands to John, Thomas and Richard Penn. This included all the Susquehanna River, eastward as far as the heads of the springs that run into said river; west to the setting of the sun; northward to the mountains called by the Nations Tyannantasacta, or Endless Hills, and by the Delawares, Kekkachtananin Hills.

"DIGGES' CHOICE."

Tradition has preserved but few names of the first settlers through the Conewago Valley. History has done no better. Historical researches ahead of us there are none;— no old papers or writings; even the original deeds are not obtainable. In Father DeBarth's time, all the books and papers kept at Conewago were taken to Georgetown.

The Father-General of the Society in Rome has a good record of the Jesuit labors in these provinces. Reports have been made up in this country from time to time, clothed in a Latin dress in presentable shape by order of the Provincial, and forwarded to the head of the Society. Some day!

In early colonial times, land, like timber, was so plenty and so cheap that large tracts were given away for the smallest service or the least consideration. In 1722, on the west side of the Susquehanna, 75,000 acres were surveyed as the Manor of Springgettsbury, for the Proprietaries of Pennsylvania, with the intention of preventing the Maryland authorities from encroaching upon lands thus claimed. Thomas Cresap, a Marylander, had a grant of 500 acres along the river, on which disgraceful scenes were enacted and great injustice done. Penn always treated righteously with the Indians, but Cresap burnt their villages and murdered the inhabitants, and acted no better with the white settlers who had crossed the river from the east. Cresap was from Yorkshire, and was only fifteen years old when he came to the Maryland Province. The Winthrops, the Penns, the Washingtons and the Calverts, all came from Yorkshire, and we would not be surprised to find that Digges and Clayborne also came from there. "The Manor of Maske" was surveyed for the use of the Proprietaries of Pennsylvania, in 1740. It was six miles wide and twelve miles long, and was located in the western part of what is now Adams County, touching the Maryland line on the south. "Carroll's Delight" was surveyed under Maryland authority, April 3d, 1732, patented Aug. 8th, 1735, to Charles, Mary and Eleanor Carroll. There were two "Tracts," containing 5,000 acres. Many difficulties arose from these special reservations, and the conflictions in titles that they occasioned were felt down to the beginning of the present century. In several instances the original settlers interfered with the surveyors and threatened their lives.

For some reason, John Digges, a petty nobleman, obtained from the proprietor of Maryland a grant of 10,000 acres, Oct. 14th, 1727. He had the privilege of taking up any unimproved lands in the Province. For this grant, Digges paid 184 pounds, 19 shillings, as pre-emption money, and a yearly rental of 13 pounds, 12 shillings, 11 pence, in silver or gold. In 1732, by the advice of an Indian Chief named Tom, Digges surveyed 6,822 acres lying on Tom's Creek, and called it "Digges' Choice." This tract took in all the beautiful Valley of the Conewago, on the Little Conewago and Plum Creeks, from the Pigeon Hill spurs to the springs that start these creeks. The original survey in 1732 crossed the Conewago and took in all the finest land adjoining on the west side.— Oct. 11th, 1732, the Maryland office issued to John Digges a patent for the land of his choice.

When the Temporary Line was run in 1732, to serve as a boundary until the border difficulties could be finally settled, Digges' land was decided to be in Pennsylvania; but his title was good, on account of a Royal Order then issued, which declared that all titles previously obtained, should hold good, no matter on which side of the Temporary Line, nor by which Province granted. Among the settlers on " Digges' Choice," were David Young, Adam Miller, Adam Weisser, John Lemmon, 1732; they were the *Kreutz-Kirche* settlers, near Littlestown, and came from the east of the river.

Andrew Schreiber purchased 100 acres from Digges in 1734, for which he paid one hundred pairs of negro shoes.— Henry Sell came in 1735; Martin Kitzmiller in 1736; Adam Forney in 1737. Robert Owings, a Catholic and one of the first settlers with the Diggeses, surveyed and laid off land for Henry Sell and Martin Kitzmiller in 1739. On this land and about this time, Kitzmiller's mill was built. Before that the settlers had to go to the Susquehanna to have their wheat ground.

Settlements were made from the east of the river as early as 1710, and by 1720 the Marylanders had pushed northward as far as the Codorus. From that time date the troubles between the Maryland and Pennsylvania settlers, ended at last by the running of Mason & Dixon's line, 1767. The claims of the Diggeses were never settled, but may be said to have died out. The land was too much mixed up in dispute to enforce them. The majority of the settlers acted honorably, as can be seen from the old deeds still preserved. Most of them held titles under Lord Baltimore first, and after the Temporary Line was run they secured titles from the Penns; then they had a Right or Deed from John Digges or his sons, which carried with it a release from the Carrolls. It is easy to understand why the title and boundary disputes continued so long in bitterness and confusion, and only a wonder that the difficulties were not more serious in their results.

In November, 1743, Digges applied to the Pennsylvania Land-Office to take up as much land as would make his tract square. This was granted on condition that he should not disturb the German settlers, complaints having repeatedly been made by them that he refused to mark his line, and was constantly changing the amount of his grant. When Digges returned he told the Germans that he had concluded an agreement with the Land Agent at Philadelphia, by which they would be compelled to give up their lands to him. This caused great excitement. Thomas Cookson, Surveyor of Lancaster County, was sent by the Governor of Pennsylvania to adjust the difficulties, but accomplished little or nothing towards that end. Officers were sent from Maryland to make arrests, but the settlers resisted them and swords were drawn on both sides. May 10th, 1749, the settlers joined in a petition to Governor Hamilton of Pennsylvania, setting forth that Digges demanded one hundred pounds for every one hundred acres of land they held under Pennsylvania titles. The killing of Dudley Digges quieted the excitement of both claimants and contestants more than anything else, and after that matters were more readily adjusted on both sides. In Feb., 1752, in an altercation between a Maryland officer and his men and Martin Kitzmiller and his sons, at Kitzmiller's house, Dudley Digges was shot by one of Kitzmiller's sons; whether accidentally or purposely, will never be known, but Kitzmiller was acquitted at the trial in Oct., when it was proven that the officer had no warrant and was in truth not even an officer. Those engaged with the pretended officer, were Dudley and Henry Digges, sons of John Digges; John Stackers, Patrick Koyle, John Seyfert and Anthony Worley. The sentiment of the people was against Maryland interference, and in full sympathy and favor with Pennsylvania authority. This applies particularly to the Germans, as certain promises had induced the Irish to desire them dispossessed of the land.

John Digges was the father of Edward, William, Henry and Dudley Digges. William Digges, who came to the colony with Lord Baltimore and attended him in several of his meetings with Wm. Penn, was doubtless the ancestor of these Diggeses. John Digges lived with the Carrolls, and it was through them that he first come to settle the Conewago Valley. In or about 1800, some of the Diggeses still lived at St. Thomas, now in Charles County, and among the names that appear are Francis, Jane, John and Henry. Certainly John Digges and his family did not come alone to the Conewago Valley, but no other names come down to us. They were Catholics. Their association and friendly acquaintance with the Indians show the work of the missionaries, and that where they worshiped, whether under the humble roof of the settlers or in the rude wig-wam of the Indian, there the roaming Shawnee emigrant and the conquered braves of the northern tribes also bowed their knee.

The remains of Dudley Digges are resting in the grave at Conewago. Not many years ago, John Aulebaugh, a citizen of McSherrystown, remembered having heard his grandfather tell of the shooting of Dudley Digges. He saw the wounded man, shot in the bowels, and attended his funeral. The sight and excitement he declared could never be effaced from his memory, and so it has come down to the present from father to son, through three generations.

Another account of this unfortunate affair, claims that Digges acted upon a process obtained from the Court at Frederick. No doubt he acted entirely in the defense of his rights and interest, and believed he was pursuing a lawful course in reclaiming his property. Circumstances were against him. When the proprietors of Maryland failed to establish their claim to the land, how could the Diggeses expect to succeed. The shooting occurred on the farm now called "Carrollton," lately occupied and owned by Francis A. Uhl. The place became a noted hostelry on the great wagon road from Philadelphia to Frederick.

Digges' widow and two children remained in Conewago (then Heidelberg) township, about a mile and a half south of McSherrystown, for several years after his death, when they removed to Frederick City, where the widow had a sister, and where she died in 1812. Her maiden name was Mary Lilly, a daughter of the first Lilly that emigrated to these parts, the ancestor of the present Conewago Lillys, whose name was Samuel, and who, in 1730, located on the old Lilly farm, above Lilly's Mill, now owned by one of his great-great-grand-sons—and that has been in the family ever since, and where a woolen factory was carried on from about 1730 until about 1830, as many of the "oldest inhabitants" will recollect.

THE CONEWAGO VALLEY.

The Conewago Valley of one hundred and fifty years ago, was a dense forest of oak and hickory that covered the broad plain, and along the banks of the creeks grew the more valuable wood and beautiful trees,—the ash, poplar, walnut, water beach, sycamore and willow. Not many years ago, the stately trunks of some of the veterans of the forests stood along Slagle's Run and the Conewago and Plum Creeks, sad and lonely reminders of the days when they were kings of the forests. Some of them measured over three feet across the stump. The Conewago Valley of to-day!—look over it: Follow the narrow strip of woodland from north to south; that marks the course of the Little Conewago: off to the west, over hills and valleys, the South Mountains limit the view, running south across the Potomac and the Shenandoah, north and east across the Susquehanna, the Schuylkill and the Delaware. In the south and the east the valley broadens out along the shadowy woodlands of my Maryland. Right at your back rise the blue tops of the Pigeon Hills, that before long, alas! will be cleared of the heavy chestnut growth which is struggling to get upward. What else? Nothing but broad fields of waving grain; large barns and houses, (barns before houses with the sturdy sons of toil,) beautiful homes and gardens,—thriving towns and villages in every direction. Everything easy, quiet and peaceful. May nothing ever mar its beauty or blight its happiness.

Hanover is the central point, on the Frederick Division P. R. W., the Hanover & Baltimore and Hanover & Gettysburg Railroads; 42 miles from Frederick, about 50 from Baltimore and twice that distance from Philadelphia; lat. 39° 46' north, long. 148° west of Greenwich. Conewago Chapel is 4 miles west of Hanover, in Conewago Township, Adams Co., Pa.; about 10 miles from Gettysburg, the county seat; 7 miles from Littlestown, 4 from New Oxford, about 22 from York, 80 from Washington, 110 from Philadelphia; in lat. about 39° 45' north, long. 0° 0' 3" west from Washington.— The Post-Office address is McSherrystown, Adams Co., Pa.

It is said that all the early attempts at Catholic colonization in these Provinces have been failures. How Conewago could have been more successful as a Catholic settlement, we cannot easily understand. Conewago Chapel is the parent church from which the Catholic religion spread over southern and western Maryland into Virginia, along the frontiers of Pennsylvania, into the very heart of its settlement, Philadelphia itself. The churches at Hanover, Littlestown, Taneytown, Bonneauville, Gettysburg, Millerstown, The Mountain, Carlisle, Harrisburg, York, Paradise and New Oxford, are all fruits of the Conewago Missionary labors. The early Catholics, scattered within the bounds of these outlying missions, once looked to Conewago for all the spiritual aid they ever received. The missionaries in their long journey over the country, kept no account of their labors, and all that has come down to us are a few scraps of paper, where a child was baptized in the Path or Cove Valleys, a death-bed attended along the South Mountains, or a sick-call here or there,— twenty, thirty miles away. Take the large and flourishing congregations at all these places, their well-built churches and schools, and houses,—take the credit of all these away from Conewago, and yet there is left a successful Catholic colony of five thousand souls; a fine, large and well-finished church,—Conewago Chapel; six hundred acres of the best land in the valley, school houses and chapels at every little surrounding village; and a large and well-established Convent School and Sisterhood at McSherrystown.

Conewago is a thoroughly Catholic settlement. From Hanover to Gettysburg, sixteen miles east to west, half of the population is Catholic; from Oxford to Littlestown, ten miles north to south, two-thirds of the population is Catholic. You can travel five miles along any road within that distance from the Chapel, and meet almost nothing but Catholics.— There are Protestant families scattered all through the valley, but they do not make up one-tenth of its population.— Though not belonging to our church, we have come to consider them very near and dear to the household of faith. All live agreeably together, associating and assisting each other as citizens, and taking part in every enterprise that concerns home or church. The few Protestants in the valley have always been good and liberal neighbors to the Catholic Church. Mixed marriages, you ask? are rare occurrences under these circumstances. Catholic teachings and associations are strong, thanks to the watchful Fathers of the church and the good Catholic mothers of the valley. Conewago has been free from all dire afflictions of Providence, and spared from all shame and disgrace into which human nature is so apt to fall. Not to say that none have fallen; no, but they have been quietly helped to rise again; and this we say, that in all the history of the valley, memory can point to no serious reflection on priest or people; no difference or disagreement in any work of the church. Her record is fair and pure. People who have always lived here do not rightly appreciate the blessings of a Catholic community. It is easier to be a Catholic here than in the mixed and busy push of the towns and cities. Yet look at the work the struggling Catholics accomplish alone in those places,—build churches, support priests and schools and contribute to every cause of religion. They have no rich establishments of any order or society to build upon. The poor are everywhere the brightest ornaments of the church. So at Conewago.

We need not transport ourselves with De la Martine (*Harmonies Poetiques*) to the neighborhood of some church in the Middle Ages, to " see the humble crowd winding its way along the pious path. It is the poor orphan who spins as she walks; it is the blind man who feels his way with his stick; it is the timid beggar whose hand holds a rosary; it is the child who caresses each flower as he passes by; it is the old man who hastens with feeble steps;—youth and age are the friends of God."

In Catholic times and Catholic countries, of which Conewago reminds us so much, one of the greatest virtues practiced was the education of the poor and an effort to start them in life. The Catholic wealth of Conewago presents not one such instance. The priests and the people had an anxious care for the poor—never a care the rich. Could only the widow and the orphan speak.

As a farming country, the Conewago Valley is one of the richest in the State. The soil is the best quality of limestone land, and very productive. There is a perfect system in agriculture, and hardly a foot of ground that has not been reclaimed and put to use. The land tenure is hereditary, and there is little of that great desire for change which has scattered Pennsylvanians over every State in the Union. The first Conewago settlers are represented to-day by an industrious and well-to-do people, many of them on the same lands which their forefathers took up. Times, and customs, however, are changing now. The restless, worldly spirit of progress and novelty has entered the precincts of this old-time retirement. The young people have caught the spirit of the age—that freedom of parental restraint unknown to their fathers and mothers, and show an unwillingness to follow the safe and steady paths which have led the generations before them to peaceful homes and plenty, and to old age crowned with humble but virtuous and useful lives. Who can tell what will be the result? The good old missionary Fathers, so suited to the times and the people, are also gone. True, we have good priests of modern education and American ways, and perhaps it is better that everything moves with the times.

One thing is certain, if the future Conewago remembers her God and her religion as faithfully as did the Conewago of the past, there is no danger, whatever may happen. The history of the church has shown that she is equal to any emergency, and suits herself to the changes of time and custom, to the revolution of governments, of nations and of ages. She goes on forever, and in her there is no change or shadow of vicissitude.

It is hard enough for those who belong to the past, and are used to the ways of ye olden times, to reconcile themselves with the changes of the quickly-passing years. They may well weep with Schiller over the times gone by, and sigh for the days of peace, the homes of their fathers, and the elysian scenes of their childhood. How they call upon Nature to mourn with them for the scenes that will never come again, and with their balmy sighing cool no burning brow;—"they are gone! gone! and may not return."

EARLY HISTORY OF CONEWAGO.

There is nothing striking or very prominent in the whole history of the Conewago Valley. Entirely an agricultural country, its history is one of hard labor, economy, peace and plenty; and that is record enough for a plain, virtuous and law-abiding people. They have tried to follow the illustrious example of their leaders, the Jesuits, whose greatest deeds are only recorded in Heaven. Patriotism was never wanting in the valley. The colonial records and the archives of the State show that old Heidelberg contributed as much or more than any of the other original townships, when called upon in time of need. It supplied men and aid in the French and Indian wars, the Revolution, 1812-14, the Mexican war and the "late unpleasantness" as we call it further South, but known here as the Rebellion.

The first claim on the land was held by the Carrolls, from Lord Baltimore. The Carrolls were an Irish family, and the elder Carroll was Secretary to Lord Powis, a leading minister in the cabinet of James II. This minister, forseeing troublesome times ahead, and having a great regard for the success and welfare of his Secretary, advised him to go out into the Maryland colony. Daniel Carroll with his father came to America in 1689, acted as agent for Lord Baltimore and obtained large grants of land. Charles Carroll, Sr., was born in 1702; Charles, Jr., surnamed of Carrollton, in 1737.

The "Releases" of the Carrolls to the lands in the Conewago Valley extend from the first settlements to the Revolution. They amounted to a mere form, for security's sake on account of the title troubles, as there is no record of any payments except the mention of certain ground rents included in the first sales of land, which probably originated with the Carrolls, descended to the Diggeses and became extinct in the McSherrys.

There must be some reason for the peaceful attitude of the Indians towards the Conewago settlers. In the western part of the county and northward, buildings were burned by them, children abducted and the settlers murdered. There is not a single instance of wrong by them in the Conewago Valley, except where in a state of intoxication they assaulted the family of Adam Forney near Hanover. There is no traditional evidence that they were feared by the people, by whom it seems they were regarded as friends. True, the western borders formed a barrier against Indian raids, and the people from the frontier settlements, in times of threatened danger from the Indians, would flee for safety almost this far into the interior. There certainly were Indians through the valley, for there are evidences to this day of their camps or villages on several places around Conewago. On account of the labors of the Maryland missionaries among the Indians, they may be looked upon as a part of the early settlers, traveling together in their explorations and living together in their settlements. There are several traditional stories handed down of the "last Indians" seen, coming to a house here or there for food, or to a blacksmith shop to have a lame horse or pony shod, and going off into the Pigeon Hills for coal when the blacksmith was out; but whether true or not, we will not say. They left here like everywhere else, pushed away by the advance of civilization, the destruction of their forests, and the absence of game, for even then bears and deer began to keep closer to the mountains. Poor Indians! the last remnant of them is crowded to the ocean's wall, and there seems to be no more room left.

The early settlement of the Conewago Valley does not differ much from that of the other parts of the State. The people coming from the older settlements of Maryland might have been a little better provided for than the poorer emigrants from the German Palatinates, the expatriated Irish and poor "redemptioners." A few of the better class were able to build substantial stone houses that stood for a hundred years and more, but the most of them built very common log houses. The settlement almost from the beginning was made up not only of farmers but of different kinds of mechanics. A little later, carpet weaving, spinning, woolen and flax industries, were very generally followed. For over a hundred years, wagoning was the great means by which trade was carried on. Grain and flour were taken to Pittsburg, Baltimore and Philadelphia, and store goods and whatever else was needed, brought back. In the proper season, shad and other fish in large quantities were hauled from the fisheries along the Susquehanna. Many a priest and student rode to and from Conewago, Baltimore, Washington and other points, with these old teamsters. Conewago was well situated with regard to the early modes and routes of travel. The wagon road from Wright's Ferry, on the Susquehanna, to the Monocacy road at the Maryland line, passed through the valley. The wagon and stage roads from Philadelphia to Frederick and from Carlisle to Baltimore, crossed each other where Hanover now stands, the first house of which was McAllister's tavern, part of it standing yet, built up in modern walls.

The country around Hanover was entirely a German settlement, while the Conewago settlement was considered Irish, and many a good old time the two elements had together.— At the first election for York County held at York Town, McAllister was the candidate of the Germans for Sheriff, and Hance Hamilton led the Irish. There was a general fight; the Irish were routed and driven from the polls, but their candidate was commissioned by the Governor. For many years a jealous spirit of rivalry existed between the two settlements; which, perhaps, was good for their growth and success. The upper part of what is now Adams County was settled by the Scotch-Irish, between 1736 and 1740. The Conewago Valley was settled by a few English families from the Province of Lord Baltimore, somewhere between 1700 and 1725, as there were births and deaths between these periods. Then the Irish and Germans came in about equal numbers, and scattered together from the "barrens" all through the valley, and westward, as one of the principal directions emigration took to Pittsburg and the western settlements, was from Conewago. English and German sermons alternated at Conewago up to 1800; after that English took the lead. German sermons might have averaged one a-month to 1850.— Fathers Enders, Deneckere and Manns preached in German once in a while after that; now German is not heard, except for a special purpose. The first English sermons were preached in the Protestant churches of Hanover in 1837. The first English papers in Hanover and Gettysburg were started about 1818. The first German paper was started in Hanover in 1769, and a German paper is still published there.

THE CONEWAGO OF THE INDIANS.

The name "Conewago" is the last connecting link between the aborigines of the valley and their successors, the present American people. With them it will continue, and may even exist after their identity shall have been obscured or lost in the deepening shadows of antiquity. Like all other foreign names and words, Conewago had to shape itself to English use, a tendency which carried everything in its way. Later in the history of the language, "young America" became afflicted with such a mania for anglicism, that the names of their fathers full of memory and meaning were ruthlessly despoiled in making them assume an English garb that fits in nothing but the ridiculous. The Conewago missionaries were of different nationalities, but the Latin tongue was to them a common language. Thus the English Conewago comes down to us from the Latin, and not direct from the Indian term.— In handling the German names in Latin, the missionaries made some amusing changes. The German names are mostly derived from solid words in that language, which sound all right when translated into English, but in writing them in Latin according to sound, they lose all significance and trace of origin. The German Koontz is given the Latin C in Cunes and the English hn in Kuhns. Thus we could note many similar changes had we the time to follow them up.

The Indian word "Caughnawaga" is said to mean "the rapids." The Germans pronounced it "Konowago;" the English and Irish, "Canawaga." The missionaries wrote it Conewago as early as 1740, placing it in the third declension.— Accordingly, those who persist in using "Cono," follow the German derivation. Conewago is the correct way as applied to the Chapel or the Creek; when meaning the township, it may be claimed that the rules of law by which it was formed have it "Cono," which is immaterial, as the name has but one origin.

As a definition of the word "Caughnawaga," "the rapids" was certainly not applied originally to the streams of that name in southern Pennsylvania. The Big Conewago drains the slope east of the Blue Ridge and flows into the Susquehanna. The Little Conewago winds through the lower valley and empties into the Big Conewago. It rises about on the dividing line between the Susquehanna and Potomac drains. Except when swollen by heavy rain or melting snow, neither of these creeks can be called swift or rapid. Since the Conewago Valley has been stripped of its forests, the Little Conewago is narrowing its banks into a mere stream, and the mills along its course have parted with the old-fashioned water wheels and put in turbines.

The original "Caughnawaga" of the Indians was a tributary of the St. Lawrence. There were no native tribes in this part of Pennsylvania;—only roving bands from the great branches of the Indian families along the bays, rivers and mountains. The number of Indians in the Provinces was not as great as many suppose. The Shawnees were a "restless nation of wanderers," who inhabited the region of Kentucky. By permission from the Pennsylvania authorities in 1698, some of them came from Carolina and settled in Pennsylvania. When in 1732 the number of Indian fighting men was estimated at 700, half of them were Shawnee emigrants. "So desolate was the wilderness," says Bancroft, "that a vagabond tribe could wander undisturbed from Cumberland River to the Alabama, from the headwaters of the Santee to the Susquehanna." From the heart of the Five Nations two warriors would thread the wilderness of the South; would go through the glades of Pennsylvania, the valleys of Western Virginia, and steal within the mountain fastnesses of the Cherokees, and after securing scalps enough to surprise their native village, bound over the ledges and hurry home.

If it is true, that "a pious rivalry" existed between the Maryland missionaries and those of the St. Lawrence, as the great American historian says there did, there must have been some means of communication. This could only come through the Fathers in the old country, or by means of wandering bands of Indians. St. Mary's was the starting point of the Maryland missionaries; Caughnawaga the "chief mission" of the St. Lawrence Jesuits. It was a Mohawk village on the Caughnawaga Creek, into which the Indians cast the body of Father Jogues, after murdering him, in 1646. Goupil and Lelande met a similar fate at Caughnawaga. When the Susquehannas poured down upon the missionary settlements in Maryland, Father Jogues received word at Caughnawaga that one of the Jesuit Fathers "had fallen amid his neophytes."— "At Caughnawaga the faith was more constantly embraced than in any other part of the Mohawk country," and here, say the missionaries, we first saw a native church and christian generosity displayed. From 1673, prayers were said at this mission as regularly as in any christian community in Europe. Fathers Bonaface and De Lamberville labored at Caughnawaga. Catharine Tegahkouita, a pious and saintly Indian maiden, was born there; and the noted chief, Tagannissoren, converted. His oratory was compared to that of Cicero by English writers, and the king of France hung his portrait in the galleries of Versailles.

The Maryland Indians consisted of branches of the great Huron-Iroquois family. The Susquehannas were the most powerful, and among them the Catholic missionaries began their labors. The Five Nations, a powerful northern confederation, had conquered almost all the surrounding tribes of Indians. The Indians in Pennsylvania were all subject to the Five Nations. They seem to have been fugitives, having no settlement of their own, but loving their wild freedom, sought to keep out of the way of the more powerful and warlike tribes. The St. Lawrence Indians were engaged in many incursions into the country of these roving bands, and the prisoners they brought in were instructed by the missionaries and every effort made to save their lives. When the Senecas and Ottawas were at war, Father Fremin instructed and baptized the prisoners brought in to die. Conestogues were frequently burned, and always instructed and baptized. They were called Gandestogues by the French, or Andastes, and were in all probability the Susquehannas. Father Fremin found some who were instructed in Catholic doctrine, and Shea thinks they might have been objects of the care of the Jesuits in Maryland. The Indian missions were from time to time broken up by the ceaseless warfare among the tribes. The Caughnawagas were subject to the Five Nations, and the mission has almost a continuous history, down to the present Sault St. Louis. Being thoroughly Catholic, (except in their murderous wars which will forever cling to them,) if there ever was any communication between the missionaries, it was through the Caughnawaga or Susquehanna Indians.— It might have been in this way that at an early day they found their way along these creeks into the Maryland missions, and left their name to the valley. Future researches in the line of the St. Lawrence missions, and the older Catholic settlements of Maryland,—St. Mary's, St. Inigoes, St. Thomas Manor, Newtown, Port Tobacco, "Hickory" in Harfort County,—will throw additional light upon the Caughnawaga of the Indians.

THE FIRST PLACE OF WORSHIP.

The course of new settlements is everywhere and at all times the same. First a few pioneer families build their humble homes and lay the foundation for others to follow.— Then arises the demand for business and professions, churches and schools. The local history of the Catholic church invariably finds the priest saying mass in a room of some of the few Catholic families, whose spiritual wants bring him among them. Thus was the Catholic religion introduced into the

Conewago Valley. The present Conewago Chapel stands on high ground, on one of the many little spurs that follow the Blue Ridge range, of which the Pigeon Hills is the largest, and the last to the eastward from the mountains, about two miles from the chapel. Beyond that the "barrens" set in, extending southward with the valley into Maryland. Similar hills, valleys and lowlands are found across the river in Lancaster County. The Little Conewago and the Plum Creek come together along the foot of the hill on which Conewago Chapel is built, the former from a direction due South, the latter a little to the East. The meadow land along these streams was grown up with dense underbrush and trees, and received its name from the man who farmed the church land, known from 1830 as "Will's Bottom," and now as "Devine's." The land had been cleared and cultivated under Father De-Barth, but suffered to go to waste again after him, until Father Enders had it given out to be cleared, drained and farmed. The present site of Conewago Chapel has been used for church purposes since 1740. This valley is the oldest settlement in the county, and here also is the oldest place of religious worship. The first Kreutz Church settlers, near Littlestown, came in 1734, and organized their church in 1747. The Marsh Creek and Great Conewago Churches date from 1740; the Bermudian Churches from 1747, and Christ Church, Huntington, from about 1750.

Settlers from Lord Baltimore's Province pushed northward through Baltimore County, and reached the Codorus almost as early as 1700. Rupp's researches through these parts of Pennsylvania, Glossbrenner & Carter's History of York County, Smith's Annals of Hanover and History of York County, all give from 1710 to 1720 as the time when this valley, the barrens and the land along the Codorus to the river, were settled by the Marylanders. Many of the Maryland settlers were Catholics, while the most of those who came into the valley from the East of the river, before 1750, were Protestants. They settled the surrounding country, and the fact that only a few Protestant families secured land in the Conewago settlement would go to show earlier Catholic claims. Digges' grant of 1727 was given conditionally, for vacant land only, and *improved land* was particularly excepted. This he plainly disregarded, since from the moment he attempted to locate his choice in the valley, he was met with opposition; and that must have come from those who had previously located there, though they may have had no right from either Province, until Digges' effort to take their land made them apply to the Maryland or Pennsylvania proprietaries for patents, and appeal to both for protection of their claims. That part of Digges' Choice to the west of the Little Conewago, was left out of his re-survey without an effort to enforce his claim, and his strongest efforts in the contest were made for the lands farther south, near the disputed boundary line; so that he left Conewago undisturbed, probably because "the improvements" had gone too far before his grant was taken up. Patrick McSherry had a large tract of land, covering all the ground around McSherrystown, and taking in the present lands owned or occupied by Sunday, Geisleman, McSherry and Croninger. He had a title from the Diggeses, but he also had patents from both Provinces and a release from the Carrolls. The earliest Protestant families adjoining the Chapel, were the Schreivers and the Slagles. Ludwig Schreiver held the land immediately to the west of the Conewago settlement proper, under Lord Baltimore's patent dated November, 1735. He built a mill near where O'Bold's now stands. The McCrearys at a later date were Protestant neighbors, John and David purchasing four tracts from Patrick and Catharine McSherry, March 15th, 1795, now adjoining the O'Bold mill property on the west. Christopher Slagle settled in Berwick Township, on Slagle's Run, adjoining the Chapel land on the north, in 1737. Slagle's Run must have been the dividing line between Berwick, Heidelberg and Manheim Townships. Henry Slagle, one of his sons, was a very prominent and useful man, occupying public positions until his death about 1802. The Slagles were farmers, millers and carpenters. One of the Slagles built Conewago Chapel in 1786-7, and when the church was enlarged in 1850, he used to come and watch the work, too old to do anything, while one of his sons was working there at the trade, to the best of our information as the contractor. Many of the old deeds in the valley are in the hand-writing of Henry Slagle. He must have been very popular with the Catholics, as the many offices he held attest. Another Protestant family adjoining the church more to the east, was the Keagys. Jacob Keagy settled on part of the Manor of Maske in 1752. The land in the possession of these older Protestant families, like that of the Catholics, hardly ever went out of their hands. These Protestants among a few others whose names have not come down to us, were good neighbors to the church, and when a little after the Revolution the present large stone building was erected, they gave their teams and lent their aid in what was then an important undertaking. These actions show their good will towards us, and we make this in acknowledgment of our respect for them.

We cannot trace all the early Catholic settlers. Many of their families have long since died out; and others were among the emigrants that drifted westward with the ever-flowing tide from here. Their descendants can be found to this day along the mountains and through the valleys of western Pennsylvania, Maryland and Virginia. They were the Catholic pioneers of those places. By 1730, there must have been twenty-five Catholic families scattered through this part of the Provinces. The records on the oldest tombstones partly preserved, show births as early as 1696 and the earliest death in 1725. They may have belonged to the older Maryland settlements.

Just as difficult is it to trace the first missionary labors in this mission. It is the gate which opened the route of travel for the missionaries into Pennsylvania, between Maryland and New York. There is a vague tradition, with hardly ground enough to record it, that the Jesuits were not the first priests to penetrate the forests of southern Pennsylvania.—The Franciscans, at an early period, and for a short time, had charge of the Maryland missions. The Recollects were with the French on the western frontier, but hardly early enough to antedate the Jesuits. The earliest missionary labor was among the Indians. Through here, on into Maryland, the Indians were more or less connected with the northern tribes among which the Jesuits were most successful at a very early date. Conewago was within twenty-five and fifty miles of some of the oldest Maryland missions; and the Indians through here being wandering subjects to other nations, probably having some knowledge and instruction from the St. Lawrence missions, the Maryland missionaries were almost sure to find their way among them. This valley is on the direct route between Maryland, Philadelphia and the north. The earliest connection and communication came through here.

The accounts of the early missionary labors in the Provinces are very meagre. We do not know what may be preserved in the archives of the Society of Jesus.

Upon the best authority it may be stated that the Franciscans, Revs. Polycarp Wicksted and James Haddock, did some missionary work through Pennsylvania and Maryland. The Franciscans were sent into Maryland by the Propaganda, but abandoned the mission about 1673-5. Rev. Basil Hobard died in Maryland in 1698, and Rev. James Haddock labored there as early as 1700, and died before 1720.

The Jesuits, Revs. Thos. Harvey, Henry Harrison and Charles Cage were in New York before 1700. Rev. Thos. Harvey was in Maryland in 1693, and died there in 1719, aged 84. Martin I. J. Griffin, Esq., who is so successfully rescuing the Catholic history of Philadelphia from oblivion, believes that Thos. Harvey is the priest spoken of in *The Records* of the Society of Jesus, (by Henry Foley, S. J., Vol. III., p. 354,) as having "*traveled on foot*" from new York to Maryland, after the suppression of Catholics in New York in 1690.

In the will of Peter Debuc, who died in Philadelphia in 1693, there is a bequest of fifty pounds to "Father Smith, now or late of Talbot Co., Md." It is the belief of several Catholic writers that "Father Smith" was no other than Rev. Henry Harrison. In the early history of this country, priests were often compelled to travel under assumed names and in various disguises.

It has been asserted that Mass was celebrated in Philadelphia before 1700, but Mr. Griffin has made close research and does not repeat the claim. Mass was celebrated there as early as 1708, probably by one of the fathers we have just mentioned.

The records of the English Province of the Society of Jesus say that Catholicity was introduced into Pennsylvania "about the year 1720," by Rev. F. Greaton and others. This declaration is repeated in two places in the Laity's Directory for 1822. Father Greaton was born in 1680, entered the Society of Jesus July 6th, 1708; was ordained and came into the Province of Maryland in 1719. His starting point most likely was old St. Inigoes. Rev. Thos. Harvey died in Maryland in 1719, and probably Father Greaton took up the work where he left off. He built the first church in Philadelphia in 1732, and labored there until 1750, being Superior of the Missions in Pennsylvania and Maryland, which were associated together. In 1750 he was recalled to Maryland, and died at Bohemia in 1752 or 1753.

If Catholicity was introduced into Pennsylvania about 1720, Conewago was the place. Besides the Indians who were friendly to the Catholics, there were births, deaths and marriages among Catholics in this settlement between 1720 and 1730. If there was a priest in the country he was here.

Many people place little confidence in tradition, but have we not our faith from tradition, as Jesus taught and the Apostles preached?

Samuel Lilly landed at Chester before 1730, and in that year removed to Conewago where he had heard the Jesuits had a settlement for some time. There was no church or priest at Chester, and for that reason he came to Conewago, where there were Catholics and where he could practice his religion. He was born in 1699, died in 1758, and is buried in the family lot in Conewago Cemetery. Miss Sally Lilly, born in 1800, and living yet, is one of his descendants. Besides her memory, which is clear and distinct, there is a record of the Lilly family preserved, so that we are not depending upon tradition to establish the fact that the Jesuits had "a settlement" here before 1730.

As an example of what tradition says upon this question, we take the testimony of Peter Smith, Esq., which we regard as equally important with the Lilly evidence. Peter Smith was a descendant of the earliest German settlers,—a very intelligent gentleman, a pious and practical Catholic and good citizen. He was born in 1794; died April 9th, 1884. He was baptized by Father Pellentz, and enjoyed a personal acquaintance and friendship with Fathers Gallitzin, De Barth and Lekeu. One of his daughters, Anastasia, is Sister De Sales, of St. Joseph's, McSherrystown. His earliest recollection was hearing it said that Father Josiah Creighton passed through the Conewago settlement in 1720, on his way to Philadelphia, dressed like a Quaker. Such intelligence could not have been derived from books, but is one of those traditional reminiscences repeated from time to time, and as a fragment of the past, is handed down through the centuries. It will outlast this print itself.

Among those who came to the settlement with the Diggeses, was Robert Owings, a surveyor. He was born in 1692 and died in 1759. He had a grant of five hundred acres, called Bear Garden, by letters patent, dated Oct. 8th, 1733, from "The Right Honourable, Charles, Lord Baron of Baltimore, and Avalon," &c., "under the great seal of said Province."— This tract bordered on Slagle's Run and the Little Conewago, and extended eastward, now three farms in possession of the Sneeringers. In the centre of the tract, on a slight elevation, was the colonial homestead of Robert Owings, Esq. It is a sacred place. There the first Mass was said, religious instruction given, and the rites of the church performed. In a Catholic Province and a Catholic settlement, Catholics thus escaped the severity of the existing penal laws. There also was the first burying ground. It continued to be used for church purposes until the log church was built in 1740 or 1741, a quarter of a mile southward, on a higher elevation, now occupied by the Chapel of the Sacred Heart. We never look over this sacred ground, hallowed by ages and consecrated by memory and associations, without being almost moved to tears. When the ancient forests yet covered the present site of Conewago Chapel, the Holy Sacrifice was being offered on this sacred spot, and the Red Man there stood in awe and admiration of ceremonies more solemn than he had ever seen in his own native solitude. A mysterious holiness surrounds the place. Nobility itself may there await the call of the great King of the Universe, and consecrated hands there be folded away in the dust of ages.

Rest in peace, O Indian Warrior! hidden foe never more will seek thee; thy warfare over, thy forests gone, thy sons no more,—no trace of chief or brave is left!

Eternal rest, poor pilgrim you! No father's dust is mingled with your own; no aged mother slumbers by your lonely side; far off your native land—dim its sacred memory,—lost, unknown, forgotten, where old ocean rolls along the sands of Time! O sweetly sleep, your work is done, your fields are green,—in peace your homes are blessed, and happy children play where first to its mother's breast your darling babe was pressed, and fondly lisped your own—a dear father's name!

O faithful shepherd, reign thou forever with the Keeper of the ransomed fold; joys divine be ever thine; heavenly peace and rest where no lambs stray and dangers threaten not the flock. Long since thy sheep were found, were sheltered, saved! Upon us, weary wanderers, look down! remember! pray!

THE LOG CHURCH BUILT.

Father Greaton was Superior of the Missions in Pennsylvania until 1750, with three Fathers assisting him. Rev. Robert Harding, S. J., came to this county in 1732, and labored through Maryland and Pennsylvania, and succeeded Father Greaton. Rev. Henry Neale, S. J., was one of Father Greaton's assistants, dying at St. Joseph's, Philadelphia, in 1748. Up to 1740, Conewago was not regularly visited by any priest, but from time to time by the several priests on the missions in both Provinces. When the Germans settled the valley around Littlestown in 1734 and 1735, they passed a "Mass-house" near a dense swamp, through which they made their way, and where their tracks could be seen long afterwards. Rev. John Ault, a late pastor of the Kreutz-Kirche congregation, wrote a full history of that settlement, in which he says that the Irish were not pleased because the Germans settled so near them in the valley. This feeling between the two elements in the valley did not come from religion or nationality, but arose from Digges' trouble with the settlers regarding the titles to their land.

At what time and under whom Conewago first became a Maryland mission, cannot be ascertained until the history of the older Maryland missions is written. According to what little knowledge we have of these, it is safe to say that Conewago was attended about once a month from a place in Harford County, Md., now or lately called "Hickory." How long such attendance dates before 1740, we are unable to say. If the Jesuits had any grant of land from Lord Baltimore, as is the common belief, it was made to these missionaries through their Superior. We would rather think that the first grant of land at Conewago was made through the Carrolls; that the greater portion was obtained from John Digges, and about one hundred acres at a much later period from Patrick McSherry. Not being able to see any of the deeds to these lands, we are not prepared to state the number of acres held, but it is generally placed somewhere about five hundred, now divided off into three fine farms.

The Germans began to push across the Susquehanna as early as 1730, and by 1740 there were a number of German families in the Conewago settlement, and a few scattered here and there in all the surrounding country. Among these people, two German Fathers were sent to labor. Rev. Theo. Schneider, S. J., a Bavarian, built the first church at Goshenhoppen, soon after 1740. He was born in 1703, and entered the Society in 1721. Rev. Wm. Wapeler, S. J., built the log church at Conewago in 1741, as near as can be ascertained. These men were "full of zeal and prudence." Father Wapeler was born in Westphalia, Jan. 22d, 1711, and entered the Society in 1728. Bishop Carroll says he converted and reclaimed many to the faith of Christ, during the eight years he remained in America. Bad health compelled him to return to Europe. He died at Bruges in 1781. The log church of Father Wapeler's time was built so as to appear as a private dwelling, so as not to be an open violation of the stringent penal laws then existing in the colonies,—the "best contrivances ever devised by the perverted ingenuity of man, for the degradation of the human soul and intellect." Thus Catholics were *permitted* to worship, not by the laws, but by public sentiment, which thus confessed its shame for the intolerant spirit of the mother country and its established church. Churches so built were called "Mass-houses," rather from suspicion than from public knowledge. The church at Conewago had three rooms, one in which services were held and two that were used for household purposes. Imagination can hardly picture the poverty of this humble place of worship. Being a Catholic settlement, with friendly Protestant neighbors, there is no record of Catholics ever having been disturbed. Father Wapeler had purchased land for a church at Lancaster at the same time, but in consequence of fears of a war with France, he became an object of suspicion, and the matter having been brought before the Council by Gov. Gordon, it was abandoned for the time.

FIRST RESIDENT PRIEST.

About this period, 1750, the missions in Pennsylvania were just becoming established and their organization was assuming definite shape. This was probably the most troublesome time for the church. Catholics were increasing in number, and scattering wherever new settlements were being formed. The missionaries were few, in a strange country and climate;—and these few mostly old and worn out. Means were wanting to carry on the work of building churches and pushing the missionary labor. It is said that up to the Revolution, only the churches in Baltimore and Philadelphia were able to make any contributions. Aid was extended through the Society in London, and some contributions to the missionary cause may have come from charitable individuals in Europe. The only record we have of this, is the report of Rev. George Hunter, Superior of the Jesuits, forwarded to Rev. J. Dennett in England, Provincial, in 1765. Conewago is called the mission of St. Francis Regis, with an annual income from the missionary plantation of twenty pounds, and twenty pounds more as aid from London. How long this aid was received, we have no way of ascertaining.

The unsettled condition of the country, the Indian troubles and the difficulties between the French and English regarding their possessions in the new world, all worked against the success of the missions. The Catholics suffered a great deal because of their friendship for the French. The suspicions of the English were unfounded, and the colonies never found truer friends than the Catholics. War was formally declared between the French and English in May, 1756. About this time it was alleged the French sent emissaries through York and adjacent counties, to incite the Catholics to rise against their Protestant neighbors. If such an effort was made. it failed. The local histories here assert that five Swiss Catholic families joined the French, but it is not likely that they were impelled by such motives. They may have had friends or relatives among the French, and moved with them into the far western settlement where the French had their headquarters.

The Pennsylvania Archives give an account of an examination by the authorities, who were suspicious that the Catholics in these missions might aid the French. Wm. Johnston was examined, and testified that he came from Naaman's Creek, on the Delaware River, to Baltimore County, Md., where he was sometime engaged in the service of Thomas Burgons and others, and attended at "Priest Neale's Mass-House." Father Neale was suspected of advocating the cause of the French against the English. When the struggle for Independence came, priests and people were among the first to sacrifice their lives and their property for the cause. It may not be out of place to state that Thos. Burgons alluded to in Wm. Johnston's examination, was no doubt the Burgoons family which at a later day Father Gallitzin rode many miles to visit in their sickness, an account of which his biographers give.

From a return made to Lord Louden, Commander of the British, April 29th, 1757, it appears that the number of Catholics in York County, such as received the sacraments, under the care of Matthias Manners, was 116 Germans and 73 Irish. It is impossible to tell how near correct this estimate was, but it is safe to say that it did not take in all the Catholics scattered through this section of the Provinces. The same enumeration gives the number of Catholics about Philadelphia and in Chester County, under Rev. Robert Harding; those in Philadelphia County, Berks, Northampton.

Bucks and Chester Counties, under Rev. Theodore Schneider; and under Rev. Ferdinand Farmer (Steinmeyer) in Lancaster, Berks, Chester and Cumberland Counties,—in all 1365.— Cumberland County extended from the Susquehanna to what is now the border line between Maryland and Pennsylvania, and Father Farmer journeyed in his missionary labors through all this section and the State, into New York and New Jersey. He was an untiring laborer. He came to Philadelphia in 1758, and died there in 1786.

Of Father Manners we know very little. He was the first priest stationed at Conewago, and his missionary field was large, taking in all this section of the States and extending westward along the mountains into Virginia. We do not know when he first came here, but he must have ministered on this mission up to 1758. It is said he was "a great man," and acted in the capacity of Provincial, but under what conditions and circumstances in the state the Society was in, we are not able to say. If even he was only Superior, there is no record to show who were his co-laborers. His proper name was Sittensperger. Why he officiated under an assumed name does not appear, but it might have been to avoid the interference of friends in the old country, who might have been opposed to his conversion, or *perversion* in their estimation, as we learn from the similar experience of other priests. At that time it was customary in both countries to translate proper names into the language of the country of adoption; and as *Sitten* in German is equivalent to *Manners* in English, Father Sittensperger may have thought it both *mannerly* as well as customary to Anglicize his name. That there was a graver cause than this, there is every reason to believe. At home at Conewago among his friends and those of the faith, he may have been known as Father Sittensperger, S. J.; but on his travels among strangers he was doubtlessly only recognized as Mr. Manners, a gentleman traveling for some purpose or other, except to the few Catholics he met, who knew him as a Catholic priest. Those were not halcyon days for the poor Catholic priests or people.

THE LOG CHURCH ENLARGED.

Since writing the last few chapters, we have discovered that Father Neale took up a tract of land at Conewago in his name. Rev. Henry Neale was an English Jesuit, arriving in this country in 1740, and doing missionary work as assistant to Father Greaton, of St. Joseph's, Philadelphia. In 1747, he took up 121 acres at Goshenhoppen, Berks County. He died in 1748, and was buried near the church in Philadelphia. This tract, no doubt, is the large body of land now held by the Society, and was then part of Digges' Choice.

Up to the Revolution the church had no head or organization in this country. The Jesuits were the principal missionary workers in the eastern States. The Society was being persecuted in Europe, and was eventually suppressed, in 1773, though it was an act of compulsion, never carried out except in appearance as a matter of policy. The members of the Society in this country continued to live and labor under their rules, as the troublesome circumstances would best permit.— They were governed by the representative of the Superior of the Society who resided in London. The Provincial or representative so appointed resided at St. Thomas' Mission, near Port Tobacco, in Maryland, still the residence of the Superiors, or so at least up to the recent formation of the tri-State province of Maryland, Pennsylvania and New York. We do not know that there is any record, giving the names and dates of appointment of the first Superiors in this country. Probably Rev. John Williams, an English Jesuit, was Superior as early as 1763; Father John or George Hunter as early as 1765, and Superior and Vicar-General in 1794, according to Scharff.— Father John Lewis was Superior some time during the revolutionary period. As we have said before, there seems to be no definite record of the early missionary priests. Baltimore itself was only a station before the Revolution, supplied once a month from White Marsh. When we compare the church to day with the missionary field at that time, we are astonished at the labor they performed and the hardships and inconveniences they underwent. Now the church has Bishops and Archbishops, a Cardinal; thousands of churches and priests; colleges, seminaries and religious institutions, and all the comforts and conveniences of a progressive age and of a powerful country. The poor missionaries left their homes and were driven from their country; they came into the new settlements, strangers among strangers, without any churches or congregations or friends, looked upon with suspicion by the people and hampered and persecuted by the laws; but they held their ground, performed a noble work in guarding the infant church and building up what is now the mightiest religious structure in America. May the church never forget her founders,—the poor, scattered Catholics, and the daring, persevering missionaries. They lived, labored and died for the faith. All honor to them, and may God increase their reward for all the ages of eternity. How much we have! how little we do! How little they had; yet what wonders did they not accomplish.

In 1758, June 9th, four priests arrived in the Maryland missions from England. They were James Frombach, James Pellentz, John Williams, but who the fourth was we are not certain. Father Christopher Andrews lived with Father Pellentz for nearly forty years, "a faithful servant," and died at Conewago Nov. 2d, 1799, at the age of nearly one hundred years. We may suppose that he was one of the company of four, but are not certain. Father Frombach succeeded Father Manners as Superior, and remained at Conewago ten years. He spent a year and a half at Lancaster, and then went to Frederick, from which place his missionary travels extended through western Maryland into Virginia, as far as Winchester. He was a model missionary priest, an example of every virtue,— mild, patient, modest, obedient, pious and zealous. His death record is entered at Conewago, Aug. 27th, 1795. He died of a contagious fever; some say at St. Inigoes, Md., which may agree with the record of his death, "in comitatu Mariae, in Marylandia."

Father Frombach was assisted while Superior of Conewago by Father Detrich, a French gentleman, during whose time an addition was built to the old church, and another small room attached thereto. Father Pellentz's name also appears, especially on the different missions, so that he most likely made Conewago his home from 1758 to 1768, and went out on the surrounding missions,—Frederick, Hagerstown and the valleys along the mountains. He succeeded Father Frombach as Superior. Father Andrews was no doubt his assistant, both on the missions and after he became Superior. It is sad to think that so little knowledge is preserved of these Fathers and their labors. We know that they rode on horseback many miles to visit the sick and minister to the wants of the Catholics, that they had to undergo many hardships and dangers, but beyond this little else is known. Whatever information may be gained from kind friends who are interested and better informed on such matters, we shall be only too glad to give later on.

THE SACRED HEART BUILT.

The Revolutionary period was one of trial and gloomy foreboding for the colonists, and especially so for the Catholics. War with the mother country cut them off from all communication or authority with the church in Europe and the head of the Society in England. There were dangers to be feared from such freedom from authority, but in greater straits than this the church had found able men raised up for its rescue. So with the infant church in the colonies. Among the few priests were men of strong mind and determined purpose,—men of example and judgment, who by their labors and their virtues inspired priests and people with confidence and encouragement. Independence, like the sun after the darkest storm, brought light and freedom and prosperity to the people; the church shared in the new life and light thus spread. Many things rendered it necessary that the church should have established authority in America, from Rome and not from London, now that America rendered her no more allegiance. Rev. John Carroll was appointed Vicar-Apostolic, consecrated Bishop in 1790, and raised to the Archbishopric in 1809.

Father Carroll visited Conewago in 1784, and administered the Sacrament of Confirmation, and again about 1811. He placed the number of communicants at Conewago on his first visit at one thousand. There are but few living now who were confirmed by Bishop Carroll. Miss Sallie Lilly, no doubt, is one of them, and there may be several more in the valley, who were born about 1800.

From this time the growth of the church was rapid everywhere, and on a sound and healthy basis. There were a few weak points here and there which caused trouble, but they deserve now to be forgotten as they served only to strengthen the church the more permanently. Diocese after diocese was formed, new Bishops and Archbishops created, and so the work is now going on successfully to-day. First Conewago was under the Bishop of Baltimore, then it belonged to the Diocese of Philadelphia and now it is in that of Harrisburg. It is subject, of course, like always, to the Superiors and Provincials of the Society of Jesus, and they to the Father-General in Rome, or wherever he may temporarily reside. In religious matters it is governed by the rules of the Church as they relate to the Orders and the Bishops in their respective dioceses.

We come now to one of the most important periods in the history of the Conewago Church, when the present stone church was built by Father Pellentz. The church was spreading and growing everywhere. The greatest trouble experienced was the want of priests, especially men of executive ability, who could by their energy and perseverance, with the limited means at hand, build suitable churches for the accommodation of the increasing number of Catholics. Conewago was truly blessed with such a man, in the person of Father James Pellentz, S. J. As a missionary he had attended to the widely scattered missions of Maryland and Pennsylvania, and as a German his services were required in more places than he could possibly render them. We find him at Frederick, at Lancaster, and intervening points; at Carlisle and through the valley to Hagerstown, and later on having in charge the border settlements along the mountains, of which he was relieved by Father Gallitzin. His principal assistant at Conewago was Father Andrews, whom he calls a "faithful servant," which implies more than we can express—the whole burden of church work at Conewago, as Father Pellentz had many outside duties and matters of business which claimed his attention. Two other priests' names are mentioned as assistants to Father Pellentz, but no dates can be given. They were Fathers Charles Sewell and Sylvester Boarman, of the Society, and could not have been at Conewago very long before Father Pellentz's death. There were other priests on the Maryland and Pennsylvania missions, who came to Conewago off and on, but were never stationed.

The building of canals and public roadways shortly after the Revolution, brought many Irish and German Catholics into the States, and wherever they went missionaries were sent among them. Conewago increased rapidly in population, and the rich farming lands brought increased wealth and prosperity. When Father Pellentz succeeded Father Frombach as Superior about 1768, the want of a larger church was already beginning to be felt. The log church must have been but a small place, with bare walls and rude benches and hardly a floor in it except around the altar and the small room attached. Everything that entered the building had to be furnished in the settlement, and the means for any kind of work were very limited. Travel was then yet mostly by horseback, so that people were depending to a great extent upon their own resources, cut off from the towns by long distances through an unsettled country.

Many of the Catholics of Conewago were then considered well-to-do, and were as intelligent and appreciative of the comforts of life as people are now. Father Pellentz saw the need of improvements, so that religion might take the lead in the growth of the country. Any steps towards carrying out his plans were out of the question, on account of the troubles and uncertainties occasioned by the war of Independence.

When peace was restored and the country attained a separate and independent existence, the future of the church like that of the land became brighter and more promising — Father Pellentz lost no time in making preparations for his great work. There was money to be collected, material to be furnished and worked out, and many things to be attended to in the erection of so large and finished a building. The stone for the church had to be quarried and dressed near East Berlin, and hauled a distance of ten or fifteen miles. The erection of the Church of the Sacred Heart was begun sometime in 1786 and completed in 1787. It stands to-day as solid and substantial as ever. We have no record of its dedication and consecration. The old log church was removed, and services were probably held in one of the rooms of the house or temporary place of dwelling. The parsonage was built at the same time, and like the church has since been enlarged and improved. There was a quaint old cupola on the church, but whether it was put up at the same time, or later by Fathers DeBarth and Lekeu, we are unable to find out. The one hundredth anniversary of the building of this church will be appropriately celebrated next year. The Fathers held a picnic in the grove adjoining the church on the 28th of July, just passed, and realized nearly $500, which will be devoted to the celebration of this anniversary. In this church, Father

Pellentz has left a greater monument to his memory than our humble pen can inscribe.

"This Father's memory is still, and will ever be, affectionately and gratefully cherished by the pastors and congregation of Conewago, as one of the most liberal, charitable and zealous of men and benefactors, and as a shepherd who laid down his life for his flock, after many weary years of incessant and successful labor, in erecting and perpetuating a church in which thousands and tens of thousands were expected and destined to worship their Maker, and save their immortal souls."

A short sketch of the church, written about 1830 by one of the Fathers, from information of one of the oldest inhabitants, has the following allusion to the present church as it then appeared: "As it respects the settlement in which it is placed, it is not too much to say that few settlements, if any, will be found in the United States composed of a more dense, wealthy, economical, industrious and intelligent population. The farm attached to the church contains about 500 acres, of probably the very best quality of land in the State of Pennsylvania. The present church is built of rough-stone, the front of a peculiar sort of red sandstone, found some miles distant from the church, of a very strong texture, and is about 60 feet long, 40 feet high and about 80 feet broad, [taking in the whole front of the building and parsonage,] with a semi-diagonal sanctuary at the east end of about 20 feet, this showing it to be one of the largest buildings for public worship as yet in the interior of the country, exclusive of towns and cities." * * * "Father Pellentz was a missionary of the most exemplary piety, of untiring zeal, of the most agreeable and fascinating manners, and certainly possessed of uncommon influence, not only over his own flock but also possessing the affection and confidence of persons of other religious denominations, else it would have been impossible for him to have erected at such an early period, and at such heavy expense, a building of such dimensions. Suffice it to say, that those few, without distinction of religious creeds, who have survived him, and who were personally acquainted with him, speak in the most exalted terms of his character and by them his memory is held in the highest veneration."

James Pellentz, S. J., was born in Germany, Jan. 19th, 1727; entered the Society in 1744, and made his profession in 1756. He filled the office of Vicar-General to Bishop Carroll in 1791, and was present at the first Council of Baltimore. He died, according to the record entered at Conewago, on March 13th, 1800, and was buried on the 15th. He was at old St. Joseph's in Philadelphia in Nov., 1765, as appears from the baptismal register.

FR. PELLENTZ TO FR. DE BARTH.

Every effort to obtain some connected account of the history of Conewago during this period, has been fruitless.—There are conflicting statements regarding the successor of Father Pellentz as Superior in 1800. If Father Brosius was Superior at all, it was for a very short time. We are inclined to think that he was not, but may have been acting as such until a permanent Superior was appointed. Between Father Pellentz and Fathers De Barth and Lekeu, there is a space of some years when there was no permanent Superior, but different priests acting in that capacity. The priests who were at Conewago about this time, attended the different missions more or less alternately, as best suited the various conflicting circumstances. The Bishop was then beginning to exercise his authority, and getting his large and scattered household in something like working order. Demands were made upon him for a German priest here, an English one there, and one for the Irish somewhere else. The Provincial of the Jesuits was Rev. Robert Molyneaux, who had succeeded Father Lewis. The church kept meeting the growing needs of the people, and laying the foundations for vast future extensions. Colleges were being founded and native priests supplied, upon whom the church was soon to depend in a great measure. The Sulpitians founded St. Mary's College, and the Jesuits that of Georgetown. Religious orders were beginning to be introduced, to aid in the increasing work of the church, and from the humble start of Mother Seton at Emmettsburg, sprang that vast religious body which is now to be found carrying on schools and asylums and charitable works everywhere. It is not our plan or purpose to enter into any details outside of our limited field, for it could not be more than a passing notice. Thanks to able and learned men, these grounds are well covered by the History of the Catholic Church in the United States, the Life of Mother Seton, History of the Catholic Church in Western Pennsylvania, Life of Father Gallitzin, and other valuable works. If only Catholics would give more encouragement to this branch of church literature!

Rev. F. X. Brosius was the young priest who came to this country with Prince Gallitzin in 1792. He was a very useful missionary. Just what time he spent at Conewago it is impossible to designate. Father Middleton, O. S. A., places him here in 1801, and at Baltimore in 1804-5. According to Mr. Griffin he was at Lancaster in 1796, where he issued the "Reply of a Roman Catholic Priest to a Peace-Loving Preacher of the Lutheran Church;" in 1806 in Philadelphia; 1807, he founded a "Seminary" or School at Mont Airy, adjoining Philadelphia; 1813, he issued at Philadelphia "The Elements of Natural or Experimental Philosophy;" 1815, at Jamaica Plains, near Boston, where he taught German to Geo. Ticknor; 1816, April 14th, his first baptismal record appears at the Cathedral, Boston, and his last on June 28th.—Then he went to Germany, or brobably first to Cincinnati, then started for Europe. His name appears as sponsor on the baptismal records of Conewago on the following dates: Feb. 7th, 1794; May 25th, 1795; Nov. 25th, 1798; Oct. 24th, 1800; Nov. 3d, 1800; April 28th, 1803.

March 2d, 1793, there is a baptism recorded, with the name of Rev. P. Erntzen given as sponsor. The "P." may signify "Father" from the Latin *Pater*. There is some doubt as to the correctness of his name, as it is impossible to distinguish the "n" from the "u." Father Middleton gives his name as "Enntzen" or "Erntzen," which latter would correspond with the record. Rev. Paul Dominic Enntzen or Erntzen was the fifth pastor of Goshenhoppen, from April, 1793, to May, 26th, 1818. The same Father was at Lebanon from 1801 to 1804.

It has also been stated by some that Father Pellentz was succeeded as Superior by Father Charles Sewell or Father Sylvester Boarman, both of whom labored at Conewago some time before and after 1800.

These priests were assisted by Fathers Cerfoumont, Manly or Maunly, Mertz, Zocchi, and others. There is mention of a Father *Zockley*, which most likely meant Rev. Nicolaus or Nicholas Zocchi, who succeeded Father Gallitzin at Taneytown. Rev D. Stanislaus Cerfoumont was a missionary priest for nineteen years, and died at Conewago Aug. 2d, 1804, aged 53. He was one of the priests present at the first Council of Baltimore in 1791. Of Father Manly nothing is known. Father John Nicholas Mertz was at Conewago in 1804,—his name appearing only once on the register of baptisms. Father Middleton places him here from Aug., 1803, to Nov., 1805; from Dec. 6th, 1805, to May 20th, at Baltimore; in 1828 at Java, N. Y.; 1829, at Buffalo; about 1836 to 1838, at Eden, and Western New York; dying Aug. 10th, 1844, aged 81. Bishop Timon wrote that Father Mertz was pastor at Conewago in 1826, for three years, and left it in 1829 for Buffalo and Eden, N. Y., "where he labored with the most untiring zeal from the year 1829 till his death."— He was a native of Germany, where he was ordained in 1791, and was received into the Diocese of Baltimore by Bishop Carroll in 1811, "by whom he was always much respected and esteemed."

We come to another name in the history of Conewago, of a man the record of whose life and labors would fill a volume itself, and that is Demetrius Augustine de Gallitzin.— He was born at the Hague, Dec. 22d. 1770. His father was high in favor at the Russian Court, and the young prince himself was destined for a soldier and statesmen, but Providence ordained otherwise. His mother was of noble birth, and to her training is due to a great extent the religious course of the Prince's life. She herself was misled for a time, but lived and died a model christian woman and a Catholic. There are many traits of character in the life of Father Gallitzin which challenge our admiration. Catholic youth should study his life. Born to vast estates and all the honors of nobility, he forfeited all and became the humble missionary, of Loretto, in the wild and distant country of the Alleghany mountains, in America. His life was a continual sacrifice of all that the world had to offer. Friends and kindred, home and country and everything, he left to become a poor, traveling missionary, living and laboring for others, with never a thought of himself. In coming to this country, he assumed the name of Herr Schmett, from the family of his mother, who was the daughter of Countess Ruffert and Marshal Count Schmetteau. From this he derived the American name of Mr. Smith, which he kept until changed by an act of the Pennsylvania Legislature. He joined the Sulpitians in this country, and was ordained a priest March 18th, 1795, and was sent to Conewago. From here he attended the missions for many miles around. The great aim and object of his life was to found a Catholic colony. Starting with a few Catholic families in 1799, when he left Conewago, he gave all his means and energies towards its accomplishment; and from this humble beginning at Maguire's settlement, among the Alleghany mountains, in Cambria County, Pennsylvania, he raised up a church and a Catholic people, cultivated the land and cleared the forests, so that at his death all the blessings of home and religion were enjoyed by thousands of happy souls, where once a lone wilderness spread its attending desolation. Father Gallitzin died at Loretto, May 6th, 1840. He visited Conewago at different times during his life, and many people yet have a personal recollection of this saintly priest. Poor, dear Father Gallitzin! When discouraged by the sad failures of life, and disgusted at the hollow deceits of the world, we recall the sacrifices, privations and sufferings of this truly noble man, we become reconciled to fate and feel that we have done nothing to entitle us to the miserable existence an unworthy life affords.

FR. DE BARTH TO FR. LEKEU.

With the growth of the country and that of towns and villages, the days of the traveling missionary were drawing to a close. In the beginning of the present century all the outlying missions had already been supplied with churches, and priests stationed at the most central points, who supplied the wants of the Catholics within their reach. So the priests of the community at Conewago had their respective fields of labor. Littlestown, York and Carlisle were the first places provided with church buildings, and where there were none, services were held at first once a month in a room of some Catholic family, where the surrounding Catholics would meet. The priests made use of the best means in their power to keep the Catholics who were far from churches well grounded in their religion, and that was "Catechism." Who does not remember the happy days when "going to Catechism!" Before schools or churches were built, the priests would give instructions at stated times wherever a few Catholic children or people could be gotten together; at the same time, baptizing, marrying, and performing all the rites of the church as necessity demanded. All the surrounding towns, villages and country places were thus visited by the Conewago Fathers. Those were days of trials for the Catholics, and the sacrifices they made to practice their religion show that the faith was strong in them. Who to-day walks ten and twenty miles to hear Mass on Sundays and holy days of obligation? With all our modern conveniences many of us are exceedingly careless and negligent in this respect. Our fathers and mothers tell us that they walked from the "barrens,"—from beyond Abbottstown and the Pigeon Hills in Paradise, from East Berlin and Pinetown (now New Chester) to the vicinity of Gettysburg, and down by Littlestown to the country below Hanover,—walked many a time from these places to Conewago Chapel to church, carrying their shoes in their hands as far as Slagle's Run or the Conewago and there putting them on, and feeling as neat and trim in linsey dress and homespun as we do to-day in silk and broadcloth. How times and customs change, while the church suits herself to every need and circumstance and goes on forever! We who are proud and haughty and religious only for fashion's sake, might learn a wholesome lesson from the simple manners and true piety of our forefathers of the "good old time." And if some writer one hundred years hence undertakes to teach his generation by the example and practice of this age, O what is to become of our boasted civilization!

Among the priests who were at Conewago from 1800 to 1820, and of whom we have nothing but mere mention, are the following: Rev. Matthew Carr, O. S. A., in 1807. He established the Order of St. Augustine in Philadelphia in 1795, and started the building of the church of St. Augustine. Rev. Francis Rolof from 1808 to 1810, who was in Baltimore in 1828. Father Marshall, in 1814; there was a Rev. Francis Xavier Marshall at Reading in 1839, and this may be the same one. Father Middleton puts the date of Father Matthew Lekeu's coming to Conewago as May 26th, 1817, and probably he labored here continuously from that time till his

CATHOLIC LOCAL HISTORY.

departure for France about 1843. Rev. P. Rantzun or Ranson was at Conewago in 1818. This was no doubt Rev. Maximilian Rantzau, spelt so himself in his will, a copy of which we have. He was born in Munster near Westphalia, Dec. 23d, 1769; died at Frederick, Aug. 7th, 1827. Father Vincent Phil. Mayerhoffer was at Conewago in 1819. There is mention of Fathers Cummysky and Stogan, as assistants to Father De Barth; Rev. J. W. Beschter is also mentioned in that capacity, but we do not know at what time he came to Conewago. A breviary preserved in the old library has the following inscription; "Ad usum J. W. Beschter, 1816."— This must have been when he was a young priest, for he died at Conewago (Paradise) more than twenty-five years afterwards. There is a death record at Conewago of Father Patrick O'Connor, July 18th, 1816. Whether he labored here any length of time, is not known. He was probably a Maryland priest.

The Revolution in France was a blessing to the church in America. What Europe lost by her wars against religion, this country gained. The Jesuits were great missionaries, teachers and statesmen, and worked for great ends. The Society of Jesus was founded as an army to battle against the enemies of religion; to fight the battles of the church against infidelity, and to stand between the powers of the world, the flesh and the demon in their attacks upon God, His church and His poor. The prayer of its saintly founder, St. Ignatius Loyola, was for continual persecution of its members, so that they might become grim warriors used to the struggles that light is bound to meet with darkness as long as time shall exist. Like the soldier, the Jesuits are trained to religious austerities from youth to the grave, and they are practiced in every mode of christian warfare. They are as learned a body of men as the world will ever see. Their school of theology is the grandest in the history of the church. As teachers they have hardly an equal, and when they once have the training of a youth his habits as a rule are formed for a life-time. No wonder that they are persecuted by the world of cruel and ambitious tyrants; for if religion is to be crushed, the Jesuits will have to be conquered first. All the intrigues of men have been brought against them in vain, and though their suppression may have been thus accomplished, themselves slandered, calumniated and persecuted, it only served to make them stronger and more powerful in the cause of religion. Defeated in one place, they turned up in another with half a nation converted to the church before their enemies knew what had become of them. Thus it seems providential that when Europe ceased to be a profitable field of missionary labor, persecution drove the Jesuits into other countries where they met with unbounded success.

Among those whose names will ever adorn the annals of the Society in America, Adolphus Lewis de Barth is not the least. Next to Father Pellentz is his memory cherished at Conewago, and his life and labors here rank with those of such Companions as Lekeu, Enders, Deneckere, Villiger and Emig, in what they have done for Conewago. He was born Nov. 1st, 1764; came to this country shortly before 1800; labored at Bohemia Manor, Maryland; at St. Joseph's, Philadelphia in 1795; at Lancaster a number of years; Vicar-General to Bishop Egan, and administrator from his death in 1814 to 1820, when he became Superior at Conewago. He remained here until 1828, when he became rector at St. John's Church, Baltimore, where now stands the beautiful church of St. Alphonsus. In 1838, his growing infirmities compelled him to retire for rest to Georgetown College, where he died a saintly death, October 13th, 1844. His name occurs at Conewago in 1807. He signed his name "L. Barth" and "Lewis Barth." He is further mentioned at Conewago in 1804, 1809 and 1815. His name is pronounced "De Bart" by the old people who knew him. It is said that he was pastor at Conewago for twenty-five years, but he could not have been such and performed his official duties to the Bishop and the Diocese. He may have been connected with Conewago and had more or less supervision, from the beginning of this century to 1828. In 1820, the pew system was introduced, and on that question there was a decided difference between himself and Father Lekeu. The sketch of 1830 says Father De Barth was the "Presiding Pastor" of Conewago Congregation, and Father Britt the "Superior of the Fathers of the same house." Be that as it may, we know that Father De Barth managed the property and all the business and papers were transacted in his name. He received power of attorney from Rev. Francis I. Neale, of Georgetown College, June 21st, 1811, for the estate at Conewago,—then already "in his possession," which had been bequeathed to Father Neale by Father Molyneaux and held by Father Pellentz, and transferred from Father De Barth to Father Lekeu in 1828. Father Neale we presume was the successor of Rev. Robert Molyneaux as Provincial of the Jesuits.

When the Society of Jesus was reorganized under its rules in this country, a number of Jesuits from Europe joined its ranks. In Russia the Order was protected and it existed there when more or less suppressed and expelled from the other countries. "That good Franciscan of the Vatican," said Frederick the Great of Pope Sixtus V., from whom the brief of suppression had been wrung,—(compulsus feci! compulsus feci!)—"leaves me my dear Jesuits, who are persecuted everywhere else. I will preserve the precious seed, so as to be able one day to apply it to such as may desire again to cultivate this rare plant."

Conewago received a part of this precious seed. Fathers Adam Britt and Michael Joseph Byrne were priests from White Marsh, Russia, and were among Father De Barth's assistants. Father Britt was stricken with paralysis while on the altar, and was carried to his room. He died July 8th, 1822, in his 81st year, after receiving all the rites of the church. Father Byrne died March 28th, 1823, and was buried on the 30th. He was a missionary in the city of Lancaster, and was aged forty-six years. Fathers Larhue and Divin were also assistants about 1822, but of them we know nothing more.

FROM FR. LEKEU TO FR. ENDERS.

There is never any rest for man in this world, no matter how long his life nor how successful his works. We are speaking of laborers, those who have been brought up busy and active at any employment. If old age or infirmity compels rest and retirement, it turns into weariness and unrest that betokens approaching dissolution. So with the Fathers who had grown old in the service of the church at Conewago. They always found something to do, and were ever planning some means of temporal and religious improvement for the community. Not one of them but what he had to be persuaded that it was necessary he should be relieved of his active duties and take the rest which age demanded, and even then compliance was only in response to authority, sacredly and religiously observed for a life-time. Poor Fathers, they loved their household as parents love their family, and their only desire was to care for it to the end.

The people of the valley at present would be surprised could they see Conewago as it was yet in 1830, and along there. Dense woods extended all around. These furnished timber for all the improvements that have since been made. The large tract of woodland reaching back to the Keagy property, and about the last belonging to the Chapel farms, was cleared out some years ago and used in the building of O'Bold's large barn, and in the new house and barn of the third church farm, on the Hanover road. We can only guess at the dates when the farm buildings were erected and the church improvements made. The old stone house, torn down when the present dwelling of James Devine was built, was probably the work of Father Pellentz; as also the old brick barn; for this can be called the homestead on the church property. There stood several small houses along the hill, that were built in the beginning of this century. Father Enders, in his time, removed an old brick house and built a new one, in which Henry Kaehler lived, now occupied by his widow and sons. Henry Kaehler was a "faithful servant" at the church for a number of years, and his sons, especially Joseph, succeeded him, attending to the stables, the grape arbor, and such work. The brother attends to the garden. Father Enders also tore down an old log house at the foot of the hill and built a new one, now used by the Fathers until the repairs of their house adjoining the church are finished. The house and barn on the second church farm, occupied by the Smalls for a number of years, were probably built by Father Lekeu, or near his time.

Father Matthew Lekeu received power of attorney from Father Neale, to manage his estate at Conewago, July 24th, 1828, just about the time Father De Barth left. He must then already have been acting as Superior of Conewago.— Father Lekeu is still well remembered by many people who went to instructions to him in their childhood. The missions grew and prospered during his management, and substantial improvements were made at Conewago, in the church and on the farms. In many respects he was "too good and easy," and when he was taken away, Father Lilly was sent on to straighten up business matters and adjust accounts. Father Matthew Lekeu was a native of Belgium, born 1788, entered the Society in 1816, and became a priest about 1823. About 1843, he was stationed at Newtown, Md. Shortly after that he sailed for his native land, where he died some years later. His name is pronounced "Leck-eu;" the German element pronounced his name short, "Leckie." He wrote his name Lekeu.

The sketch of the church written about this time, between 1828 and 1830, says Father Lekeu was assisted by Fathers Kohlman and Dougherty, S. J., "under whose administration the congregation appears in the following truly prosperous and flourishing condition: If we look at the natural advantages which the beautiful valley of Conewago presents, in regard to fertility of soil, healthfulness of climate, profusion of all kinds of produce, and the artificial improvements of towns, villages, mills and other water works, together with a ready market, we cannot but place it among the most prosperous settlements in the Union. Yet gratifying as these advantages may appear, when the congregation as a body is taken in a religious point of view, it must afford matter of still more sincere and edifying congratulation. The number of communicants at Conewago Church is supposed to be about 2400, and taking into consideration the number of infants [children], the whole number of Catholics may be estimated at between 3000 and 4000. This congregation was originally composed of the adjoining places of Littlestown, Gettysburg, Mountain Church, Carlisle, York and Brandt's in Pigeon Hills; but as small churches have been erected in each of the above places, they may now he properly considered as branches emanating from the principal or parent congregation of Conewago,—more especially as three of said places still resort to Conewago on great festivals, York and Carlisle having been allowed a separate priest, and also Pigeon Hills—Brandt's Chapel,—they may now be considered as separate congregations, under the pastoral care of Rev. Mr. Dween (probably Divin,) and Father Beschter."

Of the assistants of Father Lekeu, little is recorded. C. Paulus Kohlman, S. J., was a brother of Anthony Kohlman. They were distinguished priests. Father Michael Dougherty was born in Ireland, and made great sacrifices to enter the Society. The Provincial particularly recommended him to the care and kind treatment of his Superiors. He was a valuable laborer at Conewago, and at the neighboring missions. He was born Aug. 15th, 1791; died Aug. 27th, 1863, at Conewago. Ferdinand Helias, S. J.. labored several years at Conewago, and was then sent to Missouri. The name of Rev. J. Randanne appears about this period, but he was probably among the priests called to Conewago by the Sulpitian Seminary at the Pigeon Hills, near New Oxford. Priests also came down from Mount St. Mary's, and during vacation some priests and students would make the trip on foot; thus we find such names as Brute, Dubois, Gildea, Elder, O'Brien, and others connected with Conewago.

During the latter part of Father Lekeu's ministry, he was assisted by Fathers Barber, Kendler, Steinbacher, Beschter, Zacchi, Tuffer, Gibbons, Villiger, Hatting, Cotting, and others. Father Virgil H. Barber has a very interesting personal history, and we shall give a fuller account of his life further on. In the history of the other mission churches we shall find some particulars regarding the labors of these priests. Father Cotting built the church at Gettysburg, and attended Paradise and Littlestown a while. Fathers Beschter and Zacchi served Paradise church for a time. Rev. John W. Beschter died there Jan. 6th, 1842, and he was buried at Conewago. He was for many years a zealous missionary in Pennsylvania and Maryland; a man of a kind and good-natured disposition, and was much esteemed by all who knew him.

July 19th, 1844, an ordination was performed at Georgetown, D. C., by Archbishop Eccleston, at which Messrs. Michael Tuffer, Milesius Gibbons and George Villiger, of the Society of Jesus, received the sub-deaconship. On the day following they were ordained deacons, and on the 22d were promoted to the dignity of the priesthood. Conewago was their first field of labor.

While Father Lekeu was Superior he had pews placed in the church, of a more comfortable make than the old-time seats. He made other improvements around the church and on the farms. He had some friends in France who were in good circumstances, and they sent him a number of valuable presents, among them a fine set of vestments and a rich chime of bells. Father McElroy had at the same time procured a bell for his church, at Frederick. His bell and Father Lekeu's chimes were taken together from Baltimore to Frederick. Mr. John Lilly was sent with his wagon from Conewago to

Frederick for Father Lekeu's bells. When he arrived there Father McElroy had them already in use, and the single bell was sent to Conewago. It is said that Father Lekeu did not like the exchange, but this old bell has rendered much valuable service, and from its lofty place in the belfry of the new spire it may call the faithful to the service of the church for a century or more to come.

Father Nicholas Steinbacher, S. J., succeeded Father Lekeu as Superior of Conewago, about 1843. He is said to have been a man of great determination of purpose, and a very pious priest. He made considerable improvement in the interior of the church. He had it painted by an artist from Philadelphia, Mr. Monaschei, who also painted some of the beautiful pictures still on the walls, and made paintings for some of the mission churches. A brother of Father Steinbacher was building a church at Lancaster at the same time, and called upon him for help at Conewago, but this Father told him he had all he could do to pay for his own undertakings. Father N. Steinbacher was afterwards pastor of St. Mary's Church, Erie, Pa. The pleasure of writing a history of old Conewago is turned into regret, for the want of fuller records. Many of the priests have to be passed by with the mere mention of their name, for there is nothing to show where they came from or where they went to, and no dates to go by. Rev. Joseph Enders succeeded Father Steinbacher as Superior of Conewago, in 1847.

THE WORK OF FATHER ENDERS.

People who become dearly attached to a man, through personal friendship or on account of successful accomplishments in whatever interests them, are apt to think that after him, no more such able leader and great and good man can be found. This is a pleasing delusion, but the grandest tribute that friend can pay to a friend, or inferior to superior. History is filled with such delusions, and the world has learned by many a sad lesson that no matter how great and eminent the man in any profession, work or calling in life, there is always someone to take his place and continue what he may have begun. Soldiers, statesmen and rulers; learned prelates of the church, men of fame in the arts and sciences—all have shared but the common end of nature, yet the world moves on as fast and unconcerned to-day as if the whole universe was the work of its hand for time and eternity.

On the same principle, the good people of Conewago from time to time are favored with a Superior so kind and well beloved, such an able manager and successful laborer, that surely they say his equal will never again be had. How little did the dear friends of Fathers De Barth and Lekeu expect Conewago to be blessed with such good old priests again! The young carpenter priest who was appointed Superior in 1847, became not only such a blessing, but a greater benefactor, and as noble a father and kind a pastor as any found in the annals of the church. Father Enders! Go from one end of the extensive parish of Conewago to the other, and from old and young, rich and poor, nothing will be heard but words of praise and fondest expressions of remembrance for Rev. Joseph Enders, who was truly a father to all. The work of his hands will attest his love and devotion for Conewago when the generations now springing up shall have passed away and be known no more. The congregation is larger and more prosperous than ever; the church farms are better cultivated, and improved with substantial buildings; the Church of the Sacred Heart is well preserved and greatly enlarged, with handsome spire, marble altar and rich interior adornments; but better than all this perishable work was the saintly life, — in patience, humility, charity and resignation,—of this faithful servant, which we may hope has brought him into his eternal reward. In that communion of saints which reaches to the throne of the Most High, we trust to be remembered in the prayers of those who only lived, labored and prayed for these entrusted to their charge here below.

The want of a larger church was already felt at Conewago in Father De Barth's time. There is a drawing of a proposed improvement preserved from 1828. It contemplated additions on each side of the main building, crowned with turrets and centre spire, like many of the great churches of Europe. The first thought of Father Enders when he came to Conewago was to enlarge the church or to build a new one in some other part of the parish. There was no church then at Hanover, New Oxford nor Bonneauville. Meetings were held at Conewago and at the principal surrounding points.— The Rt. Rev. Bishop and the Very Rev. Father Provincial were consulted, and their opinions announced to the congregation. Their views were the same as those of the Superior himself and the largest part of the congregation, all agreeing that it would be best to enlarge the Conewago church. Having thus decided what to do, Father Enders made every preparation to begin the work. At a meeting of the congregation, it was decided to appoint a building committee, and the appointment was left to Father Enders. He selected Jacob Dellone, Jacob Smith, Henry Reily, Charles Will and John Busbey, representing the different sections of the parish; they met and elected Father Enders Chairman and Treasurer.— Subscription papers were drawn up on the 10th day January, 1849, and from that time the work went on successfully to its completion in 1851. The enlargement was in cross-form, 45 feet wide to transept,—which is 85 feet,—125 feet in depth and 38 feet high. The Sanctuary and part of the old church had to be removed. The new part then covered the *oldest* part of the graveyard, where several of the priests had been buried. Thus of the eight or ten Fathers buried there, there is no mark left, except of those buried since the enlargement, whose remains were placed in vaults, and inscriptions added. When the foundations for the furnaces were dug, parts of some priests' vestments were discovered. The heat of the furnace now almost necessitates the removal of the vaults from under the altar.

The church was consecrated by Rt. Rev. Bishop Kenrick, of the Diocese, Aug. 15th, 1850, assisted by seven priests and some scholastics. The sermon was delivered by the Rev. President of Mt. St. Mary's College.

The old church having been adorned with rare paintings, it was necessary that the new part should be made to correspond in interior decorations. Francis Stecher, a young German artist who had already gained some reputation as a painter, was engaged, and to his skill and taste Conewago is indebted for the beautiful adornment of its walls. The artist returned to Europe to further prosecute his studies, and visit his parents, but died there soon after his arrival. He certainly gave promise of great fame as an artist, and Conewago may well hold his name in grateful remembrance.

Father Enders continued Superior until 1862, when he was sent to Leonardtown, St. Mary's County, Md., where he acted as Superior and built a church. There were a number of priests at Conewago while Father Enders was Superior, but no dates can be given, and only such names as memory hands down to us. Rev. F. X. Deneckere came with Father Enders and spent the greater part of his life on the Conewago missions. Fathers Enders, Deneckere and Manns, constituted a happy family, and labored together for many years. Father Manns survives, and is still at Conewago. He came in 1862. Fathers Villiger, Cotting, Dougherty, Kreighton, Dietz, Rieter, Haller, and others, served from time to time at Conewago.

Rev. J. B. Cattani succeeded Father Enders as Superior about 1860 or 1862. His death-record says he was a Bavarian, born Aug. 30th, 1805, and died at Conewago Aug. 31st, 1865. Father Burchard Villiger probably succeeded him as Superior, assisted by Fathers Deneckere, Manns, Domperio,

Tuffer, and others. Rev. J. J. Bellwalder was Superior about 1869. There is nothing special to record during these years. The church-work was carried on at home by several of the Fathers, while others were out on the missions on Sundays and holidays, and whenever duty called them.

FATHER ENDERS RETURNS.

In 1870 or 1871, Father Enders was returned to Conewago as Superior. He was then beginning to suffer from the infirmities of increasing years, especially from an ulcerous sore on his leg, which caused him great pain to the end of his life. Though getting old in years, his mind and energy were as vigorous as in former days, and he began the work of church improvement at Conewago with his characteristic earnestness. In 1873, he had the old cupola removed and the present attractive spire erected. It is 80 feet in height from the comb of the roof, and is surmounted by a beautiful gilt cross, that can be seen for many miles around. The builder was Elias Roth, of New Oxford. From the upper windows of the spire a wide view of the country may be obtained.— Many of the neighboring towns are visible, and the country extending into Maryland and along the mountains to the north and west. On a clear day late in the fall, Father Deneckere was sure he could see some of the Mt. St. Mary buildings. He had a small telescope, and took great pleasure in viewing the valley from this high ground.

Father Enders made many improvements around the church. He built the two school houses, one on each side of the churchyard, when he was here the first time, and had the iron railing erected. He also enlarged the kitchen buildings, had the water brought up from a spring at the bottom of the hill, and put hot and cold water through the house, supplied from a large tank on the kitchen attic. The water was first forced up by hydraulic pressure, then by a system of water works, and now by a patent wind mill, which also grinds the mill feed and saws the wood. He planted a large vineyard after his return, and made great quantities of wine. Father Enders hardly knew an idle moment.

From the time the church was enlarged by Father Enders, he never gave up the thought of one day erecting in Conewago Chapel a marble altar. The church was otherwise a model of architectural beauty, but in this particular there was a noticeable want. This last object of his life was accomplished in 1877, when he himself went around through the parish soliciting contributions towards its payment. It is a beautiful piece of art and workmanship, and cost about $2000. The contractor was John Barth, Bel Air Avenue Marble Works, Baltimore, at one time a marble cutter in one of the school houses at Conewago. Its architecture corresponds with that of the church, being of the Romanesque or Composite order. The altar is seventeen feet in width, and thirteen and a half feet in height. The ante-pentium is formed in a crypt, supported by four columns. The marble used is Italian, Spanish, Portuguese and Tyrolese, and in its combination taste and skill have brought out the work in all its grandeur. The Tabernacle is of Carrara marble, with columns copied from those found at the ruins of Palmyra. At each end of the altar there is a pedestal, surmounted with a capital, having on its face the head of a cherub, and on each side of the Tabernacle is placed a worshiping angel.

At this period, Father Enders had a new roof put on the church, the pews repainted, and statues placed in the niches in the walls, vacant since the building of the new part. SS. Ignatius and Aloysius are on the side of the Blessed Virgin's altar, and St. Francis Xavier and Blessed Peter Claver on St. Francis' side. The church was also re-painted about 1880, and the outside walls repaired by pointing, to keep out the rain which had begun to show through on the inside and damaged the paintings.

Father Enders was assisted principally by Fathers Deneckere and Manns up to 1880. Father Deneckere attended Paradise, Oxford and Littlestown until his death, Jan. 8th, 1879. Father Manns attended the schools, the Sisters in McSherrystown and St. Joseph's Church, Hanover. Father Emig took charge of the Hanover church sometime before 1880, and is still its pastor. Father George Villiger succeeded Father Deneckere at Littlestown in 1879. He died at Conewago Sept. 20th, 1882, and was succeeded by Father Renaut; shortly after that the Littlestown church, founded by Father Pellentz and Gallitzin, was given over to the Bishop of the Diocese.

In 1880, Rev. Peter Flannigan was at Conewago, and Father Archambault attended Oxford and Paradise: Father Richards is now pastor of these places. Fathers Jamieson, Casey, Dufour, and others, were at Conewago for a short time about 1880 and after.

The crowning point in the religious life of Rev. Joseph Enders, was the celebration of the fiftieth anniversary of his priesthood, at Conewago, Aug. 15th, 1881. He himself was the celebrant of a Grand High Mass, with Father Casey as Deacon, Father Brennan Sub-Deacon, Father Archambault orator, and Father Emig master of ceremonies. The church was filled even to the aisles. The altar was specially decorated for the occasion, and the music prepared for the same. It was a happy day for all, and Father Enders received a number of presents to commemorate his golden jubilee, besides the congratulations and well wishes of thousands of his loving children. He was right feeble then already, and had to be supported by a chair on which to rest his afflicted leg, and more or less attended by the Brother while on the altar. He went to the hospital several times, but could only obtain temporary relief. He continued to say Mass to the last, though the book and everything had to be arranged for him.

He was removed to Frederick in Feb., 1884, where his declining days could be made more easy. He could not reconcile himself to the change, except in obedience and resignation which he had followed all his life; but his nature wanted active work and duty to which it was accustomed by years of labor. He complained that now he was of no use, and seemed ready and willing to be dismissed in peace like the servant of old. He died at the Novitiate, Frederick, Sept. 10th, 1884, in his 77th year, full of merits and good works. To the last his thoughts were of his old home at Conewago, where he hoped to die and be buried, but alas! the measure of his reliance upon the will of God had to be full. Conewago! Conewago! you have lost the best of Fathers, who only lived for God and His children. Gratitude should have prompted you to have gone to the very gates of the Society and begged the remains of your faithful Superior, carried them home like bereaved sons and daughters as you are, deposited them where his feet loved to stand, and kept his life and virtues in grateful remembrance, unto succeeding generations.

Father P. Forhan succeeded Father Enders as Superior of Conewago in June, 1883. He came from Frederick, and was stationed at Washington, Baltimore, and other places in Maryland during his former ministry. He is assisted at Conewago by Fathers Manns and Haugh; Father Richards at New Oxford and Paradise; Father Emig at Hanover.

Here we leave the Conewago Chapel history. It might have been much fuller had we not been compelled to write it while conducting other business, and away from Conewago; or had there been sufficient interest elsewhere to aid us in the work. Sketches of the Fathers, and scraps of local history which the want of time prevented a record in their proper place, will be given hereafter just as they come.

Farewell, Conewago, farewell! The happiest joys of my life and its saddest sorrows and vainest regrets are in thy keeping. Every foot of thy hills and valleys and streams is familiar to me, and they change not, but the scenes of my childhood are gone, and its associates scattered like the mists of youth. Every nook and corner of thy sacred place have I hunted over by day with miser care for some scrap of the past, and dreamed by night of treasures of hidden lore, and behold the meagre fruits of my labor! Time guards well the trusts confided to its care.

Conewago, farewell! Thy happy days and sorrowful chase each other in troubled hurry over the pathway of memory. Friends and dear ones have come and gone in faithful trust, true and lasting, where recreant hopes long since have perished and lie buried in misery and anguish of heart. The past has nothing in common with the present; the one knew no care; the other knows no quiet rest free like then from trouble. Where are the bright sunny days of school life, the happy faces and innocent enjoyments, the kind teachers and dear old Fathers? Look back and see sorrow mingled with gladness: the sad tolling of the bell, the mournful funeral procession winding its way around the hill; again joyful peals where sorrow echoed still; happy souls united where festive throngs made merry; Christmas chimes and Easter carols; tears to-day and smiles to-morrow, and forgotten scenes hurry on each passing hour. Why look back or why peer forward? Has not life been always thus?

Then farewell, once more, but before we part, heed my words generations yet unborn. Conewago has been as dear to us as will ever be to you or was to those before. It is not ours, nor yours, nor was it theirs. It is blessed by every sacred tie from Heaven, and as a religious inheritance guard it well, for others are destined here to find their rest. Holy and venerable is the place. Our footsteps follow the traces of hallowed lives, unworthy as we are. Soon we, too, will have passed away, and our children come and go until in God's own good time the angel's voice sound here below. Ye shepherds, while your flocks abide, watch the old building with an anxious care. "Guard it as best you may, and at *any* cost from every influence of dilapidation. Count its stones as you would jewels of a crown ; set watches about it as if at the gates of a besieged city ; bind it together with iron where it loosens ; stay it with timber where it declines ; do not care about the unsightliness of the aid ; better a crutch than a lost limb ; and do this tenderly, and reverently, and continually, and many a generation will still be born and pass away beneath its shadow."

EDUCATION AT CONEWAGO.

The first schools in the Valley like those through the county, were mostly private or subscription schools. The missionary Fathers combined the primary education of the children with their religious instruction, which was never neglected when it could in any way possible be provided. The religious instruction of the children continued to be a part of the ministry until late years, when Sunday-schools and parochial schools relieved the priests to a great extent of that labor. Catechism is now taught in the schools, and one of the Fathers visits them once or twice a week to give catechetical instructions and to prepare the children finally for Confirmation and Communion.

Very little is known of the early educational interests of Conewago. Joseph Heront taught a school near the Pigeon Hills before 1800, where afterwards the Sulpitian Seminary was located. Colleges were just then being established, and he may have had a preparatory course in the higher branches, or for the young men of the Valley whose parents were in good circumstances and who desired to give their sons all the educational advantages then possible, for they were limited compared to what they are now. Father Brosius taught a school at Conewago about the period of 1800, but of what nature or how long kept up, we do not know. There were schools at the church then, taught sometimes by the Fathers and at others by a lay teacher or a Brother, up to the time when the parochial schools were started. When Father Deneckere first came to Conewago he established a school in which the higher branches were taught, something in the order of a preparatory school for those who might have a vocation for the priesthood. This school was taught by himself with the assistance of a Mr. Gross. In 1868 or 1870, Father Deneckere started another preparatory school in the school houses then standing in the churchyard, and one of which has since gone to ruin and been removed. He had as high as eighteen scholars at that time, and kept it up until a while before his death. There are several of his students now novices in the Society. During Father Bellwalder's Superiorship, Ed. S. Reily, Esq., taught a select school at the church; he also gave lessons in algebra and mathematics to Father Deneckere's scholars. David Smith, Esq., taught a winter school at the church for several years after Father Deneckere's death. For some years satisfactory arrangements have been made with the Directors of the Free Schools in the parish, by which competent Catholic teachers were employed and the larger scholars sent there. The Free Schools, generally, had only a few scholars of their own, and in some instances they were willing to provide a Catholic teacher and pay him out of the school taxes, of which the Catholics contributed almost the entire amount, besides keeping up their parochial schools. This arrangement was allowed by the Fathers only for the larger boys,—the girls and smaller boys attending the parochial schools.

In Irishtown there is a Catholic school building and

church combined, called St. Peter Canisius, built in 1868. Mass is occasionally said there. Francis Noel taught the school for a number of years, and was succeeded by Mr. Topper.

A Catholic School was established at Mt. Rock a number of years ago, a frame building having been erected on the free school lot above the hill. Miss J. M. O'Neill taught there. A stone church building and school house was erected in 1869, on the second hill west of Mt. Rock, on land given by Charles Smith, and called St. Charles. Miss O'Neill taught here awhile and was succeeded by the Sisters from McSherrystown, who are the present teachers. These schools have a large number of pupils. The parochial schools were started when Rev. Burchard Villiger was Superior. Father Manns was the leading spirit in the Catholic School question for a number of years, and gave religious instructions in them once or twice a week. About 1860, Mass was said in a private house at Whitestown, along the H. & G. R. R., now discontinued. In the last few years steps were being taken to build a school house at Flatbush, between Littlestown and Bonneauville.

The Sisters of Charity were established in McSherrystown, by a Board of Trustees, in 1834. They arrived June 20th, and opened their school that month. They were from St. Joseph's, Emmettsburg, and the School was dedicated to St. John the Baptist. Sisters Anne and Agnes were the two first Sisters. They met with such success that application was made to Rev. Mr. Hickey, then Superior of the Sisters of Charity, for more assistance, and Sister Mary Cecilia was sent to aid them. After that four or five Sisters were employed. Their house became too small for the increasing number of scholars and boarders; an unfinished house was purchased from Mr. Slagle for $2200, and their work continued, until the academy building was destroyed by fire in 1840. The house was rebuilt by the trustees and sold with five acres of ground to a branch of the Ladies of the Sacred Heart, by whom it was enlarged and successfully conducted until 1851, when they left and located at Eden Hall. The Sisters of St. Joseph then purchased the house and lands, and the institution received permanent life and success. They were incorporated Aug. 31st, 1854, under the title of the McSherrystown Novitiate and Academy of St. Joseph. They have made many improvements and purchased several additional tracts of land. It was managed for a number of years by Mother Mary Magdalene, who died Aug. 22d, 1876, and was buried on the 25th,—Bishop Shanahan and eight priests attending. She was succeeded by Mother Ignatius, who is raising the standard of the institution in every way, enlarging the scope of its work and making such additions to the buildings and property as necessity demands. Their objects are educational and charitable; the reception of Novices, the education of young ladies, teaching, visiting the sick, and the care of orphans.

Since the consecration of the Rt. Rev. Bishop Shanahan, St. Joseph's Convent has become the Mother House for the Sisters of St. Joseph in the Diocese of Harrisburg. It was formerly a branch of Chestnut Hill. A large number of Sisters are employed here in the various departments of the Sisterhood. Several of the Sisters reside at Hanover and teach the parish school at that place. Others teach the Mt. Rock and McSherrystown parochial schools. The boarding school at the academy is conducted by the best teachers in all the higher branches. A department for the instruction of the blind has been provided, under an experienced member of the community.

The school is furnished with all the facilities for educational purposes. It is located in the Valley of the Conewago, well known for its landscape beauty and healthfulness. The buildings are large and roomy, and the grounds laid out in walks, yards, and orchards. The land is farmed and used for dairy purposes, thus providing the best products of farm, garden and dairy for their own maintenance.

The want of additional buildings was felt several years ago, and efforts were made to erect them. The chapel was too small for the community itself, yet many of the old and infirm people of McSherrystown were accustomed to hear Mass at the Convent. A priest from Conewago Chapel says Mass every morning for the Sisters. The erection of the new building was begun in May, 1883, and completed in May, 1884. It adjoins and communicates by a two-story corridor with the Convent proper, and covers a site 55x65 feet, three stories and attic in height, with pointed turrets. The architecture is of the semi-Gothic, and was designed by Mr. J. A. Dempwolf, of York, Pa. The building is entirely devoted to the work of education, and the accommodation of the pupils. The rooms are well ventilated and thoroughly heated throughout. The study-hall, dormitories and recreation halls are spacious, and furnished with every appliance for the health, comfort and convenience of the pupils. The Convent property includes thirty-four acres of ground. The recreation grounds of the Academy are extensive, and consist of a fine lawn, walks and groves. The property known as Capt. Brogunier's lot was purchased in July, 1880, at a cost of $1246; and the Ginter lot was bought in June, 1884, for $3000. The cost of building the Academy, exclusive of expenses for drainage, paving walks and such improvements, is $12000. This does not include the valuation of the original buildings, just the cost of late improvements. New day-school buildings have also been erected.

Conewago has not given many sons to the church, but her daughters in religion are numerous. Of those born at Conewago who became priests, we can only name Bishop Timon, Fathers Shanefelter, Shorb, Miller, Sullivan, Marshall, (I think,) two of the Lillys, and Brothers Rimbaugh, Marshall and Gulden. There may be a few others. It is impossible to name all the Sisters. McSherrystown received quite a number, and many made their profession elsewhere. The Fathers at Conewago were instrumental in many of them being able to carry out their intentions of becoming religious, for there were in some instances great obstacles to overcome. In the correspondence of the Fathers, the most touching tributes of gratitude come from such of their spiritual children who have been counseled and assisted by them in the direction of a religious life. Happy souls!

THE "SEMINARY FARM."

The Sulpitian Seminary at the Pigeon Hills has a very important connection with the Catholic Church in the eastern provinces. Many eminent bishops and priests studied at the Pigeon Hills and spent their vacations there. Its history, like that of other old land marks of the church, is lost, and we can only give a general sketch of it as a religious institution. The place is at the foot of Pigeon Hills, in Oxford Township, about five miles north of Hanover, and still goes by the name of the "Seminary Farm." The land was originally taken up by warrant from the proprietaries of Pennsylvania, issued July 26th, 1750, to Henry Gearnhart, (or Kingheart, illegible in old deed,) and descended to the Lorimores. It contained about 273 acres, and was conveyed to Joseph Heront, April 4th, 1794, for one thousand pounds, gold and silver, which would seem to have been a very high price. He improved the property, opened a select school and called it "Herontford." To this day, Joseph Heront is spoken of by the older people of the Valley as a monk and a priest, but we are not sure that he was either. Father H. F. Griffin, one of the oldest Sulpitian priests living, informs us that Mr. Harent, or Heront as spelled in the old deeds, was an exile from France during the first French Revolution, and that he was a private gentleman, but may have studied for the priesthood after he left Pigeon Hills. The Laity's Directory of 1822, records the death of a Rev. Joseph Heront in 1817, in the Island of Martinique. This may have been "the monk of Herontford," as he certainly was, from what we can learn, a very intelligent, seclusive and pious man. Local tradition says he sailed for France, his native land, and died on the way. His name is last mentioned in the deeds about 1810.

John Tessier inherited "Herontford" by the last will and testament of Joseph Heront, recorded in the office of the Register of Wills for Baltimore County, liber W B, No. K, folio 419. Father Griffin thinks Mr. Heront was not related to Mr. Tessier, but bequeathed his farm to the Sulpitians on condition that they should pay some outstanding debts. The lands of Nicholas Bittinger, James McTaggart and Frederick Myers, adjoined the Heront property. Frederick Myers was the grandfather of Rev. Father Myers, dec'd, of pious memory in the Diocese of Baltimore. It was through Joseph Heront, and by his means, that Father Myers became a priest.

On the Feast of the Assumption, 1806, the Abbe Dillet, a Sulpitian, founded at Pigeon Hills "a college intended to give a religious education to boys, whose piety and qualities seemed to show a decided vocation for the priesthood." Pupils were received on the recommendation of their confessor. Conewago furnished some of the students. The Sulpitians had a Seminary in Baltimore, St. Mary's, founded in 1791, and Pigeon Hills was the preparatory school for this Seminary. About 1807 or 1809, Rev. John Dubois founded St. Mary's College, Emmettsburg. In the spring of 1809, sixteen scholars were transferred from Pigeon Hills to the Mountain School.

June 3d. 1830, the "Seminary Farm" was conveyed by deed from John Tessier, president of St. Mary's, Baltimore, to Lewis Regis Deluol, his successor. He also came in possession of an adjoining tract, the deed of which he obtained from Thomas C. Miller, Sheriff of Adams Co. This latter tract was no doubt the property of Francis Marshall, who was very intimate with Father Deluol, and whose history is not very plain. Father Griffin knew him well, and thinks he was of German origin more than French, probably from Alsace. His name is signed to various old deeds and conveyances, and he wrote it " Franz Marschall." He was no relation to the Marshalls of Conewago, as far as we can learn, and most likely came to the place through some of the priests who were from his own country. In their old age, through the mismanagement of one of their children, misfortune overtook them. The farm was sold and bought by the Seminary. Father Deluol allowed the old couple to live on it as their own till the day of their death. There were several other old families of Marshalls, of which Francis and Joseph were descendants. They were doubtless French people, and may have come to that vicinity with the Noels and Dellones, who settled there from France about the beginning of the 1700 era. There was a Father Marshall, a Brother and a Sister Marshall, but to what family they belonged we are not informed. Francis X. Marshall was educated at Mt. St. Mary's, and ordained at the Dominican Convent, Perry Co., Ohio, A. D. 1824 or 1825. Father Griffin was present at his ordination and served his Mass. He afterward returned to Maryland, and was stationed in Alleghany County.

Father Deluol fixed up the Seminary property as a retreat for students during vacation. There was a fine chapel there and buildings for the students; with large gardens and orchards. The premises were laid out in walks and lawns, and everything made attractive and inviting. The students had good times there, and like boys will be, made things lively in the neighborhood. Mr. Peter O'Neill, then at the Conewago Chapel, did the hauling back and forward and lived at the Seminary a while. He was their friend and helped them in their pranks and amusements, or out of them rather, by fixing up things when anything was wrong or complaints made. It continued to be used by the students in the summer until 1849, (so generally given,) when St. Charles College took its place. The deed from Father Deluol to Henry Eichelberger is dated 1847. Once every year, on St. Ignatius Day, the services at Conewago were conducted by the priests and the students from the Seminary, who would march over to the Chapel in grand procession. Many men, afterwards distinguished ecclesiastics in the Catholic Church, visited the Seminary and Conewago at that time. Father O'Brien was Prefect of the Seminarians. Father Chance, Professor and afterwards President of St. Mary's, gave lectures to the students during vacation. Father Elder, successor of Rev. Chance as Bishop of Natchez, and other priests, made their retreat at the Seminary. Father Eccleston was there, afterwards Bishop of Baltimore.

When the Reign of Terror drove the Trappist Monks from their native land, they resolved to seek an asylum in America. A party of them, eight or ten priests and nearly twenty lay brothers, under the guidance of Father Urban Guillet, embarked at Amsterdam, May 29th, 1803, for Baltimore. They proceeded to Pigeon Hills, and remained about a year, going from there first to Kentucky, then to Missouri, and other places, finally we believe returning to their native country, though there are several monasteries of that order now in America. While at Pigeon Hills they dug the well on the "Seminary Farm." The traditional idea that Joseph Heront was "a monk," very likely comes from his association with these Trappists. It is to be regretted that this place, so dear to the memory of the church, was allowed to come into the possession of strangers. A railroad runs near it now, (through one of the fields, we believe,) on to Abbottstown and Berlin, and it is a valuable property.

The students to whom it was once a dear home, would know it no more. It was the home of the exile and the sacred enclosure of the religious; what is now a common farm-house was once the temple of the Lord, where the Holy Sacrifice of the Mass was daily offered. Alas! how Time leaves every barrier broken down in its way.

THE PARADISE CHURCH.

The Catholic Church, at first called Brandt's Chapel or Pigeon Hills, in Paradise Township, York Co., about one mile north of Abbottstown, has a very interesting history, but much confused. Exercising even the best judgment, it would be difficult to give a clear sketch of the church.— Here we passed nine years of our childhood, and are as well acquainted with the parish as at Conewago. In the settlement of the country at an early date, several French, a few Irish and a number of German Catholic families located near the Pigeon Hills, around Abbottstown and towards East Berlin. At one time the church was right flourishing in numbers, but later on many families removed to Conewago and elsewhere. The early Catholics attended church at Conewago Chapel.

Probably the first Mass said in the neighborhood was at Abbottstown, by Father De Barth, in the beginning of the present century. Mass was occasionally said in the house of Wm. Jenkins, a prominent Catholic of that place. The Jenkinses were probably a Maryland family, but not related to those at Conewago. There are few descendants of the family; none that we know. One son died about forty years ago, and is buried at Paradise Church. One of the Reilys living in the West married a daughter of Wm. Jenkins, and one of the sons of Baron de Beelen married another. The

Wises were among the oldest Catholic families; the property now owned and occupied by the Clunks was their homestead, and there Mass was said at stated times.. This might have been about the period of 1800.

Among the first Goshenhoppen settlers was the Brandt ancestry from Germany. From there Frederick Brandt removed to near Abbottstown, but at what date we have been unable to discover. His tract of land, now the Paradise church property, is called "Brandtsburg" in the patent from the Commonwealth, a full title to which he obtained June 28th, 1809. The same tract had been granted by warrant from the Proprietaries to Matthias Bouzer, dated Oct. 28th, 1746. Frederick Brandt paid $460.73 into the Treasury of the State, which with the moneys paid by Matthias Bouzer, gave him a clear title to the land. The original grant was bounded by lands of John Abbott, Nicholas Bittinger, Wm. Mummert, John Jacobs, Wardle Kexer, and contained 235 acres, 87 perches, and allowance of 6 per cent. for roads.

Frederick Brandt was an intelligent and industrious man, and a good Catholic. He had no children, and no relatives on his side according to his will. Mrs. Brandt's maiden name was Keens; she had two brothers, John and Jacob, and her sisters were Catharine Dellone, Eve Heidler, and Magdalene, whose married name we do not know, but the grandmother of Gregory Dellone's wife. Frederick Brandt built the house now on the church farm; part of it was used for a chapel before his death and after, until the stone church was built about 1844. Brandt's mill was one of the first in that neighborhood; the site and old water courses are yet to be seen. Frederick Dellone hauled the stones for the mill when he was eigteen years old. Fathers DeBarth and Lekeu and their assistants attended the Paradise Catholics from time to time.

Frederick Brandt made his will Feb. 9th, 1815, "being of advancing age." He left his personal property to his wife, with whose "advice and consent" he determined to appropriate his real estate for the benefit of his religion and his country; "for as God has not blessed us with any offspring, and our brothers' and sisters' children being very numerous, the said estate could be of very little use to them if equally divided among all, and to favor some more than others would naturally produce jealousy and perhaps enmity." Therefore he bequeathed his dwelling, plantation and mills, and a five acre tract lately purchased of Clement Steuthabeker, to his wife during her life or widowhood, and after her death then the same to Rev. Francis Neale of Georgetown College, "his heirs and assigns for ever, in fee simple, in order to establish thereon as soon as convenient a school or seminary, or any other house of education for the purpose of bringing up youth in useful literature and christian piety;" or if more advisable, for a school or Noviceship for the reception of young men destined for the ministry of the Gospel in the Roman Catholic Church. He desired the property to be used for such purposes and no other, "and that it be never sold, mortgaged or alienated in any manner, either in whole or in part, for debt, security, or any other reason." He then provided that two boys, the preference to be given to those of relations, be educated either at the school to be established there or at Georgetown, out of the revenue from the farm, exclusively for the priesthood, and thus always to have two boys provided for. The entire purpose of his will seems to have been twofold, first the education of youth for the ministry, and after that the performance of worship on the said plantation. The executors were Michael Dellone, Wm. Jenkins and the testator's wife. Witnesses, Franz Marschall, Michael Strausbaugh and John Brieghner, Recorded in York, Jacob Barnitz, Register. There is a codicil dated Jan. 26th, 1820, in which he bequeaths to Rev. Francis Neale a five acre lot purchased of Isaac Latschaw, and appoints James McSherry Executor in place of Wm. Jenkins, dec'd. John L. Gubernator wrote the will.

After the death of Frederick Brandt, the widow managed the farm, and priests from Conewago kept up religious service in the chapel of the house. She made her will Oct. 20th, 1829, in favor of Rev. Francis Neal and Rev. Francis Dzicrozynski, in accordance with the will of her husband. She had a schedule of articles excepted, signed by Rev. Matthew Lekeu, who on behalf of the devisees agreed to the conditions of the will, which made allowance for her support and maintenance on the plantation until her death. March 9th, 1839, she executed another writing, by which she conveyed to Rev. J. W. Beschter all her household goods and schedule of exceptions, for which Rev. Mat. Lekeu was accountable, and released him from further obligations. In this writing, all the articles in the front room and second room, which she occupied, were excepted. It is witnessed by F. W. Koehler and Jeremiah Harman. The relations of Mrs. Brandt were somehow under the impression, whether by word or promise, that the $200 worth of goods held by Mat. Lekeu were to become the property of Mrs. Heidler after Mrs. Brandt's death, but there is no provision to that effect in any of her legal transactions.

In 1848, Aug. 10th, Rev. Thos. Mulledy and Wm. McSherry, of the District of Columbia, purchased of Magdalene Brandt five acres of land for $200; Rev. J. W. Beschter, witness. This lot had been confirmed by the Commonwealth unto George Dressler, by letters patent, dated Jan. 7th, 1792; and sold in 1815 to Michael Dellone and Catharine, (Keens,) his wife, who sold to Magdalene Brandt, Sept. 9th, 1828. Mrs. Brandt died about 1840; the provincial's notice for the usual suffrages is dated Oct. 1st, of that year. The relations became very much dissatisfied with the provisions of the will. Frederick Brandt's will is a plain document, repeatedly expressing his demand that religious worship should always be maintained on the farm, and that the property should be permanently vested in the successors of Father Neale as the legal representatives of the Society of Jesus, and that the revenue be exclusively devoted to educational purposes in the ministry of the Catholic Church, and the keeping up of the property. As far as the establishment of the school is concerned, there is a provision in case of impossibility to establish or maintain one, for a time, but the ultimate object remains the same. The property is valuable, well located, with good buildings, a new barn having been lately erected, and the soil yields good crops. Some years ago it was almost surrounded by dense woodland, but the most of it has now been cleared out. The Jesuits, living in communities, can not serve this parish with much advantage. There would be sufficient income for a resident priest, but for the educational provisions, and such a one could build up a prosperous congregation at Paradise.

When the disposition of the property was in question after the death of Mrs. Brandt, some correspondence was carried on between the Society and Bishop Kenrick, who in certain events inclined to make a Diocesan Seminary there, but the location then was not convenient, there being no railroads near, and outside of the establishment of a school he considered as too formidable the gratuitous education of two students. The Society, in October, 1840, through Rev. Francis Vespre, expressed a willingness to relinquish its right to the property, could any other legal claim be established that would insure the carrying out of the will as far as the good of religion was concerned.

The letter from Bishop Kenrick to Rev. N. Steinbacher, authorizing him to bless the new church, is dated Feb. 18th, 1845. Since the death of Mrs. Brandt the Paradise farm has been under the management of the Superiors of Conewago, who have it farmed. Mr. Allwine was the tenant under Father Lekeu, and after him Lewis Will lived there, about the time the church was built. Since then it has been occupied by the Bradys. Paradise, Littlestown and New Oxford formed a charge until recent years, with alternate

Sundays at the former and latter places, and on week days and certain festivals and odd Sundays at Oxford. Now Paradise and Oxford are attended by Father Richards, with early Mass and High Mass alternating. The Paradise church is a fine stone building, with large yards and graveyard. The church was built about 1843 or 4, by Mr. Kemp, contractor. Messrs. Frederick Dellone, Peter Noel, J. J. Kuhn, and others solicited subscriptions and aided in the work. Father Manns attended about that time, or shortly after the church was built. Mary Dellone (of Peter) had willed money for a bell, which was procured, leaving considerable money over. Father Manns insisted that the money was left for a particular purpose for which it should be used, so another bell was added and two bells were placed on the church. Father Beschter was pastor of Paradise several years and died there. Fathers Dougherty and Cotting attended occasionally while having charge of the Gettysburg church. Father Steinbacher was a true friend to Paradise, and took great interest in the congregation, and so did Father Deneckere after him, who served from about 1860 to his death, when Father Archambault succeeded him. Fathers Sacchi and Villiger were there for some time about 1850, and other priests from Conewago, as best suited the arrangements of the Superiors. Father Deneckere started a summer school there, taught by Misses Shane, Fink and others, but the congregation is too widely scattered to keep up a parochial school. Conewago was the burying place of the Paradise church for many years. Mrs. Elizabeth Hair is said to have been the first person buried at Paradise. As far as we know, no priests have been born at Paradise, though Fabian and Michael Noel and F. X. Brady, of Father Deneckere's school, are now novices in the Society, and Jos. Strubinger died a Seminarian at Frederick some years ago. A number of young girls have become Sisters. Catharine Dellone (Sister Ann), daughter of Fred. Dellone, went to be a Sister Dec. 5th. 1849, at Emmettsburg, and died July 16th, 1851, at Cincinnati, where she was buried. Henrietta Wise, in religion Sister Bona, and two Misses Kuhn, probably of the Berlin family, became Sisters; also, Minnie Koehler (Sister John the Baptist), Salome Noel (Sister Josepha), and Annie Brady (Sister Francis); the latter three took the veil at McSherrystown. Mary Shane also became a Sister.

After the death of Mrs. Brandt, Paradise was disturbed and excited by mysterious noises and appearances, that were attributed to supernatural agencies. The Brandt will matter was assigned as the cause of such unusual happenings, and it excited a great deal of interest. Mrs. Brandt's figure in life was well known to every person in the parish,—a little, old woman, bent under the weight of years, and after her death imagination only needed a ghost story to set it in active work. There is no doubt, however, that there was room for serious thought, and it was so considered by the priests. The mysterious actions were mostly confined to an old cupboard in the priest's room,—which served as a sacristy,—in which the vestments were kept. Father Steinbacher was a man of determined purpose, but failed to account for the disturbances by which he was troubled. At night he would call Mr. Will into his room, and stay together part of the night without hearing the least alarm, but as soon as he was alone the troubles were renewed. Mrs. Will, who then waited upon the priests and took care of the rooms, assures us that Father Steinbacher subjected himself to rigorous fasting and continual prayers, until his health began to suffer and he was taken away. Father Deneckere came soon after him, and made inquiry into the Brandt will affair. He then started a school at Conewago, in which he placed boys from Paradise, and besides he applied some of the revenues of the Paradise farm to the education of young men for the ministry. From his time on nothing more was heard of the disturbances. The old cupboard was placed in a rear cellar of the house where it yet stands or has decayed, like all else ever connected with it. Perhaps this account would have rested as well with the past, but the recital of such facts, attested by people of good character and reputation still living, can do no harm. The church daily asks for eternal rest unto the dead.

We say on page 89, that Mrs. Brandt had three sisters, and name one Magdalene; that is a mistake. Her own name was Magdalene. The third sister's name we are not able to give. Most of the families mentioned were intermarried, and it is almost impossible to trace the names and connections of a century ago. Also on page 91, the date of the purchase of the five acre lot from Mrs. Brandt by Fathers Mulledy and McSherry is given in some of the first pages printed as 1848, when it should be 1838 where not so.

THE LITTLESTOWN CHURCH.

Littlestown is one of the oldest of the Conewago missions. The first Catholics in the valley around Littlestown attended services at Conewago Chapel, but were provided with a place of divine worship at an early period, they being the oldest religious congregation in the town. Erdman's Geography and History of America, published in Germany at the close of the last century, notes the existence of a Catholic Church at Littlestown; and so the Boston "American Gazetteer" of 1797. The Fathers at Conewago, beginning with Fathers Pellentz and Gallitzin before 1800, attended the Catholics at Littlestown, and the church was supplied from that place until the fall of 1884 or spring of 1885, when it was given over to the charge of the Bishop of the Diocese of Harrisburg. The first priest under the Bishop was Father Gormerly, then stationed at Bonneauville, which two parishes were intended to be combined; but both desiring resident pastors, Father Crotty, of Columbia, became the first pastor under the secular administration.

The first building used as a church, was situated on the northern corner of the lot, afterwards used as a burial ground. This building, occupied as a dwelling, was converted into a church about the year 1791. The Trustees at that time were, Patrick McSherry, Joseph Flauth and Henry O'Hara. After the death of Father Pellentz in 1800, the Littlestown Church was attended by Fathers DeBarth and Lekeu, and their assistants. The present brick church was built in 1840, Michael Dougherty, S. J., being pastor; and the trustees were, Henry Spalding, John Shorb, James McSherry, Jacob Rider, Dr. J. A. Shorb, Jacob Baumgardner, Joseph Fink and Joseph Riddlemoser. The old frame weatherboarded church was sold to Joseph Aker, Sr., and turned into a house on the Littlestown and Taneytown road.

From that period there was a succession of pastors from the Conewago Fathers, among others Fathers Joseph Dietz, F. X. Deneckere, George Villiger, Peter Manns, Father Reiter. Father Deneckere attended Littlestown for nearly twenty years, and died there Jan. 8th, 1879. Father Villiger succeeded him, dying a few years later. Father Renaut was then assigned to the charge for a short time, and was the last pastor attending from the Society.

A very fine brick school house was erected in 1867, by Rev. Father Deneckere. The first teacher was Miss Mary Wilson. She was succeeded by the following teachers: Miss Ellen Heath, Joseph Smith, Frank Addelsperger, Miss Mary Fink, A. J. Smith, Miss Emma Shorb. The school is largely attended, and is under the direction of the pastor of the church. The interior of the church is very neat and attractive. The congregation seems to be growing slowly, and is composed of a right well-to-do class of people. One of the oldest Catholic families in the town is that of Hon. Wm. McSherry, the name of his father, James, and that of his grandfather, Patrick, appearing in this record. The Shorbs are also among the older families, and there are others, descendants of the early Catholics.

The Littlestown Catholic congregation was incorporated by the Pennsylvania Legislature, April 19th, 1840, under the title of "The Congregation of St. Aloysius." The incorporators and trustees were, F. X. Deneckere, S. J., J. A. Shorb, Henry Spalding, Joseph Fink, Jacob Baumgardner, Hon. Wm. McSherry, Sebastian O'Bold, Jacob Marshall, Andrew Little.

THE HANOVER CHURCH.

St. Joseph's Church, Hanover. is one of the most flourishing congregations connected with Conewago. Hanover being a growing town and a local railroad center of considerable importance, the church property is a valuable addition to the Society, and may in course of time be further improved by the Jesuits. Conewago had on several occasions been selected as the site of some Jesuit institution and as often abandoned for want of railroad facilities. Hanover is easy of access from any direction, is surrounded by a prosperous agricultural community, and located in a healthy climate and in a beautiful section of country.

At an early date there were a number of Catholic families, mostly Germans, settled in and around Hanover, attending church at Conewago Chapel. When Father DeBarth came, he exerted himself in every direction to provide places of divine worship, around which Catholics would be induced to locate and grow up into congregations. From about 1822 to 1826, he said Mass occasionally in a shop or old school house, on a lot owned by the Jesuits, along the alley east of Baltimore Street, now in possession of Luther Weigle, Wm. Grumbine and Henry Trone. Peter O'Neill, living with Father DeBarth at that time, remembers accompanying him to Hanover on such occasions. Besides, Mr. S. Althoff is informed by an old gentleman who has lived all his life in Hanover. that when a boy, he, with another lad, found the door of this old building open, and they entered. They found a few pennies in a drawer, which they appropriated to their use; and further remembers that there were benches and an altar in the old building at the time.

After that we have no knowledge of Mass being celebrated in Hanover until about 1863, when a large room in the house of Jacob Hildt, on Carlisle Street, was used for that purpose by Father Domperio. Mass was continued to be said there and instructions given to the children, until 1864, when it became too small and the desire for a regular place of worship prompted such action as would secure that need. Rev. J. B. Cattani was then Superior of Conewago, to whom the trustees of the M. E. Church of Hanover conveyed their lot and church building on Baltimore Street, 60 feet front and 25 feet deep, for $900, in trust for the Catholic congregation. Rev. Father Manns became pastor, and services were held on the first and third Sundays of the month. He also started a Catholic school there, which soon had a large attendance. To this Father the Conewago settlement is greatly indebted for the establishment and support of parochial schools, under adverse circumstances and with many obstacles in the way of starting them. The first teacher of the Hanover school was A. J. Smith, succeeded by Miss Alice Dellone. The Sisters from McSherrystown took charge of the school in 1873; Sister Rose, present Mother. School had been kept in the old church building for a while; now part of the Sisters' house, a fine building between the old and new churches, serves for that purpose. The ground occupied by this house and the new church, 90 feet front and 257 feet deep, was purchased by Father Enders for $4500.

The congregation gradually grew stronger in numbers. In 1865 an addition was made to the church, 35x40 feet, at a cost of $2,145. A cupola was also erected, and a bell costing $945, and weighing 1834 pounds, placed therein. The church, when dedicated, was called St. Joseph's. Then already the congregation desired more regular services. In Feb., 1874,

CATHOLIC LOCAL HISTORY. 99

a numerously signed petition was addressed to the Superior of Conewago, asking for the regular Sunday service at Hanover.

Rev. Father Manns continued as pastor until 1877. During this year, Rev. Father Jamison attended St. Joseph's for several months, and delivered lectures in aid of the new church, then proposed to be built. Rev. Father Enders, the venerable Superior of Conewago, also ministered to this congregation every alternate Sunday, during the close of Rev. Father Mann's pastorate. Rev. Father Emig, the present incumbent, became pastor in the fall of 1877; since which time the congregation is attended more regularly—there being the entire church service on Sundays, and Mass nearly every morning during the week.

The old church becoming too small, and being also needed as a school building, it was concluded to build a more creditable place of worship, and to carry on the work in accordance with the means that could be commanded, so that when finished it would also be paid for. This resolution, we believe, has been faithfully carried out so far, through the great perseverance and energy of the venerable pastor, Father Emig. The building was begun in the spring of 1877. The corner-stone was laid Sept. 16th, of that year. There were nearly three thousand people present. A procession, with St. Joseph's, St. Mary's and St. Patrick's I. C. B. U. Societies, of York; the Citizens' and Spring Garden Bands, in line, marched through the principal streets. Father Clarke, of Loyola College, Baltimore, delivered the address. The Fathers present were: Revs. Enders, Deneckere and Emig, of Conewago; Revs. Clarke, of Baltimore; Pape, of York; Shanahan, of Bonneauville; Boll, of Gettysburg; and Koch, of New Freedom. The corner-stone is of marble, with the inscription "1877." The building Committee consisted of Rev. Joseph Enders, Chairman; Joseph Dellone, Vice-President; Dr. J. P. Smith, Treasurer; Wm. Overbaugh, Secretary ; Joseph Althoff, John Clunk, Joseph Brockley and Ambrose Schmidt.

Only the foundations were raised in 1877. The building was put under roof in 1878, the brick-work of the tower erected, and the bell removed from the old belfry into the new steeple, which is 154 feet in height. The interior of the church was partly finished that year. The building is 130x50 feet, with a neat yard in front and a large rear lot.

The new St. Joseph's Church was dedicated on All-Saints Day, 1880. The Fathers present were : Very Rev. R. W. Brady, Provincial of the Society of this Province ; Very Rev. M. J. McBride, Vicar-General of the Diocese of Harrisburg, (Bishop Shanahan being absent in Rome); Rev. Louis J. McKenna, of York ; Rev. Hugo Magevney, Professor of Sacred Eloquence in Woodstock College ; Revs. J. B. DeWolff, Ed. McGurk, Dewitt; Rev. Joseph Enders, Peter Flanagan and Francis Casey, of Conewago Chapel ; and Rev. J. B. Emig, pastor of St. Joseph's. Father McBride performed the ceremony of dedication. A Grand High Mass followed; J. B. Emig, Master of Ceremonies ; Father DeWolff, Celebrant ; Father Casey, Deacon ; Father Flanagan, Sub-Deacon ; Father Magevney preaching a very eloquent dedicatory sermon, from the Third Book of Kings, " Building, I have built a house for thy dwelling, to be thy most firm throne forever." The choir rendered the Kyrie, Sanctus and Agnus Dei, from Bollman's Mass ; and at the Offertory, " *Justus ut Palma*," by Lambilotte. The cost of the building up to its dedication was $17,000. The pews are of very fine finish and style, and cost $1200. The interior of the church is roomy, and is now very attractively finished and furnished. The windows have stained glass ; a handsome set of station paintings grace the walls; neat altars for St. Joseph and the Blessed Virgin, and a fine main altar, with two sacristies.

A large organ, and other embellishments, make the church all that could be desired, and one that will compare favorably with the finest in the Diocese. St. Joseph's is the crowning work in the life of Father Emig, a monument to his judgment and labor, and a credit to the liberality of the congregation.

The Catholics of Hanover buried at Conewago until 1875, when a large Catholic Cemetery was laid out on the west side of Baltimore Street, adjoining Mt. Olivet. Four acres were purchased for this purpose in 1875, at a cost of $800.

Dr. J. P. Smith, a very wealthy and prominent Catholic of the congregation, died a few years ago, leaving all his means to the town for a public library. At that time Father Emig, aged and infirm, was going almost from house to house in his efforts to raise the money to build a church.

Mrs. Mary Smith, *nee* Dellone, died about the time it was proposed to build a new church, for which she left $1000, and $700 for Sanctuary purposes.

St. Joseph's Catholic Beneficial Society was organized March 7th, 1882, Charles Losman, President. J. A. Renaut succeeded him. The membership is 56.

Mary Elizabeth Barnitz, in religion Sister M. Elizabeth, daughter of Daniel J. and Maria L. Barnitz, joined the Sisters of St. Joseph at McSherrystown, in 1875. Anastasia Hair, Sister M. Gertrude, daughter of Joseph and Caroline Hair, joined same order in 1874. Elizabeth Hildt, Sister Anacleta, daughter of Jacob and Elizabeth Hildt, became a religious in 1867, with the Sisters of Notre Dame, near Baltimore. There is another daughter of the same family a Sister of Charity, received about 1857 or 1858.

THE NEW OXFORD CHURCH.

New Oxford is not quite half way between Conewago and Paradise, and the Catholics living there belonged to the Conewago congregation before they had a church of their own. The Conewago Fathers taught catechism in private houses there, long before the church was built. Mr. Jacob Martin donated a lot on Carlisle Street for a church, which was erected thereon in 1852,—Rev. F. X. Deneckere being the attending priest. The building is of brick, 75x35 feet in size. It was enlarged and improved several years ago. The church is under the invocation of the Immaculate Heart of Mary. Father Deneckere had charge of the Littlestown and Paradise Catholic Churches at the same time, holding services at those places on alternate Sundays, and at Oxford only on a week day at first and on certain holy-days. Fathers Reiter and Cattani also attended New Oxford the few years that Father Deneckere was away from Conewago, after which he returned and continued his attendance at Oxford until his death in 1879. New Oxford and Paradise were then formed into a charge under Father Francis Casey, with services on alternate Sundays at each place. Father Arthur Archambault succeeded him, until about 1884. There was a young German Father then in attendance for a few months. Father Richards is the present pastor. A parochial school was established in 1862, by Father Deneckere. The following are the teachers in successive order: Mrs. Trayer, Miss M. J. Felix, Joseph Smith, Miss Wager, John F. McSherry, E. G. Topper. School was held in the church until 1877, when a school building was added. Over one hundred scholars attend. The church membership is between three and four hundred.

THE BONNEAUVILLE CHURCH.

Bonneauville is a small village midway between Conewago and Gettysburg, and about four miles from Littlestown. Among the early settlers of the surrounding country, were many Catholics, who then belonged to Conewago. After churches had been built at Littlestown and Gettysburg, some attached themselves to those places, but for a number of years no strict line divided the congregations, and people went to the church nearest and most convenient. An effort was made about 1850 to build a church at Bonneauville: the undertaking was then thought too great for the Catholics, and was not advised by the Bishop or the Conewago Superior.— Rev. Basil A. Shorb became the founder of the Church of St. Joseph at Bonneauville, the corner-stone of which was laid Aug. 1st, 1859. He was born near Littlestown, educated at Mt. St. Mary's, and ministered to several congregations before he chose Bonneauville for his field of labor. He had considerable inheritance, and donated much of it to the church work in which he was engaged. It was through him, and by this means, that he obtained the necessary encouragement from his Superiors to form a congregation and build a church at Bonneauville. He died April 4th, 1871, in his sixty-first year and the thirty-first of his ministry. Father Pope succeeded him, and built a large brick school-house near the church in 1873. Sisters were engaged as teachers for a time. A house was purchased for their use, but was sold again after they left. The school had a large attendance. James W. Gubernator taught a short time. Miss M. Martin teaches this year. Father Pope's management was not as prudent as was demanded by the ordinary circumstances of the congregation. He was enterprising in other directions, and succeeded in having a daily mail established, changing the old-time name of "Bonaughtown," and that of the Postoffice, "Square Corner," to the more modern name it now bears. The congregation passed through many trials about this period, partly from want of prudent management. Father McIlhenny succeeded and was followed by Father Shanahan. Father Gormerly is the present pastor. There is a fine parsonage adjoining the church, and several lots are owned by the congregation. The church belongs to the Harrisburg Diocese. In Nov., 1879, a mission was given at

St. Joseph's by Fathers Bausch and Kolp, of Boston, during which a mission cross was erected on the east side of the church. A cemetery was laid out about 1870, with a vault in the center for the burial of priests. There rest the remains of Rev. Basil A. Shorb, founder and first pastor of St. Joseph's. The churchyard served as a burying ground until the cemetery was secured, into which most of the bodies were then removed. When a boy we served Mass at Bonneauville, and also at Paradise and Conewago; we shall never forget the fear entertained for Father Shorb, but in many ways he was a kind man, whom the Bonneauville Catholics will ever gratefully remember.

THE GETTYSBURG CHURCH.

For many years the Catholics in and around Gettysburg attended divine service at Conewago, a distance of about twelve miles. They were few in number in the beginning of the present century, and not possessed of much of this world's goods, but were devoted to their religion with that characteristic devotion of Catholics the world over, which induced them to go to Conewago to hear Mass on Sundays and holy days of obligation, notwithstanding the distance or inclemency of the weather. The erection of the first church building was commenced about 1826, on ground given by Jacob Norbeck on Washington Street. The church was built under the direction of the Superiors of Conewago Chapel—first Father Louis De Barth, then Father Matthew Lekeu; though it is not certain that Father De Barth visited Gettysburg often, as he left Conewago in 1828 for St. John's (now St. Alphonsus') church in Baltimore. The church was not yet completed in 1831, for on the 18th of May in that year, during a heavy thunder storm, the church was struck by lightning. "The fluid passed down the cupola and the wall of the church to the front door, marking its progress by forming a groove to the ground. A plasterer and several other workmen were prostrated, and remained unconscious for some time.

The congregation at Gettysburg, while it belonged to the Jesuits of Conewago, had no *regular* pastor. Conewago had many missions to supply— more so then than now—to which ministers were sent according to the best convenience and judgment of the Superiors. Father Michael Dougherty officiated at Gettysburg alternately with Father Leckeu, who was Superior of Conewago until 1843. After him came Father Joseph Dietz, and some of the older members remember Fathers Kendler, Geo. Villiger, V. H. Barber, and F. X. Deneckere among the priests who held services in the old church at Gettysburg, between 1831 and 1850. The new brick church on High street was built under Father J. B. Cotting, in 1852. Father Brocard, as Provincial, authorized Father Enders, Superior of Conewago, to build the Gettysburg church. The agreement between George and Henry Chritzman, John Gilbert, (or Gailburt), A. B. Kurtz, David Ziegler and Joel B. Danner, and Fathers Enders and Cotting, is dated Feb. 10th, 1852. John Martin, Nickolas Codori, Joseph Smith and Jacob Case were the Building Committee. The contractors were to receive $3870, and the old material. Payment was made in full, June 27th, 1853. Up to this time the church was under the jurisdiction of the Jesuits, who also supplied a small congregation at Millerstown. These churches were then handed over to the Bishop of Philadelphia, and were formed, with the Mountain Church, into a charge—the minister being resident at Gettysburg. The congregation was now served in turn by Rev. Messrs. B. A. Shorb, L. J. Miller, A. McGinnis, until 1860. Rev. Joseph A. Boll became pastor soon after the battle of Gettysburg, and as such serves yet. Gettysburg and Fairfield form the present charge—the mountain church having been later joined to the Chambersburg charge—and is under the jurisdiction of the Bishop of Harrisburg. A handsome parsonage was built nearly opposite the church in 1870 or 1871, and about three years ago a fine school building was erected. The name of the church is St. Francis Xavier's. Father Boll traveled through Europe and the Holy Land, in 1881 or '82. On his return he delivered several lectures on the subject for church benefits. Several years later he was appointed to the Lebanon church, but shortly after he was returned to Gettysburg again.

THE "MOUNTAIN CHURCH."

St. Ignatius' Catholic Church, better known as the Mountain Church, is situated in the Buchanan Valley, five miles from Graeffenburg, near Mr. Kimple's Mill, on the road to Corwell's. It is about ten miles west of Gettysburg, in Franklin Twp., Adams Co., almost on the Franklin County line. This church was originated by a Mr. Lostetter, who gave 150 acres of land, and the money to build a church was collected through the adjoining counties. The corner-stone was laid Oct. 10th, 1816. There was an old Catholic graveyard on the tract long before the church was built. The first settlers of the Valley were Irish and named their estates according to the baronial system of Great Britain. Mr. F. Cole's tract was originally called "Armagh." The first church consisted of nothing but the walls, a table being used for an altar. Mr. Lostetter failing in business, the tract was sold at Sheriff's sale, and was purchased by the Jesuits of Georgetown and Conewago Chapel. The first services at this place were held in Mr. Andrew Noel's house. The ministers serving this congregation from Conewago Chapel, were, Revs. Louis De Barth and Matthew Lekeu until 1829; Rev. Michael Dougherty from that period until about 1840; Rev. Father Kendler in 1843; Rev. Joseph Dietz from 1844 to 1850; Rev. Father Cattani then attended the congregation for a short period; Rev, J. B. Cotting from 1850 to 1853; Rev. F. X. Deneckere until 1858. These Fathers also attended Gettysburg and Millerstown, the latter congregation being few in numbers had as yet never been asked to contribute anything for the support of the pastor. They now petitioned the Bishop of the Diocese of Philadelphia to supply them with a pastor, which was complied with on condition that Gettysburg, the Mountain Church, and Millerstown formed one charge—the pastor to reside at Gettysburg. The ministers supplying the charge from this time (1858) were, Rev. Messrs. Basil A. Shorb, to 1859; L. J. Miller, 1860; A. McGinnis until 1863; Joseph A. Boll from 1864 to 1873. The congregation was then connected with the Chambersburg charge—Path Valley, Waynesboro', Chambersburg, and the Mountain church—J. M. Boetzkes and D. A. Riley serving from 1873 to 1875. and T. J. Fleming and Joseph Kaelin from that time until 1880, and since that time attended by the Chambersburg priests. Services were held once a month under the Jesuits, and since then twice a month. Father Cotting was desirous of selling the land, but Mr. George Cole suggested that it be laid out in lots, and sold only to Catholics, in order to strengthen the congregation and keep them together, which was accordingly done, in lots of ten, fifteen and twenty acres. Messrs. George Cole and John Brady purchased eight acres of woodland, and donated it to the church, to be used only for supplying firewood. The first repairs of the church were made by Father Dietz, who built the first altar. Father Cotting put pews in the church, procured a bell and an organ, and made other improvements. Father Fleming repainted, and otherwise remodeled the church during the summer of 1880.

THE TANEYTOWN CHURCH.

This is the oldest town in Carroll Co., Md. It was laid out about the year 1750, by Frederick Taney, who came from Calvert Co., Md. He was a Catholic, and a member of the family of Roger B. Taney, the late Chief Justice of the U. S. Supreme Court. By the way, Roger B. Taney, Catholic, and Anne P. C. Key, Baptist-Protestant, (a sister of F. Scott Key,) were married Jan. 7th, 1806, by Rev. Nicholas Zocchi, Pastor of St. Joseph's Church, Taneytown. As far back as 1790, there are records of Mass having been celebrated at private dwellings by Fathers Frambaugh, Pellentz, Brosius and Cerfoumont, S. J., all of whom came hither from Conewago. Prince De Gallitzin, who was ordained by Bishop Carroll, March 18th, 1795, although a Sulpician, was located for a time at Conewago, and also attended this mission, as well as Hagerstown and Cumberland in Md., Chambersburg, Path Valley and Huntingdon, in Penn. Rev. A. A. Lambing, in his History of the Catholic Church in Western Pennsylvania, says that Father Gallitzin left Taneytown and went to the Alleghany Mountains because he was opposed to the pew-rent system. This statement is inaccurate, for pews were first rented here in 1876, when the present St. Joseph's Church was built. Previous to that time the subscriptions for the support of the priest, (and they were very meagre,) were collected by the Trustees.

Prominent among the early Catholic settlers hereabouts, were the Taneys, Coskerys, Brookes, Hughes, Spaldings, Boyles, Elders, Adlespergers, Diffendals, Gougers, Toppers, Riffles, and others. About 1796, Mr. Brookes built the first Catholic Church here, at his own expense. It was of brick, made near the town. Father Gallitzin was the first pastor of St. Joseph's. From a letter of Bishop Carroll to the Rev. Pastor, dated Washington, March 1st, 1799, (Brownson's Life of G. p. 111,) we infer that Father Gallitzin left here about that time. From 1799 to 1804, Taneytown was again attended by priests from Conewago. Rev. Nicholas Zocchi, a secular priest, was born in Rome, Italy, in 1773, and was ordained at Milan, probably in 1797. He came to this country and was appointed pastor here in 1804. He is said to have been a priest of great learning, and remarkable executive ability. In addition to the places mentioned, he visited Martinsburg, Va., (now W. Va.) and Westminster, Md. At the latter place, in 1805, he built a neat brick edifice, called "Christ Church;" the first church, a frame structure, was built in 1785, four acres of land having been given to the Catholics by John Logston, after the Revolutionary War. The church built by Father Zocchi, made way in 1866 for the present handsome brick church, built by the zealous and beloved Father John Gloyd, P. P.

After a pastorate of 41 years, good Father Zocchi died at Taneytown, Dec. 17th, 1845, and was buried here on the 20th inst. The celebrated Rev. Dr. McCaffrey, then President of Mt. St. Mary's College, preached the sermon. The funeral was the largest ever seen here,—Catholics and Protestants coming in their sleighs from all parts of the county. One may form some idea of the extent of his labors, when it is known that at least twelve priests are employed on those missions. It is true that Catholics and Churches have multiplied, but Father Zocchi had to travel over that vast territory in the interest of the few Catholics (comparatively speaking) scattered over his several missions. It was certainly no small labor to go a distance of 150 or 200 miles at times to attend a sick call, especially as the journey had then to be made on horseback or in some unwieldy conveyance.

From the death of Father Zocchi until the close of the year 1851, this mission was served by the secular priests, Flautt, McCaffrey, D. D., Elder, of Mt. St. Mary's College; and Rev. Messrs. Stelzig, Tapput, and Krutel, Redemptorists, of Baltimore. Frequent visits were also made by Father Dietz, S. J.

In Dec., 1851, Rev. Thos. O'Neill was appointed pastor,

and remained in charge until Nov., 1862. He also attended Westminster and New Windsor, in the same county. At the latter place, in 1861, he built St. Thomas' Church. Leaving here in 1862, Father Tom became pastor of St. Paul's Church, Ellicott's City, where he remained several years, zealously discharging his duties. He then retired to Mt. St. Mary's College, where he died Nov. 21st, 1874, aged about 72 years. A tall marble monument, of beautiful design, marks his grave, placed there by his friend and executor, Rev. John Gloyd.

In Nov., 1862, Father Gloyd succeeded to the pastorate here, and in 1869 removed to Westminster, which then became the headquarters of the mission. This was done in accordance with the wishes of Archbishop Spalding,—Westminster being the county-seat. In May, 1871, Rev. R. W. Hazeland, a native of England, was appointed assistant to Father Gloyd, and they attended Taneytown, Deer Park Chapel, and St. Mary's, Union Mills, Carroll Co. Father Hazeland left for the West in Jan., 1873, and was succeeded by Rev. Casper Schmitt, who was ordained in Baltimore, Dec. 21st, 1872. In Nov., 1873, Rev. John T. Delaney was made assistant to Father Gloyd; and in 1876, St. Bartholomew's, Manchester, was added to the missions. This church was built by the Redemptorists, and served by them until placed under the care of the priests at Westminster. In Jan., 1879, the mission was divided,—Father Gloyd retaining charge of St. John's, Westminster, and St. Bartholomew's, Manchester, while Rev. John T. Delaney took charge of St. Joseph's, Taneytown, and St. Thomas', New Windsor. He is a kind and zealous Father, deeply interested in his church work.

The present church at Taneytown was built in 1876, when the old church built by Mr. Brookes was torn down. The church is a neat brick building, 40x70, and was erected by Father Gloyd, who raised the amount necessary for its completion before the work was begun.

CATHOLIC LOCAL HISTORY. 111

The remains of Father Zocchi rest in the cemetery at Taneytown. A plain marble monument about five feet high, marks the spot and has the following inscription: Sacred to the memory of Rev. Nicholas Zocchi, late pastor of Taneytown Catholic Church, who departed this life Dec. 17th, 1845, in the 72d year of his age. Christian, say "May God have mercy on his Soul."

Rev. Henry B. Coskery, V. G., D. D., who died in Baltimore in 1872, was born here in the house adjoining the parochial residence, July 19th, 1808. He was ordained at Baltimore in 1834, and in the same year assigned to missionary duties in Belair, Md. In 1837, he was transferred to Ellicot's Mills, and there built St. Paul's Church, and discharged the various and laborious duties of the missionary priest in the most edifying and efficacious manner. In 1839, he was called to the Cathedral by Archbishop Eccleston, and in that important field labored late and early for 32 years. He died Feb. 27th, 1872, and was buried at Bonnie Brae Cemetery.

A sister of his, Matilda Coskery, became a Sister of Charity, and died a few years ago at St. Joseph's, near Emmitsburg. She was a Sister fifty years and more, and was born here March 25th, 1805. Sister Helen Josephine (Swope), now at St. Joseph's, was born here April 11th, 1826. Sister Elizabeth (Case), born near Taneytown, Oct. 13th, 1832, and died at New Orleans. Josephine Baumgartner, born near Taneytown about 1830, became a Sister of Mercy in 1849. Matilda Sullivan, born near Taneytown, also became a Sister of Mercy.

Pastors of St. Joseph's, Taneytown: Demetrius A. De Gallitzin, born on the Hague, in Russia, Dec. 22d, 1770; ordained at St. Mary's Seminary, Balto., March 18th, 1795; died May 6th, 1840. Rev. Nicholas Zocchi, born at Rome, Italy, 1773, ordained about 1797, at Milan, died Dec. 17th, 1845, at Taneytown. Rev. Thos. O'Neill, born in Ireland about 1802, ordained in Balto. 1830; died at Mt. St. Mary's,

Nov. 21st, 1874. Rev. John Gloyd, born in Montgomery Co., Md., Oct. 22d, 1831; ordained at St. Mary's, May, 1858; now pastor at Westminster. Rev. John T. Delaney, born in Balto., Feb. 1843; ordained at St. Mary's Seminary Dec. 21st, 1872; now pastor of St. Joseph's, Taneytown.

THE WESTMINSTER CHURCH.

The church property at this place, consisting of four acres, was donated by John Logston. Upon this a frame church was built about the year 1789. There is nothing to show who had charge of the church at that early period; probably the Fathers from Frederick and Conewago. The second, called Christ's Church, a brick building, was erected by Rev. Nicholas Zocchi, in 1805. This venerable priest was ordained when he was twenty-two years and six months old. He visited Westminster once a month on Sundays until his death in 1845. The entire mission was then without a resident pastor until 1851. During this interval, irregular visits were made by different clergymen— Revs. John F. Hickey, Henry Myers, Joseph Dietz, Francis Krutel, and others. In 1851, Rev. Thomas O'Neill was placed in charge of the mission, with residence at Taneytown. He was succeeded by Rev. John Gloyd in Nov., 1862, who also resided at Taneytown until Westminster was made headquarters in 1869. The third, St. John's Church, brick, was commenced in 1865, and dedicated Nov. 22d, 1866. Mr. John Orendorf gave all the bricks for the building. The assistants until the mission was divided in 1879, were Revs. Richard Hazeland from 1871 to 1873, Casper Schmidt from 1873 to 1874; John T. Delaney from 1874 to 1879. The parochial school house was built in 1872. Rev. John Gloyd is the present beloved and zealous pastor.

THE FREDERICK CHURCH.

Many Catholic families, among them the Carrolls, were connected with the earliest settlement around Frederick Town, now in Frederick Co., Md. When first founded it was in Baltimore Co., and was an important point on the principal stage routes which then traversed the country. Frederick is an old Catholic mission, and being the location of the Jesuit Novitiate, has a very interesting history and should have valuable records. All that we are able to give is taken from Scharf's History of Western Maryland.

Many Catholics had settled on Carroll's Manor, on the Monocacy, at the close of the last century. They were attended by Rev. John Dubois, from Mt. St. Mary's. The ground on which the original chapel was built, was deeded to Father John Hunter, by John Carey, Oct. 2d, 1765. Frederick was attended by priests from St. Thomas' Mission, near Port Tobacco, for a long time the residence of the Superior of the Jesuits in Maryland. From this was supplied all the adjacent country, from the headwaters of the Potomac to the Eastern Shores. The German Fathers from Conewago also attended the mission at Frederick. The first residence and chapel were built in 1763, by John Williams, an English Jesuit, who came to the Maryland Missions June 9th, 1758, with Fathers James Frambach and James Pellentz. He returned to Europe about 1774. There is reason to believe that Father George Hunter succeeded Father Williams. He was Superior of the Jesuits in Maryland in 1765, and Superior and Vicar General in 1794. Father James Frambach was pastor of Frederick in 1773, according to Campbell. He had the whole of Western Maryland and part of Virginia, and traveled far, visiting the sick and administering the Sacraments. Many a time he slept near his horse, on the banks of the Potomac and its tributaries, and early in the morning was up and off again. He was succeeded by Father James Walton, an Englishman, who came to Md. in 1776, died at St. Inigoes 1803, aged 65. The chapel was then attended by Father Dubois. The residence forms part of the Novitiate. The small chapel of Father Williams was for nearly forty years the only place of worship for the Catholics of Frederick. The Jesuits remained during the Suppression. Father Dubois began to administer at St. John's about 1792. He also attended the Western Missions, Hagerstown, Cumberland, Martinsburg and as far South as Winchester. Scharf says he "was for a long time the only priest between Baltimore and St. Louis." We do not wish to contradict the celebrated historian, but Father Lambing's Researches furnish much information on early Catholic settlements. The Conewago Fathers themselves attended the western missions from Frambach's time, 1760, to Father Gallitzin's, 1800. The history of the Carroll families in Maryland would also throw additional light on early Catholic missionary work.

Father Dubois began the erection of a church at Frederick in 1800. It was of brick, 82x45 feet. The building was partly torn down and changed in 1859, and has since been used for other purposes. After he removed to Emmettsburg in 1806, he visited Frederick once or twice a month. Francis Maleve, S. J., took charge in 1811. He had the church repaired in 1812, as the congregation was then increasing. He was born Dec. 1, 1770, a native of Russia. He belonged to the order of St. Francis Assisi, but when the Order was dispersed he labored as a Secular priest. Father Maleve entered the Society in Russia in 1804: came to this country while a Novice, and took his last vows June 29th, 1815. He commenced the building of St. Joseph's Church on the Manor, about seven miles from Frederick, which was completed in 1820. The lot and part of the funds were gifts from Charles Carroll of Carrollton. Father Maleve died Oct. 3d, 1822.

In 1821, Mr. Coale gave land on which to build a church,

at Liberty, twelve miles from Frederick. The old church was torn down several years ago and a new one built by Gen. Coale, a son of the donor of the original lot.

Father John McElroy took charge after the death of Father Maleve. He built churches and schools, and is well remembered for his zealous labors in the cause of religion. He died in 1877 at the Novitiate. He was the oldest priest in America, aged 95 years, having been born in the town of Innis Killin, Ireland, in 1782.

In 1824, five Sisters came to Frederick from Emmettsburg, and were lodged in a log cabin. St. John's Academy was opened Jan. 3d, 1824. In 1825, a larger establishment was built. Rev. P. W. Walsh was assistant in 1825. A church was built at Petersville in 1826, on land given by Mr. West, a Protestant. Aug. 7th, 1828, St. John's Literary Institute was begun; opened in 1829. It has given many great men to religion and the professions. The new church was contemplated as early as 1830. The corner-stone was laid in 1833. It was finished after many difficulties in 1837, consecrated April 26th. The steeple was completed in 1854, by Burchard Villiger, S. J. Father Peter Kenney was Superior at that time. Father Wm. McSherry succeeded him. In 1833, a large addition was made to the residence. A wing and the chapel were added by Father Samuel Barber. Improvements were made by Father Brocard, and in 1859 by Father Parasce. The Sisters' building was burned down in 1845, and was rebuilt. In 1839, Father James Ryder was assistant to Father McElroy, and teacher of French and writing. Thomas Lilly, S. J., succeeded Father McElroy in Sept., 1845. The assistants were Revs. George Villiger, Stonestreet, Meredith, Jenkins, Finotti, and Bogue. In 1846, the Sisters of Charity withdrew, and the Nuns of the Visitation from Georgetown took their place. In 1848, Rev. Charles H. Stonestreet succeeded Father Lilly. The assistants were Revs. Bogue, Finotti and Ciampi. When Rev. Stonestreet had charge, Rev. Francis Dzierozynski, a saintly man, died there. He was a native of Orsani, in Poland, born June 3d, 1777. Father Thomas Mulledy succeeded in 1850. After him came Revs. Villiger, Barber, Hippolyte Deneckere, Blenkinsop and McAtee; the two latter, with M. Tuffer, S. J., being there in 1860. From 1853 to 1860, the assistants were Revs. Bogue, Duddy, and Tuffer. Father Sourin was in charge from 1860 to 1870; the assistants were Revs. O'Kane, Smith, Jenkins, Ciampi and Fulmer. After an absence of twenty-five years, Father Stonestreet returned as parish priest.

THE HAGERSTOWN CHURCH.

This sketch of Catholicity in Hagerstown is nothing more than the interesting and valuable data collected by Father Jones when he was pastor, and left by him as a church record. The Hagerstown Church was long attended by the early missionaries of Conewago, Taneytown and Frederick. A very full and interesting history of the church might be written from these records, but as it serves our purpose of preserving names and dates, we give them as they appear:

The deed of the old Catholic graveyard, from Jonathan Hagar to Rev. James Frambach, for three lots (Nos. 319, 320, 321,) in Hagar's addition to Elizabethtown, is dated Aug. 16th, 1786, recorded in liber E, folio 38. The deed of the present church property, from Adam Miller, of Bedford Co., Pa., to Luke Tieman, of Baltimore Co., Md., Charles Carroll, Denis Cahill (priest,) James McClellan, John Adams, James McCardell, Jos. Clark and Wm. Clark, of Washington Co., and to the survivors and their heirs in trust, is dated May 25th, 1794; recorded in liber H, folio 847 to 849; property given for the nominal sum of five shillings. From this time until about 1820, the church was at first served by Father Cahill and other priests who did missionary work in the country bordering the Potomac and Shenandoah; after them by Father Zocchi, of Taneytown, and the Frederick and Mountain priests. Father Cahill left Baltimore for Ireland in the spring of 1806, and died there in 1817. As a missionary priest his labors were equal to those of the Conewago Fathers and Maryland Jesuits, and we regret that so little information of his life can be obtained.

Rev. Timothy Ryan took charge of the Hagerstown church in 1822. The old log church, which stood where the main building of the " presbytery " now stands, was removed and a new church built. The corner-stone was laid July 4th, 1825. He attended the congregation while the Chesapeake and Ohio Canal was being built, and labored during the cholera of 1833 ; died June 2d, 1837. Rev. Geo. M. Guth succeeded until 1844, latter part, when Father Henry Myers came. He took charge of Hagerstown and the missions Aug. 15th, 1845. In this year he was taken seriously ill, and received the last Sacraments from Rev. Charles Stonestreet, S. J.

The deed of the Williamsport church is recorded in liber I N, No. 10, fol. 110, and is from Robert Lemon, executor of Peter Light, to Rt. Rev. F. P. Kenrick and his successors, for $1,000 ; dated Dec. 8th, 1854, delivered to Father Myers Sept. 4th, 1856.

Rev. Joseph Maguire was assistant to Father Myers in 1851, and died Sept. 18th, 1852, buried in front of the church where a monument marks his grave. Father Myers left about Nov., 1857 ; Rev. George Flaut left in July, 1858 ; Rev. Edmund Didier left Sept., 1861 ; Rev. John Gloyd attended from Hancock until Dec., 1861, when Rev. Malachy Moran, O. S. B., took charge. He left about the middle of 1864, succeeded by Thos. McDonough, S. J., from Frederick ; Rev. Aloysius Janalick, S. J., left in the summer of 1865, and was succeeded by Rev. Ed. Didier, who remained until May 7th, 1868.

1867, Aug, 17, deed from Charles Tieman and G. R. Tieman his wife, to Rev. Ed. Didier, James I. Hurley, Jacob A. Wright, Jerome B. McClery, Jacob H. Wills and John Eck, trustees of St. Mary's Church at Hagerstown, which includes church property and priest's house. The survivor of the original trustees of May 5, 1794, was Luke Tieman, and from him the legal title descended to Charles Tieman. Deed from Dennis and Margaret Galvin, of St. Louis, to same trustees, for the school house, afterwards sold to C. V. R. R. for depot, is dated Aug, 21st, 1867. The deed for all the church property, from the trustees to Most Rev. M. J. Spalding, and his successors the Archbishops of Baltimore, is recorded in liber I N, No. 18, fols. 693 to 696. The church property became invested in Rev. Ed. Didier and five trustees, according to article 26, sec. 88 to 101, of the Public General Laws. The number of trustees was increased to seven and the pastor. By the agreement of March 25th, 1875, Rev. J. M. Jones, J. F. Smith, Jacob A. Wright, P. M. John, H. H. Keedy, James I. Hurley, C. B. Boyle and W. F. Orndorf became trustees.

Rev. John M. Jones became pastor May 7th, 1868,— Father Didier leaving the next day for St. Peter's, Baltimore. Father Myers introduced the new pastor at High Mass. There was then need of church and house improvements, furniture, and repairs, which were made by degrees. The mission then consisted of Hagerstown, Williamsport, Boonsboro, and Smithburg. Clearspring was given to Rev. M. Daush, of Hancock. First Fair held in Lyceum Hall in Nov., 1868; the proceeds, $1900, expended in repairing church and furnishing house. Gas was put in the church in May, 1869. June 6th, 1869, mission commenced by Revs. Wayrich, Gross and O'Donohue, C. S. S. R. Wayrich was an eloquent speaker. There were several converts and 320 Communicants. The congregation gave the missionaries $180 at their departure. Rev

Michael Daush left Hancock in the spring of 1861, when Father Jones was given the whole mission, including Little Orleans, afterward attached to Cumberland, with Rev. Chas. Damer as assistant. The Booonsboro church was built by Dr. Josiah Smith, with money left by Dr. Otho Smith.

Aug. 22, 1869, Forty Hours, Fathers T. Lee and John Kain, of Harper's Ferry, assisted. Festival held in Williamsport; $175 cleared; expended for organ; congregation there small and poor. Dec. 22d, Jubilee began in Hagerstown, Revs. Richard Barry, of Harrisburg, and F. Fields, of Chambersburg, assisted; 280 Communicants; Jubilee followed at Hancock and Clearspring—180 Com. at former, 49 at latter place. June 16th, 1870, Corpus Christi; began addition to church in Hagerstown, Mr. Frederick, Baltimore, brother of Father Frederick, architect; Oliyer, contractor. Old school house and lot sold to C. V. R. R. for $3000; rest of money raised by subscription. Mission divided in Nov., Father Ryan took Hancock, Father Jones the rest. Jan., 1871, church in Hagerstown dedicated by Father Myers, who said High Mass; Rev. D. Lyman preached; Forty Hours followed held by Revs. S. F. Ryan and John Kain. While church was being repaired, Mass said in Miss Eliza Monahan's house, Franklin Street. Easter morning this year, 105 Communicants. Sept. 28, 1871, Rev. J. M. Jones returned to St. Peter's, Balto. Rev. D. DeWulf succeeded; Rev. S. F. Ryan changed from Hancock to Cumberland about this time.— Rev. C. Damer appointed to Hancock. 1873, Sept., Arch. Bayley administered Confirmation. 1874, Jan. 25 to 29— Rev. J. J. Kain, of Harper's Ferry, gave mission at Williamsport; when Rev. John Boetzkes, of Chambersburg, assisted; 72 Com. 1873, July 21st, Father Myers died at St. Vincent's, Baltimore, buried on the 24th. 1873, Oct. 14— Rev. Jones returned to Hagerstown as pastor; Rev. DeWulf left next day for St. Matthew's, Wash. 1874, Jan. 12 to 13, Dr. Chapelle, of St. Joseph, Baltimore, gave two lectures for

Altar Society. Aug. 28, Sisters of St. Joseph came to open school; small house rented for them from Mr. Keerl. Mother Liguori taught small boys; Sister Angela, head of the school; Sister Basil, small children. Sister Winfred, lay. Sister—"all strangers to each other and to us." Congregation furnished house, paid $200 rent, $200 to Sisters and $200 to Chestnut Hill for Novitiate; Priest has all responsibility of collecting money and attending to material prosperity of the school. This was the arrangement made by Mother St. John and approved by Arch. Bayley.

1874. Fair Oct. 13; $1089.05 realized; went to pay $1300 debt remaining from church repairs. Jan. 19, F. X. Boyle, of Washington, lectured for benefit of school. Sisters moved into new house, purchased from Mr. Ogilly at a cost of $6,750. Additions made in summer of 1875. Property held in name of Trustees. Sept. 17, Arch. Bayley confirmed at Hagerstown, and at Williamsport. Miss Eliza Monahan died in November; left $1000 for marble altar; money was needed at the time and put in school building. [Father Manley, present pastor, intends to have marble altar erected in accordance with bequest.]

1875. Upstairs of priest's house improved. Sept. 19 to 26th, Revs. Wayrich and Oberhart, C. S. S. R., gave mission. Fair in Williamsport Dec. 23d; proceeds $700; congregation began to tear down church, walls were giving away; Arch. Bayley added $100; men gave their labor free; church so far completed fourth Sunday in July, 1876, as to have Mass for the first time; during building services were held in public hall. Mr. Eli Stake generously undertook building, without charge for his work; congregation worked well, and gave according to means; dedication deferred to spring of '77 for want of funds.

1876. Strawberry festival held in Hagerstown, June 10 to 13th; $145.14 made. July 4th, bell rung for Centennial, and High Mass. July 19, picnic for Williamsport church,—$147.96. Aug.— addition of second and third stories to school building at Hagerstown; cost $300; Heil contractor. Nov.—Fair in new church, Williamsport, $562 realized; good fair, well conducted; Mrs. Barry obtained herself all articles on her table. Christmas,—James I. Hurley presented Hagerstown church with handsome pair twelve-light candelabra.

1877. Easter, 106 Communicants. April 2d, concert by Dr. Dielman; cleared $42.25. April 29, Williamsport Church dedicated by Rev. J. J. Kain, of Wheeling, W. Va.; Mass by Rev. Desire De Wulf; Rev. S. F. Ryan, Deacon; Thomas Fleming, Sub-Deacon; present, Revs. J. O'Sullivan, [now Bishop of Mobile,] and C. Damer. Mercadantes Mass in B flat; Bishop Kain preached, Heb. xii., 22-24. In evening, Rev. J. O'Sullivan, of Westernport, preached in Hagerstown. May 6,—Forty Hours same place, Father Watterson, Mt. St. Mary's, preached; Rev. C. P. O'Connor, from Overbrook, and Revs. Gloyd and Kaelin assisted. Nov. 25,—St. Catharine's Day; great flood of Potomac; water higher at Williamsport than since 1852; houses and barns and C. V. R. R. bridge swept away. Oct. 3d,—bell tolled from 9 to 10 P. M., for death of Arch. Bayley; news of his death not received until evening. Last of Sept.,—collected $100 on Williamsport Church debt, balance $300. Oct. 13th,—High Mass of Requiem at Hagerstown for Arch. Bayley. Nov. 27,—fair for Sisters' school; almost all articles came from Rev. C. P. O'Connor and from Visitation Convent, Georgetown, and from Sisters of St. Joseph. Dec. 25,—Rev. Jones, pastor, sick; Rev. Fowler sang Mass.

1878. Rev. J. P. Casey came as assistant at Hagerstown, March 2d; left April 22d. Rev. John M. Jones went to Europe, May 4th; returned Sept. 20; Charles Stonestreet, S. J., supplied. New Missal purchased in Oct., for $22. New cope and white vestment arrived from Toulouse, France. Thanksgiving Dinner in Williamsport cleared $67. Dec.—Rev. DeWitt, S. J., of Frederick, assisted at Christmas; new vestments used for first time. Dec. 23d, new furnace put in

Williamsport Church at a cost of $110.

1879. March 11th, Forty Hours at Williamsport, Revs. Fleming and Damer assisted. May 4th, Arch. Gibbons confirmed 61 at Hagerstown, 23 converts; preached in evening on the Infallibility; large attendance. Sixteen persons entertained at dinner by pastor. Very Rev. O'Connor sang Mass. May 5th, 19 confirmed at Williamsport, 5 converts. Mr. Victor Cushwa gave dinner to Archbishop and clergy. May 11th, Forty Hours at Hagerstown; sermons by Revs. C. Damer, J. O'Sullivan, and T. Lee; Rev. J. Kaelin finished Devotions; Jubilee followed; Sermon in German, about the last here, by Rev. Smith, of Frostburg; 300 Com. During month of Oct., Rev. Jones resigned on account of ill health; acceptance from Feb. 1st, 1880; Rev. J. A. Frederick succeeded. 1879, Dec. 25th, C. Stonestreet, S. J., assisted; Dec. 28th, fine sermon by the same, on the Immortality of the Soul. 1883, Jan. 25th, Rev. H. Voltz succeeded Father Frederick; introduced Jan. 28th. May 20th, Forty Hours, present Revs. Gloyd, Delancy, Meade and McKeefry; 230 Com. June 28th, Commencement of St. Joseph's Academy. July 15, began new story on school building. Sept. 4th, fair for school; proceeds $1500. Sept. 4th, Dr. Josias Smith, trustee, died; buried on the 7th, large funeral. 1884, Feb. 10th, Mission by Lazarist Fathers, Lefevre and Krabler; 400 Com. April 10 and 11, office of Tenebræ for first time in many years. April 13th, Easter, meeting of church members; decided to put new roof on church and another story on house; improvements begun in May, completed in June. July 27th, Arch. Gibbons preached and confirmed. 1885. Rev. Henry Voltz left Jan. 16th; was succeeded by Rev. D. Manley; who was met and welcomed by members of the congregation and Father Meade, of Williamsport. Father Manley is an earnest and prudent worker, and a kind priest. During the summer of 1885, he said Mass at Pen-Mar, a summer resort on the Blue Ridge. The Hagerstown Mission is now divided; Rev. Manley attending points nearest Hagerstown; Rev. Meade those near Williamsport, and Rev. Peter Weider at Hancock.

"Father Myers was one of the most highly esteemed pastors of the church." He was born at the "Seminary Farm," Conewago, Adams Co., Pa., in 1806; studied at St. Mary's, Baltimore; educated by the Sulpitians, and ordained in 1830. He was stationed at St. Patrick's Church, Washington, then at Cumberland where he built a church. After laboring twelve years at Hagerstown, he went to Pikesville, Balto. Co., Md. In 1860, he succeeded Rev. Leonard Obermyer as pastor of St. Vincent de Paul's in Baltimore, and died there in July, 1873. The Hagerstown missions are also greatly indebted to the labors of Father Jones, whose memory is cherished with love and veneration.

Among the church improvements in 1870, was the erection of the present beautiful steeple, crowned with a large cross.

YORK AND OTHER CHURCHES.

York, a growing city on the banks of the Codorus, in York Co., Pa., is a place full of historic interest. The Continental Congress, driven from Philadelphia by the British invasion, retired to "York Town," Sept. 30th, 1777, and held its sessions there until June 27th, 1778. Here was printed the first Continental Money; Philip Livingston, one of the New York delegates, died here June 11th, 1778, and was buried in the German Reformed graveyard; John Hancock resigned his presidency of Congress at York, and Henry

Laurence elected in his place; early in Nov., 1777, Col. Wilkinson brought despatches to Congress at York, announcing Burgoyne's surrender; Lafayette was appointed to the command of a division in the Continental Army, and Baron Steuben's offer of service was accepted here. While in session at York, an unsuccessful attempt was made by Gen. Conway and others to displace Gen. Washington and put Gen. Gates in his place; Lafayette discovered and exposed the plot. "Pulaski's Legion" made York its place of rendezvous while preparing to march South; leaving York in March, 1779; Count Pulaski fell in an unsuccessful assault on the British at Savannah, Oct. 3d of that year. A battalion of French troops known as "Armand's Legion," was quartered at York from Jan. to Nov., 1783. We have a copy of a letter of thanks from the citizens of York, to "Brigadier Gen. Armand, Marquis De La Rouerie," for the kind services, aid and protection of his troops to the country and to the town, dated Nov. 18th, 1783; and his reply to it dated the 19th, when he says his troops and himself are preparing to return to their country, and offer their services to America whenever in need of assistance, signed "Armand, Marquis De La Rouerie." Mr. Griffin, in his recent sketches of Catholicity in Philadelphia, makes mention of Count Armand, and if we mistake not, says he died at that place. Another distinguished personage at York at that time and afterward, was Baron de Beelen Bertholf, Belgian minister to this country, also a Catholic, of whom we will be able to give further particulars. There is no record that there were any Chaplains with the troops quartered at York. The Catholics at that time were attended by the Conewago missionaries, at first every sixth week, and later every fourth Sunday.

April 17th, 1750, John Moore entered his name for a lot marked No. 295, in the general plan of the town of York, founded and situated on the east side of Beaver Street, containing in breadth north and south, 57 feet and 6 inches, and in length to a 20-foot alley, 230 feet. June 20th of the same year, Moore sold to Casper Stillinger, who built a dwelling house on the lot. The property passed from the possession of the Stillinger heirs to Joseph Smith, May 4th, 1776, who purchased it for the use of the Catholic congregation, presenting it to that body and for that purpose. The house was converted into a place of religious worship and used as such until 1810, when the old stone dwelling was torn down and a brick church was built on the same site. A deed was given to perfect the title, by Hons. John and Richard Penn, by their attorney John R. Coates, "to the Reverend Thomas Neale, (should have been Francis, Provincial of the Jesuits at that time,) in trust for the Roman Catholic Congregation of York Town," dated June 2d, 1808, for the nominal sum of five shillings, conveying Lot No. 295, on Beaver St., York, to Rev. Thomas (Francis) Neale, in trust, &c., "it being the same lot whereon a chapel is erected." The first resident priest at York was Rev. Lorence Huber, who came there in Dec., 1819, and remained six months. Rev. George D. Hogan came in the summer of 1820; Rev. P. J. Dween in the summer of 1822, and was there yet in 1834. The name of the church was St. Patrick's. We have been unable to obtain the names of succeeding priests. In 1850, Rev. Father Hatting, from Conewago, built a Catholic Church at York. He was probably the last of the Jesuits attending that place. When Fathers Enders and Deneckere were first sent on the Conewago missions, they attended York; so did Father Cotting and others. In 1860, Rev. Silvester Eagle was pastor of St. Patrick's, and Revs. Mat. J. Meurer and John Vollmeyer in charge of the Immaculate Conception church. In 1877, Father Kennedy was pastor of St. Patrick's, and John Geo. Fape of St. Mary's. There were different pastors at various times, whose names we have not. The Catholic Church at York is very flourishing. Besides churches and pastoral residences, there are large and well attended schools, taught by the Sisters; and three strong Beneficial Societies. There are several missions outside of York. Father Huber is pastor at Shrewsbury. Rev. Pape is still pastor of St. Mary's. He has just completed a very handsome church at a cost of $47,000. The corner-stone was laid May 25th, 1884. The church was dedicated May 25th, 1885. The dedicatory services were conducted by Rev. J. F. Shanahan, Bishop of Harrisburg. A Grand High Mass followed, Rev. Koppernagle, of Harrisburg, Celebrant, assisted by Rev. Louis Grotenmeyer, of Lancaster; Rev. Michael Reily, of Columbia; Rev. J. A. Huber, of New Freedom, Master of Ceremonies. Rev. Joseph Wissel, of Annapolis, who was a former pastor of both York churches, preached a sermon in German. There were present the following clergymen: Revs. J. G. Pape, Pastor; James Gormley, of Bonneauville; J. A. Boll, of Gettysburg; Wm. Pieper, of Columbia; John Koeper, of Williamsport; Clement Schleuter, of Chambersburg. The church is of brick, built in the Gothic style; 129 by 57½ feet, with two side towers 70 feet each and a centre steeple of 185 feet. The interior has stained memorial windows, three altars, is tastefully ornamented and furnished with steam heat and a $3,000 organ. The new church walls were built up around the old church, in which services were held at the time. Father Pape is a hard-working priest.— He visited Europe several years ago. Rev. John Shanahan was the late pastor of St. Patrick's, resigning in Aug., 1885, and going to Rome to further prosecute his studies in philosophy and theology. Rev. O'Reilley, of Shamokin, succeeded in September.

A sketch of St. Mary's, prepared by a committee of St. Patrick's Society,—Messrs. J. C. Maguire, Henry Boll, J. H. Garrety, John Mayer, Wm. Chambers and M. M. Little,— furnishes us with the following facts in the history of that church. The Germans were long deprived of the blessings of religion in their native tongue, and were often obliged to go to Conewago and Baltimore to make their confessions.—

Rev. Shorb, an American of German parentage, was pastor of St. Patrick's for a short while, with great satisfaction to the Germans. Bishop Kenrick sent a German from Conewago, Rev. Jacob Cotting, in 1851-2. Bishop Neuman separated the two congregations. The Germans then purchased an acre of ground on the Baltimore pike for a cemetery, which was blessed June 27th, 1852. At the same time, a lot, 140 feet front and 220 deep, was purchased on South George Street, for a church, the corner-stone of which was laid July 25th, of that year. By the united efforts of pastor and congregation, a brick church, 42x80 feet, was erected by Oct. 25th, when the august sacrifice of the Mass was celebrated in it for the first time. An organ and a bell were procured in 1853. A school-house was built soon after adjoining the church. Rev. Cotting came twice a month. Rev. J. Wachter, a newly ordained priest, a Tyrolean by birth, became the first resident pastor July 4th, 1853. He was a faithful and zealous pastor, and was assisted by Rev. F. Rudolph, who attended the country missions. In 1843, through the efforts of a Catholic gentleman named Muller, from Baden, Germany, a church was built at New Freedom, nineteen miles south of York. Bishop Kenrick gave the building of it to the Redemptorists. Revs. Kronenberger and Neuman, (afterwards Bishop of Philadelphia,) had charge of St. John's Church, New Freedom, for several years. It was then attended from St. Mary's, York. In 1850, the few Catholics around Dallastown built a substantial stone church, which was served from the same place. After the removal of Rev. Kuntzer from York, Rev. Wachter was assisted Rev. F. X. Tryer, who succeeded him at his death in 1859. Rev. Tryer was a native of Switzerland; he was succeeded by Rev. M. Meurer, a native of Wurtemburg, who remained until Oct., 1861. Rev. Joseph Hamm, from Baden, succeeded him, and in 1863 built a two-story brick parsonage adjoining the church, at a cost of about $4,000. Rev. B. Baummaster, a native of Muenster, had charge from 1866 to 1868. In Nov.

of that year, Rev. J. G. Pape, also a native of Westphalia, was transferred from Ashland to York. In 1869, he built a new brick school-house on the lot in the rear of the church, and this year completed a magnificent new church edifice.—He is a very active and energetic man, both in spiritual and temporal matters. The Sisters of St. Francis, of Philadelphia, have been in charge of the school, which has a large attendance. They have been faithful teachers.

The Diocese of Philadelphia was divided in 1868, when that city became an Archiepiscopal See. At the formation of the Diocese of Harrisburg, Rev. J. F. Shanahan was consecrated its Bishop, over which he now presides. The diocese was extensive enough, but poor in churches and religious work. New congregations were organized, churches built, schools established and priests ordained, and now everywhere are evidences of his zeal and labor. For a number of years the good Bishop has been trying to establish a Diocesan Seminary, and we trust his object will be accomplished before he is called to his reward. We know very little of the early Catholic history of Harrisburg. It came within the limits of the missions already outlined, and whatever Catholics were scattered through this section of the Cumberland Valley, were ministered to by the early Jesuit missionaries. St. Patrick's Church was built in 1826, by Rev. Michael Curran. Rupp, in his history of Dauphin County, about 1840, says it is a beautiful edifice, with a handsome tower and a large bell, situated on State Street, between Second and Third. Its size is about 50x75 feet, and cost $7,000.—It was consecrated Oct. 2d, 1827, by Rt. Rev. Henry Conwell, Bishop of Philadelphia. St. Patrick's became the pro-Cathedral in 1868, and was enlarged and improved in 1874, dedicated July 12th, five Bishops being present and a number of priests. Rev. John Foley succeeded Rev. Curran.—A German priest from York attended the Germans for a time. They have a church now. Father Koppernagle labored very hard in its interest. There is also a church at Steelton.

Rev. Pierce Mather was pastor of St. Patrick's for many years. He was a priest of more than ordinary zeal and ability; a learned and generous man, well-known in religious circles, and at his death the church paid him distinguished funeral honors by the presence of many priests and several Bishops. He was born April 6th, 1812, near Clonmel, Ireland; studied for the priesthood under Bishop Kenrick; ordained May 25th, 1837. He labored at Harrisburg from that time until the arrival of Bishop Shanahan in 1868, when he was sent to Norristown, where he died Dec. 28th, 1873.— Father Mather improved or rebuilt partly the church at Carlisle. He may well be ranked with the most zealous and faithful missionaries of Southern Pennsylvania.

The Conewago Jesuits had a lot and chapel at Carlisle, long before 1800. Sherman Day, in his Collections, says the Jesuits had a small log church there. The present brick church was built in 1807, and enlarged in 1823. There is an old graveyard attached to the church, and no doubt many interesting facts of Catholic history might be gathered from the place. It was occasionally visited by the Fathers on the Catholic missions in Western Pennsylvania. In 1869 Father Kelly attended Carlisle from Chambersburg. The present pastor is Rev. McKenna.

There is a fine brick parsonage adjoining the church.— The church bears evidence of age. Rev. Huber, of the York missions, has lately been transferred to Carlisle.

The early Jesuit missionaries also had a log church at Chambersburg before 1800, where the present stone church stands, built in 1812. There are several old missions belonging to the Chambersburg charge, one in Path Valley, at Waynesboro, The Mountain Church, and at adjoining towns. The present pastors are Revs. Schleuter and Kaelin.

THE KEYSER CHURCH.

Keyser is situated on the B. & O. R. R., 215 miles from

Baltimore. It was formerly called New Creek, and was a place of little note until the B. & O. made it their Second terminal division in 1874. The Catholic mission was opened by Rt. Rev. J. O'Sullivan, Bishop of Mobile, Ala., then pastor of Westernport, five miles west of Keyser. Owing to a want of priests in his diocese, Bishop McGill could not supply either Keyser or Piedmont, a large and prosperous town across the Potomac River from Westernport. Father O'Sullivan began the erection of a little church in Sept., 1874. At that time, Mrs. Thompson, a widow with six orphans, were the only Catholics in the town. Terence Corrigan and Daniel Maloney then lived about a mile east of the town. These three families comprised the congregation. The carpenter work was begun Sep. 14th, and the first Mass was said Sep. 20th. The little church stands almost on the very spot where Col. James A. Mulligan, Twenty-Third Illinois Volunteers, Irish Brigade, erected a temporary chapel during the late war, in which Dr. Butler, of Chicago, officiated. Rev. H. J. McKeefry, of the Richmond Diocese, took charge of the congregation Dec. 19th, 1875, then numbering 225 persons. During his pastorate, besides paying off a debt of $443, Father McKeefry enlarged the church to twice its original size, and erected a parsonage. He also organized a school, which he himself taught for five months. This good priest suffered many privations, for shortly after his arrival the terminal division of railroad was removed back to Piedmont, leaving scarcely a dozen families to maintain a priest. But this true shepherd remained with his little flock, when finally the railroad shops were again located at Keyser. After a successful pastorate of nearly three years, Rev. McKeefry was succeeded in Oct. 1878, by Rev. P. Fitzsimmons, assistant pastor at Staunton, Father McKeefry taking his place. During Rev. Fitzsimmons' pastorate the church at Paw-Paw, Morgan Co., (Keyser is in Mineral Co.,) West Va., 48 miles east, was assigned to Keyser as an auxiliary mission. After carrying on the work of his predecessors for nearly two years, Father Fitzsimmons was called to his eternal rest Aug. 4th, 1880. He is buried in St. Joseph's Cemetery, Martinsburg, where a neat marble stone marks his last resting place. After an interval of eight months, Rev. P. J. Hasty, assistant pastor of Lynchburg, Va., was called to take charge, April 15th, 1881. This brilliant young priest, after a stay of four months, was removed to St. Vincent's Hospital, Norfolk, where he died Dec. 30th, 1881, from the effects of the amputation of his right leg, rendered necessary by an abscess from blood poisoning. In Aug., 1881, Rev. Eugene Mahony, assistant at Martinsburg, became pastor, who, during the short period of his stay, eight months, built a handsome parsonage and school house, the greater part of the work being done by himself in person. He was recalled to his own Diocese, Brooklyn, in April, 1882. May 29th, 1882, Rev. H. J. Cutlor took charge, and remained until Jan. 3d, 1883. He paid the remaining indebtedness, $700, incurred in building the Pastor's house and the school house. Jan. 3d, 1883, Rev. Cutlor was transferred to Norfolk, as assistant to Rev. M. O'Keefe. On the same day, Rev. J. Frioli took charge of Keyser, and has proven a faithful and worthy pastor, still presiding, Oct. 12th, 1885. In the Summer of 1882, a mission was started in Elk Garden, a mining town, 13 miles from Piedmont, on the W. Va. C. & P. R. R. Father Cutlor said Mass there several times. This mission is attended from Keyser. A church, 30x55 feet, was built there in the Fall of 1883. There are now 52 families, numbering about 270 souls. Besides Paw-Paw and Elk Garden, Catholic families, eleven in number, in Hampshire and Hardy Counties, W. Va., are ministered to several times a year by the Pastor of Keyser. During all these years, from 1876 to the present, a Catholic school has been maintained in Keyser, though the number of school children never exceeded 35. It is now taught by Miss Bee Ahern, of Martinsburg, where she was principal of the Catholic School for a number of years, and also at Winchester. The Keyser congregation now numbers 51 families, and about 250 souls. At Paw-Paw there are eleven families and fifty-three souls.

The Catholic church in West Virginia is just in its missionary state, but great progress is being made everywhere. The Diocese of Wheeling will one day be an important one. There are several fine churches in Wheeling, and a large religious scholastic institution at Mt. de Chantal. At Parkersburg, Charleston, Clarksburg, Weston, Morgantown, Fairmont, and at most of the towns in the State, are flourishing Catholic congregations and zealous laborers. For want of missionary priests in the early settlement of this Little Mountain State, the church lost many of its faithful. Quite a number of Catholic families from Southern Pennsylvania settled through the Eastern Panhandle counties in the latter part of the last century and the beginning of the present. The Maryland and Conewago Jesuits followed them up as long as possible, but increasing age and labors, and removals by death, in course of time confined the limit of their ministry east of the Blue Ridge. The children of these emigrants, some in Hampshire and adjoining counties, drifted away from the faith through the negligence of their parents and the want of religious instructions. The seed of faith is still there, and being now cultivated by good laborers, will bring an abundant harvest to the church.

We have not time to extend our researches much farther. At Grafton, Taylor Co., 100 miles from Keyser, the Catholics are well established. St. Augustine's was the first religious organization in the town. Father Dillon celebrated Mass there in 1853. A church was built in 1856, and Revs. Cunningham and Malone visited the Catholics in the surrounding communities. The first church is now used as a parish school for the girls, and the first parsonage is now occupied as the Sisters' Home. Rev. Malone died and was buried there in 1867. Revs. Duffy and Welsh succeeded. Father Walters, a wealthy priest, built the present fine church at his own expense in 1872. He died several years ago. Rev. Keleher took charge in 1879. Since that schools, societies and church work generally, have been carried on very prosperously.—There are a number of Sisters at the Home, Mother Staney, Superior. Sister Genevieve conducts an excellent music department.

THE MARTINSBURG CHURCH.

When the Diocese of Richmond was divided in 1850, Martinsburg and a few adjoining churches in West Virginia fell to the old Diocese, and are now under the jurisdiction of the Bishop of Richmond, Va. There were Catholics among the first settlers of the Shenandoah Valley, who crossed the Blue Ridge into Virginia from Maryland and Pennsylvania as early as 1750. Many of the early Catholics families have died out or removed farther Westward, and not a few turned their backs upon the religion of their fathers from wordly motives. There have been many converts to the church since the first establishment. The first missionaries through here came from Frederick, Taneytown and Conewago. Fathers Frambach, Gallitzin and Zocchi rode a circuit of two hundred miles before 1800, which extended to Cumberland and south to Winchester. There is a tradition that French priests traveled through this valley, doing missionary work among the Indians. We have not been able to trace anything positive of them, except in regard to the Abbe Jean Dubois, who landed at Norfork in 1791, traveling from there to Frederick and on to the mountains where he founded Mt. St. Mary's. It is evident that he said Mass in the house of the McSherry's, who were among the first Catholic settlers of this valley; and also with a family in the vicinity of what is now known as Orleans Church, where there was an old log church at an early day. The tradition of the French priests may also refer to Braddock's expedition, and the French and Indian wars at that time, and later to the French allies under Washington, as many of the troops in those wars traversed this country, and where there were French soldiers there were Catholic priests.

Another priest who did active missionary work through this valley, from Hagerstown to Winchester and from Frederick and Middieway to Martinsburg and West, was Rev. Denis Cahill. Business transactions also called him here as early as 1800, as some of the law proceedings in the Berkeley Courts will show. He celebrated Mass in a private house from time to time, until the spring of 1806, when he left for his native Ireland. It is said the first marriage celebrated in Martinsburg was by Father Cahill, and that it caused considerable interest among Protestants, who at that time yet entertained peculiar ideas about the appearance of Catholic priests. It is very likely, therefore, that he also said Mass in Martinsburg, either at the McSherry's or at the house of John Timmons. It is the supposition of some that Father Carroll visited this section, but there is no record of his labors except at Middleway. Richard McSherry, Sr., had a homestead near there, called "Retirement Farm," which was a well-known stopping place for the missionary priests before 1800. He was born in 1747, died in 1822. Wm. McSherry was also born in that year, died in 1834; they were probably brothers' children. Richard McSherry, Jr., lived in Martinsburg, nearly opposite the present Catholic Church. The Catholics were attended occasionally by priests from Frederick and Hagerstown. Mass was said in the house of John Timmons for the period of nineteen years, probably from about 1810 to near 1830.

From the time Father Cahill left, 1806, to about 1820, we can ascertain nothing definite, but are of the opinion that several priests on the Maryland missions passed through the valley occasionally. In those early days before there were churches or congregations, the missionaries had different points through the country which they visited, where Mass was said, and baptisms and marriages and other ceremonies of the church performed. These places were mostly the houses of well known Catholic families. Priests from Georgetown may have been occasionally called to these places by sickness or death. The name of Anthony Kohlman is remembered by some.— He was Superior of the Maryland Missions in 1817, and Rector of Gonzaga College in 1821. From the baptismal registers we gather some names and dates, which are reliable as far as they go. The missionary field to which Martinsburg belonged, was extensive, and it is not likely that the priests were resident anywhere much before 1840. To give some idea of the extent, there are entries of baptisms, marriages and deaths at the following places, taking them as they come: Harper's Ferry, near Clarksburg, Valley River, North River, Bath, Upper Dam, Martinsburg, Leetown, Dugan's, Waterford, Smithfield, Sleepy Creek, Hillsboro, Shepherdstown, Boland's, Winchester, Lovettsville, Loudon Co. Frederick Co., Washington Co., Warren Co., Romney, Hampshire Co., Berkeley and Jefferson, Front Royal, Strasburg, &c. This was especially the field covered by Father Whelan, though Father Plunkett yet attended many of these places. Is there not a priest or anyone in the Virginias who will do justice to the life and labors of Richard Whelan? For many years he kept the faith alive from the Ohio to the boundaries of the Potomac and the Shenandoah. He traversed hills and mountains, through rain and shine and cold and heat; many a death-bed was gladdened by his presence, many a heart made happy and a soul saved through his labors. Great and grand was his charity, sincere his life and disinterested his sacrifices, for he sought no temporal reward and received no earthly pay. He is the Frambach or the Gallitzin of the Virginias. Though a stranger to us in a strange country, his life's work challenges our admiration.

The first record is that of Rev. James Redmond, May 30th, 1819, and his last Aug. 13th, 1821. In 1820, Father Redmond married a couple "in the chapel room." Whether he commenced the building of the old stone church, is not known. Rev. John Mahoney's name appears in 1822. Then there is no record until 1834, in which year are the names of Revs. Geo. Flautt and Francis B. Jamison. In 1835, the latter baptized eight children, slaves, the property of Miss Ann O'Neal, of Montgomery Co. Rev. Richard Whelan's name appears Jan. 3d, 1835, and continuously until 1840. In 1838, there is the name of an assistant, Rev. Jos. Strain. Rev. P.

Danaher signs himself temporary pastor in 1841. Rev. John O'Brien pastor from 1842 to '44, and occasionally in '45, 6 and 7. Rev. Jos. H. Plunkett was pastor continuously from 1844 to 1851; from that year until 1853, Rev. Andrew Talty was with him; from that time until Jan. 5th, 1856, Rev. Plunkett's name appears alone. Sept. 19th, 1845, baptism in Moorefield by Bishop Whelan. After he was Bishop of Richmond he traveled through Western Virginia more like a missionary than a Bishop, and there are baptismal and marriage records by him as Bishop on many of the missions. There is the signature of Rev. A. Grogan once or twice from 1848 to '52. The only Jesuits whose names are found are Fathers Ciampi and Bague, about 1850. Rev. Father Leitte sighed in 1854. Bishop McGill baptized Joseph Plunkett, of Mobile, in 1851. Rev. L. E. Leonard took charge Feb. 1st, 1856, remaining a few months. Rev. Andrew Talty was pastor from that until 1860, with the names, occasionally, of Revs. Plunkett and W. Kenney. Rev. Thos. A. Becker was pastor from Jan. 1860, until 1863. So much for the records.

The date of the erection of the first church building is put by some at 1828; others make it 1830, by Father Redmond. He must have been a Virginia priest, as his name is strange to us. There were about fifty Catholic families here, who aided liberally in the work, as did also their Protestant friends. The church cost about $4,000, and was located on the ground of the present Catholic Cemetery. He was called to Rome, before the church was completed. He died there, much beloved and regretted by the Catholics of Virginia.

Rev. Patrick Kelley was appointed Bishop of Richmond when the Diocese was formed in 1820. He resided at Norfolk. The Laity's Directory of 1822, says that the Catholics of Martinsburg, Winchester, Bath, and Shepherdstown were formerly attended by priests from Maryland, but in the future would be in charge of the priest stationed at Winchester.— Rev. J. B. Gildea attended the missions from 1830 until 1835. Besides completing the Martinsburg Church, he built St. Peter's at Harper's Ferry, and St. Vincent's in Baltimore. His name is not on the records. Rev. Richard Vincent Whelan took charge in 1836, remaining four years. He was a noble priest and a true missionary. He was the second Bishop of Richmond, consecrated March 31st, 1841. In 1846, he visited Wheeling, and seeing the great need of laborers in the vineyard at that place, he never returned to his See. He became the first Bishop of Western Virginia, and labored, died and is buried at Wheeling. Rev. John McGill became Bishop of Richmond in 1850. The Rt. Rev. James Gibbons, now Archbishop of Baltimore, succeeded him in 1872. Bishop Keane is the present prelate in charge of the Diocese, a very eloquent and learned man, much beloved by priests and people. Rev. John Kain succeeded Bishop Whelan in the West Virginia Diocese. His parents resided in Martinsburg, where he spent his childhood years. He had three sisters, one living, one in religion, and another one died from the fright of soldiers entering the house during the war. His aged mother has just been buried at Wheeling; she was in her 81st year, and came to Martinsburg from Ireland fifty years ago.

Rev. J. O'Brien succeeded Father Whelan as pastor at Martinsburg, about 1840, and remained seven years. Rev. J. H. Plunket was sent in 1845, who commenced the erection of the present St. Joseph's Church on South Queen St. The subscription paper is dated Feb. 17th, 1850. The cornerstone was laid in 1850. The church was dedicated Sept. 30th, 1860, by Bishop McGill; it cost about $40,000. It is a very substantial building, with a beautiful marble altar. The plan of architecture provided for a steeple, the massive stone front at the church being intended for its foundations.

It is said that the old church at Martinsburg was built by Rev. J. B. Gildea; he may have finished it. St. Peter's Church, Harper's Ferry, was built by him. He attended Martinsburg and the missions along the canal route. He died in Baltimore and is buried under the altar in St. Vincent's Church. This priest frequently said Early Mass at the Ferry, then rode on horse back to Martinsburg and said Late Mass. The Frederick priests attended Harper's Ferry for many years. It is related that some fanatical Virginians in pursuit of Rev. James Frambach, S. J., made him swim his horse across the Potomac, under fire of their guns. As we have seen, Harper's Ferry was served by many priests who attended Martinsburg and the other missions. So was Shepherdstown, which has never yet had a church, services being held in private houses. An effort is now being made to build a church. Rev. Denis Cahill said Mass there before 1800. Among the late pastors of Harper's Ferry, are Revs. Kain, Van de Vyver, O'Reilley; and Wilson, lately from Petersburg, Va. He has several missions in Loudon, Frederick and Jefferson Counties.

The ground for the cemetery and old church at Martinsburg, was given by Richard McSherry. His house was a home for every one in need; priests and people, all found in him a friend. Mrs. McSherry, (the Anastasia of Wizard Clip,) would send word far and wide to gather together the few Catholics, so they could receive the Sacraments. His charity was unbounded; many a poor Irishman owes his start in life to him, and she was equally good to poor girls.

Among the priests who occasionally attended Martinsburg from the Western Maryland missions were Revs. Flautt, Jamison and Myers, and perhaps others. Rev. John O'Brien left the Virginia Missions about 1858, and went to Lowell, Mass., where he died. The Sisters of Charity were established in Martinsburg many years ago, probably under Rev. Whelan; they left for want of support, as the congregation was small and poor. One of the Sisters, (Victoria we believe,) died and was buried here, but whether she was afterwards removed to Emmettsburg we can not ascertain. Father Whelan was a hard worker. He fenced in the graveyard, and laid a stone walk from Pendleton's corner to the churchyard gate. With his own hands he made the large double cistern, still used at the new church. Unlimited was his care for the poor, for whom he solicited in person, and with his own arms would take them wood and supplies,—when going to say Mass in early winter mornings, some poor widow would find an armful of wood at her door when she awoke. He would give when he was in want himself. Father Plunkett was also a faithful missionary priest. He began the stone work of the present church; for want of means work was suspended and the walls covered over. He was removed to Portsmouth; where he built, or partly so, a large church, and died there, much beloved by all who knew him. Rev. Andrew Talty, his assistant at Martinsburg, finished the church here as far as funds would allow. He put wooden steps before the church, which were replaced with stone by Rev. J. J. Kain, who also finished the basement. During the War it was used by the Jessie Scouts for a stable for sixty horses, and the sacristy rooms were used as prisons. Capt. Kyd Douglass was confined there six months. The church was only used twice by the soldiers, as the wooden steps were too frail and inconvenient. Rev. Talty died in Washington, in the hospital. Bishop Becker was a convert under Father Plunkett; he was baptized in Winchester, made his First Communion at the Ferry and was confirmed in St. John's (the old church,) Martinsburg, Nov. 6th, 1853, by Bishop John McGill. Bishop Kain was confirmed by the same in 1851. He was born "near Bath," (probably near North Mountain,) May 22d, 1840. His parents were Jeremiah and Ellen Kain. He was ordained about 1866. Bishop Becker was sent through the lines to Baltimore by Gen. Stevenson, for praying for President Davis.— He was ordained in Rome about 1860;-became Bishop of Wilmington in 1868.

There is mention of Rev. E. O'Flaherty having been sent to Martinsburg in Jan., 1856, but nothing is known of him here.

Rev. Oscar Sears succeeded Father Becker. He remained until compelled to leave by ill health, when he went to Lynchburg, where he died Oct. 30th, 1867. He was a convert.— The present parsonage was purchased when he was pastor, in

1866. Father Kain succeeded. He improved the church in many ways; built the stone steps, finished the basement so it could be used for school rooms, frescoed the church, established parochial schools and paid off many debts. He built the present church at Berkeley Springs, which is also an old Catholic mission. - It was famous for its springs before the Revolution, and the Carrolls, Washington and other great men visited the place. There was a brick church there before the present one was built, and before that an old log church.— There was a Jesuit priest named Brady had a property there, known as the priest's place. Some Sulpitians were also there years ago. It is now attended several times a month by Rev. H. J. McKeefry, from Martinsburg.

Rev. P. J. O'Keefe was for a time the assistant of Father Kain at Martinsburg, and succeeded him. Ill health compelled his removal. Rev. J. Kelley, of Richmond, took charge Jan. 19th, 1874; he continued the good work and paid off some of the debts. He was succeeded Nov. 8th, by Rev. C. Van Quackelburg, of Natchez, Tenn. He built the church at Paw-Paw, and made many improvements in Martinsburg. He returned to Natchez in 1877, and died there of Yellow Fever. He is kindly remembered as "Father Charles." Rev. John Docherty, of Warrenton, Va., followed and remained until 1880; paid off considerable of the debt, and was much beloved and respected by the people. He is now stationed at St. Patrick's, Richmond. Rev. O'Donohue was an assistant of Father Kelley, and remained with Father Charles; he was appointed pastor of Warrenton and surrounding missions.— Rev. J. B. O'Reilley then came for a short period. He then became pastor of Harper's Ferry, and is now at Winchester, where he succeeded the learned Dr. O'Connel, Secretary of the late Council of Baltimore and now Rector of the American College at Rome.

Rev. H. J. McKeefry, the present pastor, came from Norfolk in 1881. He was born at Kilsea, County Derry, Ireland; took his classical course at Visnage College, Belfast;

studied philosphy and theology at St. Vincent's College, Pa., and was ordained at St. Mary's Seminary, Baltimore, by Bishop Becker, June 28th, 1871, for the Richmond Diocese. He is a young man, full of energy and zeal in his church work. He is a prudent manager, a successful financier in the raising of money and the payment of purchasing and building property,—abilities that may point him out in course of time for more important ecclesiastical stations. He is well liked by his congregation, who work together with him in perfect harmony in all church work.

Years ago there were a good many Germans in St. Joseph's congregation, but since the building the B. & O. R. R. the Irish form the greater part of the congregation. Their native fidelity to the church shows itself here. They are mostly poor workers on the railroad and in the shops, but in raising a church subscription we have seen poor men subscribe far more than they were worth. We note this in voluntary testimony to their liberality and their true Irish faith, which have always challenged the admiration of the christian world.

In 1883, the Judge Hall property was purchased for $5,000; improvements costing $1500 were made and the school building remodeled this summer at a cost of $700.— Through the perseverance of the pastor and the generosity of the congregation, the whole amount has been paid. The parochial school was long taught in the basement of the church; among the teachers were A. S. Goulden, D. C. Westenhaver, Mr. Kennedy, Miss B. Ahern, Miss Mary C. Doll, and others. The Sisters of Charity, from Emmittsburg, took charge Sept. 1st, 1883. The school is very successful, there being about 200 children in attendance. The Sisters have a large music class, and teach other higher branches. They have an institution beautifully situated, and every advantage and requirement for a boarding school for young ladies. The church membership is 1500. There is a large Sunday-school attached to the church; also Sodality of the Blessed Virgin, Sanctuary

Society, St. Joseph's Cadet Corps, St. Patrick's and St. Joseph's I. C. B. U. Societies, a Widows' and Orphans' Fund Society, Knights of America, and a Catholic Drum Corps. Adjoining the church is a two-story residence for the pastor, which has been greatly improved this year. St. Joseph's Cemetery is a large burying ground, fronting Norborne.— Many of the old Catholics of the Valley are buried here.— There is a priest buried there, noted in the Keyser Church record.

A number of missions have been given from time to time at St. Joseph's: by the Jesuits Bernard Maguire and C. King, 1866; Fathers Shea, Gaveney and another Jesuit in 1868; Revs. Sourer, Kreuss and Furley in 1870, when a mission cross was erected in the church; Revs. Ratki and Keitz after that; Revs. Elliott and Smith, four years ago; and two years ago by Revs. Doyle and Brady, Paulists. The Forty Hours were held Oct. 4th, 1885; Revs. McKeefry, Frioli, Weider, O'Reilley, present. Bishop O'Sullivan preached in the evening. There were 450 Communicants.

Besides Berkeley Springs, the pastor of St. Joseph's occasionally says Mass at Rock Gap, in Mr. John Neary's house and at Mr. Michel's, in Morgan Co.; at Charles Minghinni's and Mr. Thomas's, in Back Creek Valley. Berkeley Co. The erection of a steeple, according to the original design of St. Joseph's, is now in contemplation.

This valley has given to religion a number of priests and sisters. Francis Patrick Duggan, a well-known Baltimore priest, was born near North Mountain, educated at St. Charles and St. Mary's Seminary. John Joseph Kain, now Bishop of Wheeling, was born along the B. & O., near North Mountain, and his pious mother carried him from there to church at Martinsburg. She was a noble christian woman, true to the country of her birth in faith and every virtue. His father was injured on the railroad and is buried in St. Joseph's Cemetery, so is his sister; steps are being taken to remove their remains to Wheeling where the mother is buried. Bishop

Becker, though born in Pittsburg, spent his early life in the Shenandoah. John Boler, priest, was born near Kearneysville. August, son of Charles Thumel, now preparing for ordination, was born in Martinsburg. Michael Ahern, student at St. Charles, also born here; and Anthony McKeefry, student there, born in Ireland, is a brother of the pastor of St. Joseph's. James O'Farrel, Wm. Lynch, Edw. Tierney, and John Hagan, priests, were born at Harper's Ferry.— Father Tierney was educated at the Propaganda and ordained at Rome. Wm. Dubourg, son of Richard McSherry, born in Martinsburg in 1824, a Novice of the Society of Jesus, died at Georgetown in 1845, and is buried with his fathers in St. Joseph's Cemetery. Bernie Doll, brother of Mary Cecilia, a Sister, was born in Martinsburg. He deserves notice as a christian hero. During an epidemic of Yellow Fever at Shrieveport, La., he gave up a good business, accompanied the parish priest in his attendance upon the sick, and died at the bedside of the Yellow Fever patients. Sept. 7th, 1862, Albert, third son of Charles Carroll, of Carrollton, was shot by the Confederates, near Darkesville, Berkeley County, and buried at St. Joseph's Cemetery, Martinsburg, Sept. 9th. Rev. M. Costello, D. D., was at Harper's Ferry in 1860, and visited Winchester monthly, Martinsburg occasionally. He was a promising young Irish priest, educated at All-Hallows; died at Harper's Ferry Feb. 17th, 1867, and is buried there.

The following young ladies of the parish became Sisters: Rose McGeary, Sr. Elizabeth of the Good Shepherd; Evaline Blondell, dec'd, Sr. Redempte, received at Philadelphia; Caroline Piet, dec'd, Sr. Samuel; Rose Dunn, Frederick, Sr. Paula; Ella Montague, Sr. Genevieve; Maggie McDonald, Emmittsburg, Sr. Rose; Mary C. Doll, Visitation, Wilmington, Del., Sr. Bernard; Ella Kain, St. Joseph's, Wheeling, Sr. Joseph; Susan V. Cunningham, Emmittsburg, Sr. Loretto; Mollie O'Connors, Emmittsburg, now at Mt. Hope, Sr. Agnes; also a Miss Neumann, niece of Father Plunkett, and a Miss Timmins. Bridget O'Leary, North Mountain, received at

Frederick, Sr. Madeline. Mary Hall, a convert, daughter of Capt. Hall, Supt. U. S. Armory, Harper's Ferry, joined the Sisters of Mercy at Wilmington, N. C., as Sr. Elizabeth.

For considerable information concerning the Martinsburg Church, we are indebted to Mrs. Helen Scharman, a descendant of Anastasia McSherry, nee Lilly, mention of whom is made by Father Finoti, in his Clip book. She is an intelligent woman, having an extensive knowledge of early local church history, through tradition from her grandmother and mother, and from personal recollection. The old Missal used by Prince Gallitzin on his missionary travels, is in her possession.

The Catholic church is strongly established at Cumberland, Md., both in numbers and church institutions and property. The Sisters have fine buildings there, and the Capuchins a large monastery. Father Frambach, S. J., did missionary work at Cumberland as early as 1780. The first church was built in 1794. The old church, St. Mary's, was torn down in 1850, and Carroll Hall built. The new church is of brick, Ionic order of architecture, is called St. Patrick's and was built under Rev. Obermeyer. In 1866, St. Edward's Academy was built, in charge of Sisters of Mercy. Rev. F. X. Marshall pastor in 1833; Rev. Henry Myers in 1837, and for a number of years. He was greatly beloved and respected by Catholics and Protestants. Rev. B. S. Piot assistant from Mt. Savage until 1852,—Leonard Obermeyer, pastor. 1853, Rev. John B. Byrne, assistant. 1855, Rev. P. B. Lenaghen; 1856, Revs. James Carney, Michael O'Reilley; 1859, Rev. Geo. Flautt, Rev. Edw. Brennan, assistant; 1860, Rev. Edw. Brennan; successors, Revs. Edmund Didier, Father Barry, James Casey, Charles Damur, F. S. Ryan. 1881, Rev. F. Brennan; Rev. J. Mattingly, assistant. Father Brennan died there several years ago; he was a very able and popular priest; Father McDivitt succeeded him. There are a number of small missions in the surrounding mining regions.

Some BIOGRAPHICAL SKETCHES.

Remember your prelates, who have spoken to you the word of God, considering well the end of their conversation, and imitate their faith. Jesus Christ yesterday and to-day and the same forever.—HEB. XIII., 7.

THE MISSIONARY PRIEST GALLITZIN.

The following is from Chap. XI of MACLEOD's Devotion of the B. V. in North America; partly taken from a Discourse on the Life and Virtues of Father Gallitzin, by Very Rev. Thomas Heyden:

* * * As early as 1795 there was one Father Smith who was missionary for an enormous district in Western Maryland, Virginia, and Pennsylvania. There, for forty-one years, he toiled in humble faithfulness; from thence his soul ascended to the judgment which his life had merited. It will not be uninteresting to consider some points in the life of this servant of Mary, this glorious, although unrenowned pioneer of her honor in this country.

This Father Smith, missionary of Hagerstown and Cumberland in Maryland, of Martinsburg and Winchester in Virginia, of Chambersburg and the Alleghany mountain sweep in Pennsylvania, and thence southward; of far more, in a word, than what now constitutes the entire diocese of Pittsburg; this rival of Gomez in the south, and of Father Chaumonot in the north; this founder of Our Lady of Loretto in the *centre* of the continent, was not always known as Father Smith. In his own country, the vast Muscovite empire, then ruled by the Czar Alexander I., he was known as the Prince Augustine de Gallitzin. His father, Prince Demetrius Gallitzin, was ambassador of Catherine the Great to Holland, at the time of the missionary's birth. His mother, the Princess Amelia, was daughter of that famous Field-marshal Count von Schmettau who illustrates the military annals of Frederick the Great.

The young Gallitzin was decorated in his very cradle with military titles, which destined him from his birth to the highest posts in the Russian army. High in the favor of the Empress Catherine, his father, a haughty and ambitious nobleman, dreaming only of the advancement of his son in the road of preferment and worldly honor, was resolved to give him an education worthy of his exalted birth and brilliant prospects. Religion formed no part of the plan of the father, who was a proficient in the school of Gallic infidelity, and the friend of Diderot. It was carefully excluded. Special care was taken not to suffer any minister of religion to approach the study room of the young prince. He was surrounded by infidel teachers. His mother, a Catholic by birth and early education, was seduced into seeming Voltairianism by the court fashion of her native country, and her marriage with Prince Demetrius confirmed her habits of apparent infidelity; we say apparent, for she retained, even in the salons of Paris and in the society of Madame du Chatelet, a fervent devotion to Saint Augustine, that grand doctor of the Church who had been a great wordling and heretic. After the marriage of the elder Gallitzin with the Princess Amelia, he brought her to Paris and introduced her to his literary infidel friends, especially to Diderot, in whose company he delighted. This philosopher endeavored to win the princess over to his atheistical system; but though she was more than indifferent on the subject of religion, her naturally strong mind discovered the hollowness of his reasoning. It was remarked that she would frequently puzzle the philosopher by the little interrogative—why? And as he could not satisfy her objections, she was determined to examine thoroughly the grounds of revelation.—Though having no religion herself, she was determined to instruct her children in one. She opened the Bible merely for the purpose of teaching her children the historical part of it. The beauty of revealed truth, notwithstanding the impediment of indifference and unbelief, would sometimes strike her—her mind being of that mould which, according to Tertullian, is naturally Christian.

A terrible illness called her mind back to God; she saw the truth and beauty of the Catholic faith, and she returned to the protection of Mary on the Feast of St. Augustine, in the week following the Octave of Our Lord's Assumption.

It is to the happy influence and bright example of his mother, to whom, under God, we must mainly ascribe the conversion of the young Demetrius. As the illustrious Bishop of Milan, St. Ambrose, consoled the mother of Augustine, when he used to say "*that it was impossible for a son to be lost for whom so many tears were shed;*" so we may believe that the pious Furstenberg, her son's tutor, cheered, in a similar manner, this good lady, in her intense solicitude for a son whom she so tenderly loved.

At the age of seventeen the young prince was received into the Church. He was, in the year 1792, appointed aid-de-camp to the Austrian General Von Lilien, who commanded an army in Brabant at the opening of the first campaign against the French Jacobins. The sudden death of the Emperor Leopold, and the murder of the king of Sweden by Ankerstrom, both suspected to be the work of the French Jacobins who had declared war against all kings and all religions, caused the governments of Austria and Prussia to issue a very strict order disqualifying all foreigners from military offices. In consequence of this order the young Prince de Gallitzin was excluded. Russia not taking any part in the war against France, there was no occasion offered to him for pursuing the profession of arms for which he had been destined by military education. It was therefore determined by his parents that he should travel abroad and make the grand tour. He was allowed two years to travel; and lest, in the mean time, his acquirements, the fruits of a very finished education, might suffer, he was placed under the guidance of the Rev. Mr. Brosius, a young missionary then about to embark for America, with whom his studies were to be still continued. In the company of this excellent clergyman he reached the United States in 1792.

The next we need see of him is as a seminarian with the Sulpicians in Baltimore, November 5, 1792. In this moment of his irrevocable sacrifice of himself to God, the feelings of his inmost soul may be gathered from a letter which he wrote at the time to a clergyman of Munster, in Germany. In it he begs him to prepare his mother for the step he had finally taken, and informs him that he had sacrificed himself, with all that he possessed, to the service of God and the salvation of his neighbor in America, where the harvest was so great and the laborers so few, and where the missionary had to ride frequently forty and fifty miles a day, undergoing difficulties and dangers of every description. He adds, that he doubted not his call, as he was willing to subject himself to such arduous labor.

Father Etienne Badin was the first priest ordained in the United States; Prince Gallitzin was the second, and he, as early as 1799, was settled for life in the then bleak and savage region of the Alleghanies. From his post to Lake Erie, from the Susquehanna to the Potomac, there was no priest, no church, no religious station of any kind. Think, then, of the inevitable labors and privations of this missionary; and again understand how the devotion to Mary has spread over North America.

During long missionary excursions, frequently his bed was the bare floor, his pillow the saddle, and the coarsest and most forbidding fare constituted his repast. Add to this, that he was always in feeble health, always infirm and delicate in the extreme, and it was ever a matter of wonder to others how the little he ate could support nature and hold together so fragile a frame as his. A veritable imitator of Paul, "he was in labor and painfulness, in watching often, in hunger and thirst, in fasting often, in cold and nakedness."

When he first began to reside permanently on this mountain, in 1799, he found not more than a dozen Catholics, scattered here and there through a trackless forest. He first settled on a farm generously left by the Maguire family for the maintenance of a priest. A rude log-church, of some twenty-five or thirty feet, was sufficient for a considerable time for the first little flock that worshipped according to the faith of their fathers on the Alleghany. He commenced his colony with twelve heads of families; he left behind him when he died six thousand devotees of Mary.

But the population grew rapidly, allured by the saintly reputation of Father Smith. It was he who purchased enormous tracts of land, who built the grist and saw mill, he who found himself oppressed by debt in his old age. Of course he expected his father's inheritance, and when that prince died in 1808, he was pressed to quit his beloved Loretto and go to claim his rights in Russia. His mother and friends urged him to come; his prelate was on the point of commanding him; but when he met Bishop Carroll, he gave reasons for remaining among his flock which that prelate could not in the end refute. He stated that he had caused a great number of Catholic families to settle in a wild and uncultivated region, where they formed a parish of a considerable size; that the Legislature had proposed to establish there a county-seat; and that numbers still continued to flock thither. The bishop at length fully acquiesced in his remaining, as he could not send another in his place. The apostolic missionary then wrote to his mother, that whatever he might gain by the voyage, in a *temporal point of view*, could not, in his estimation, be compared with *the loss of a single soul* that might be occasioned by his absence.

Had he gone, it would have been in vain, for the Emperor and Senate of St. Petersburg settled the question by disinheriting him for "having embraced the Catholic faith and clerical profession."—Nevertheless, he hoped to share with his sister, who had inherited all. And she did supply him, until the ruined German Prince de Solm, whom she had married, made away her fortune as he had done with his own. Then came his days of debt, dreariest of all days to men. But he lived so that none should suffer but himself. He neither ate nor drank nor was clothed at the expense or loss of any creditor or others. His fare was often but some black bread and a few vegetables; coffee and tea were unknown luxuries in those times. His clothing was home-made and of the most homely description; his mansion was a miserable log-hut, not denied even to the poorest of the poor.—With the prodigal son of the Gospel, but in a most meritorious and heroic sense, he could say: "How many hired servants in my father's house have plenty of bread, and I here perish with hunger!"

"Being now," he says, "in my sixty-seventh year, burdened, moreover, with the remnant of my debts, reduced from $18,000 to about $2,500. I had better spend my few remaining years, if any, in trying to pay off that balance, and in preparing for a longer journey."

On that Loretto of his love he expended, from the wreck of his fortune, $150,000.—So is it with the servitors of Mary. Three centuries ago, they gave their bodies to be burned, their heads to the scalping-knife, their finger-joints to the teeth of the Iroquois; later, they gave their lives and fortunes, counting them as nothing if so they might win souls to Christ.

Let his friend and biographer tell the secret of it all, and thus show what a Muscovite prince can have in common with this book:

"As he had taken for his models the Lives of the Saints, the Francis of Sales, the Charles Borromeos, the Vincents of Paul, so like them he was distinguished for his tender and lively devotion to the Blessed Virgin; and he lost no opportunity of extolling the virtues of Mary. He endeavored to be an imitator of her *as she was of Christ*. He recited *her rosary every evening among his household*, and inculcated constantly on his people this grand devotion, and the other pious exercises in honor of Mary. The church in which he said daily Mass, he had dedicated under the invocation of this ever glorious Virgin, whom all nations call blessed. It was in honor of Mary, and to place his people under her peculiar patronage, that he gave the name of Loretto to the town he founded here, after the far-famed Loretto, which, towering above the blue wave of the Adriatic, on the Italian coast, exhibits to the Christian pilgrim the hallowed and magnificent temple which contains the sainted shrine of Mary's *humble house in which she at Nazareth heard announced the mystery of the Incarnation*, and which the mariners, as they pass to encounter the perils of the deep, or return in safety from them, salute, chanting the joyous hymn, *Ave Maris Stella!* For, like St. John, he recognized in her a mother recommended to him by the words of the dying Jesus: "He said to the disciple, behold thy mother!" And so, when the frame was worn out in her service and her Son's, he went up to see her face on high.

JAS. PELLENTZ, S. J.

Of this worthy missionary priest, we have little more to add, except the record of his death. He began preparations for the building of the Church of the Sacred Heart at Conewago in 1785, and completed the walls and roof in 1787; Fathers De Barth and Lekeu had pews put in, stone steps erected in front, procured bell and large organ; cupola put up, and made other improvements.—Father Steinbacher had the interior painted. Father Enders built school houses, put up iron fence, made cruciform addition, with paintings, erected steeple and marble altar, and made great improvements on all the Chapel property. Father Pellentz

also built the house adjoining, and the old farm buildings, besides several smaller log houses along the hill that have long since disappeared.— His name is spelled "Pellentz," but wherever found on the old writings it is "Pellantz," doubtless from the German. He is buried under the church which he built, but all trace of his grave is lost. The nearest that can be ascertained is towards the south wing, and there is no telling but what his remains have been disturbed by the construction of foundations and the digging of a gangway towards the front of the church to put in the furnace and heaters.— The record of his death is in Latin, as are all the early records and may be thus rendered: On the 18th of March, of the year 1800, at half-past seven A. M., died James Pellentz, and was buried on the 15th. He dies in peace, by the grace of Him who by his death regenerated him. Not death, but life, rather should it be called. The name of Pellentz has many claims to consideration. A stranger in a foreign land, he erected this house and church, and with zeal and devotion he made it the object of his life to gather men within the fold of the Church.

CHURCH OF THE SACRED HEART.

Taken without the steeple, so as to look like the old church before improved. At first it had a small wooden cross on the front peak of the roof. Near the top of the front wall is a stone with the figures 1787 cut in. Below a circular scroll work with the letters I. S. H., is a heart cut in stone or marble.

JAMES FRAMBACH, S. J.

This was the companion of Father Pellentz. His name is spelled "Frombach" and Frambach; the first probably correct; the last most generally used. The extent of his missionary labors cannot be comprehended. His death record is entered at Conewago, probably because he labored there so long, or it may be that the priest who ministered at his death was either a Conewago priest at the time or afterwards, as few of the entries were made at the time of death, but seem to have been entered or copied very irregularly in every way. We infer that the priests on the missions before 1800 kept their records something like memoranda just as they went, and these were brought together later, some at Conewago and some elsewhere perhaps, and entered by other hands. He died at St. Inigoes, Md., and if we are correctly informed, nothing marks the place. The record reads: On the 27th of Aug., 1795, died Father James Frombach, professed of the Society, at the age of 73. He lived here for ten years, a year and a half at Lancaster, and later at Frederick. He came to America in 1758, from the Province of Lower Germany, with Father Pellentz and two other Jesuits. He traveled the country, strengthening tepid christians; and was a source of edification to all by his devotion, zeal, meekness, obedience, modesty and patience. He suffered for years from ulcerations of the legs and arms, and finally, full of merits, he died of a contagious fever, in St. Mary's County, strengthened with all the rites of the Church.

Father Finotti says, that owing to the scarcity of Catholic books in the early days of this country, he copied the whole of the Roman Missal, preserved, he thinks, in Georgetown College. The same is said of Theodore Schneider, S. J., the first priest of Goshenhoppen.

Some descendants of the Baxters, (who lived somewhere between Hagerstown and Frederick in early times, and which was a stopping place on Father Frambach's travels,) now belong to Father Manley's mission at Hagerstown. They relate as a tradition from their grandmother, that Father F' traveled on horseback and stayed all night at their house. After it had been noticed for a long time that his clothes were very poor, they made a suit of homespun and laid it on the bed in his room. When he came again he went to his room, but returned immediately to the kitchen, and said that somebody's clothes were on his bed. Being told that they were for him, he exclaimed, "A new suit for me! well, then I must go and try it on." When he came down again, he walked up and down the kitchen floor, very much overjoyed that he had better clothes to wear. This shows the pious humility and humble sincerity of that truly noble missionary priest.

BISHOP JOHN TIMON.

About the year 1790, Edw. Reily, Sr., came from Ireland and settled on a tract of land adjoining the estate of Samuel Lilly. It was close by the Conewago, which winds through the valley with many a curve and crook.— At that time, the lands along the creek were covered with heavy timber,—

remnants of the old forests yet remain. The great, clumsy wheels of an old mill creaked in the quiet stillness of the night, and from the rippling waters rose a heavy mist that disappeared over the tree tops, with the earliest rays of the morning sunlight. It must have been a wild and romantic place.—Even now, the broad fields, bordered with woodland ; the sounds of a dashing waterfall that drives a mill near by ; and large farm buildings scattered around, form a scene of rural beauty, the grandest in the valley. Just over the hill-tops, about a mile away, rises the beautiful spire of old Conewago.—In 1796, the father of Bishop Timon came from Ireland and with his mother the Bishop. They lived in a log house, adjoining the residence of Edw. Reily, probably the temporary home of the Reily family until they had built themselves a house. There was born the future Bishop of Buffalo. John Timon, Feb. 12th, 1797. In 1802, they moved to Baltimore, and afterwards to Missouri. About 1830, after the death of Barney, a brother of Edw. Reily, the log house of Bishop Timon was moved up to the public road and made a home for the widow, Margaret Reily, grandmother of the writer. About the earliest recollection we have is of the old log house, with its dark looking cellar and crumbling walls. It was torn down about 1860, and the logs used in building an old stable on the same lot, after the death of Daniel Reily, the property of Lewis Will. It has been enlarged since, but the old part yet remains. Father Timon was ordained priest by Bishop Rosatti in 1825. He became a great missionary priest in Missouri, Texas, and other States. Many touching incidents of his missionary life are related. He was an able man, a good speaker, and kind and generous to a fault. His vocation was a missionary life, and it was never his ambition or his will to be elevated above an humble missionary priest. As a Bishop he had trials, troubles and tribulations, but he passed through them all with that spirit of right and duty which governed him in early life. He was consecrated Bishop in 1847 ; died April 16th, 1867 ; and was buried under the altar of the Cathedral in Buffalo. He visited Conewago once or twice during his life.—once about the year 1856, when the name of this saintly priest and noble prelate was conferred upon us, to bear it, the most unworthy. The life of Bishop Timon is worthy of study and of imitation. Conewago is blessed in having given him birth.

GEORGE VILLIGER, S. J.

No priest had more devoted friends on the Conewago missions than "Little" Father Villiger. His disposition was so gentle and amiable that he could never have given any offense. He was born in Switzerland, Sept. 14th, 1808, and died at Conewago, Wednesday morning, Sept. 20th, 1882, and was buried there Friday morning following, at 8 o'clock. He entered the Society Oct. 4th, 1838, and came to this country in 1843. He was ordained at Georgetown by Archbishop Eccleston, July 22d, 1844, and sent to Conewago. The Paradise, Gettysburg, Millerstown and the Mountain territory comprised his mission, and there he labored faithfully for a number of years. Wherever a few Catholics could be found, he was sure to hunt them up, instruct their children and keep the faith in them alive. He was full of zeal and energy in his sacred calling. He served several Maryland missions, and was Superior at Bohemia from 1862 until 1878. Father Villiger was a good scholar, and always ready to give a reason for the faith that was in him.—His "Letters to a Protestant Minister by a Catholic Priest," give a clear exposition of the doctrines of the Catholic religion. After the death of Father Deneckere, he was sent to Conewago again, and attended Littlestown until his death. Age and years of active labor were then already laying a heavy hand upon him, but like a true Jesuit warrior, he would rather die at his post of duty than surrender God's peace be with him. May that generation with whom his memory is most dearly cherished, never forget to breathe a prayer for the repose of the soul of their spiritual father in days gone by,—he who taught them their catechism, prepared them for the Sacraments of the church, which he administered to many.

PETER MANNS, S. J.

He was born in the Diocese of Limburg, Province of the Rhine, Germany, June 25th, 1810, and studied there. He lived in the Archdiocese of Cologne. Studied twelve years, theology and philosphy five years. Entered the Society March 20th, 1858, and was ordained June 17th. He labored in Maryland and Massachusetts, and was sent to Conewago June 4th, 1862. His health, which was rated "middling" when entering the Society, has been failing for a number of years, and he walks with perceptible pain and diffi. culty, for he is getting old in years as well as in the labor and service of God. The schools were his especial object for many years. In matters of discipline and morality he is unusually strict; and, though his ideas and views are not in harmony with the progress of the age, no one hereafter or even in this world, will regret having followed his advice. In piety and humility he is worthy of imitation; the lives of the saints are his daily spiritual food, and it is their example he tries to follow. If he has faults, they are not of the mind or heart nor intention. He expects to be judged by his conscience, and scrupulously follows its dictates. If he has suffered much for it, his reward will only be the greater. The Society has learned men and popular priests, but it has no more faithful worker than Father Manns. His spiritual children are numbered by the thousand, and it may be truthfully said that he is always in his confessional. A scrap of a report to his Superiors, for the first few years he was on the Conewago missions, carries out our estimate of his labors: Confessions at Littlestown 1200, at Paradise 8306, at Conewago 6200; General Confessions, of which he was a great advocate, 309; sermons 282; Catechisms 484; converts 9; Retreat to Sisters 1.

F. X. DENECKERE, S. J.

Father Deneckere left all to follow Christ. He was of a distinguished family, and his whole appearance and carriage were in keeping with his princely blood, but he labored among the humble and lowly with the same zeal and charity as though he were the poorest of them. His family, with the exception of one brother, were all religious. Two of his sisters were nuns of Notre Dame, Paris; and a brother, who died young, was also a

Jesuit. Bishop Guy De Neckere, of New Orleans, was his uncle. They were a family of saints. His love for his faith we have already seen in his works. His sermons were most sublime, and his perfect style of oratory inspired every one with awe and devotion. A man of his eloquence and ability would never have been sent to retirement at Conewago, except to give his active mind and wonderful energy the necessary occupations on a laborious mission, that best assured their safety. His disposition and temperament were too excitable to come in contact with a jarring world. Yet he was the kindest of men, the truest of friends, and self-sacrificial of all he possessed, dying in the very performance of his duty. He was born in the Diocese of Bruges, Flanders, Feb. 2d, 1810; and died at Littlestown, Adams Co., Pa., Wednesday, Jan. 8th, 1879, at 5 o'clock P M. He entered the Society in the Diocese of Ghent, Sept. 16th, 1844, and after his ordination was sent with Father Enders to the Maryland missions.

He was a great teacher and student all his life; he was a good French scholar, and his favorite authors were those of his own nationality. He seldom or never spoke of himself, and all we heard from him of his own life was that he spent his vacations at school. As a boy he was fond of the innocent amusements of youth, and when a teacher in his old age, nothing gave him greater pleasure than to assist in making the play-time of the scholars exciting and amusing, always planning something new for their enjoyment. He was exceedingly strict and systematic in all things. Nothing was too laborious for him, if it added to the greater honor and glory of God and the salvation of souls, or aided in making the ceremonies of the church or its religious devotions still more grand and inspiring. He had a saintly devotion to the Blessed Virgin, and her rosary was his constant companion. He had a great aversion to criminals, and would not remain at the church during the burial of any who had taken their own life, or those who died refusing to be reconciled to their God. His solicitude for the conversion of sinners was unbounded. He was called from the school-room one day to attend a dying man who for years had neglected his duties; but all efforts to reclaim him had been fruitless. He left the man, ordering that he should be sent for at once if he showed signs of returning grace. He came back to the schoolroom, leaving his horse in waiting, and with his scholars he went up to the church before St. Francis Xavier's altar, (his favorite place.) to pray. A little after noon, word reached him that the dying man had relented and sent for him. Had he been a boy of sixteen years instead of an aged man, he could not have reached his carriage any quicker, and as we watched him going out the road it seemed every minute as if his carriage must be dashed to pieces at the rate he was driving. The object of his prayers and solicitude for years, was reconciled to the church; and the joy and happiness it gave him could not be concealed the remainder of that day. Father Deneckere practiced the confidence in that supplication in prayer which he taught by word of mouth. His first recourse in all things was to prayer. For years, the Processions of the Blessed Sacrament on Corpus Christi were the dearest objects of his devotion. No time or labor was spared to make them grand and inspiring, and great was his sorrow and regret if anything interfered with their success. One year, Corpus Christi morning dawned with many indications of showers, as characteristic of spring days as snow-storms are of fall weather. Everything was in readiness for the Procession to start, and thousands of people were waiting, yet the black clouds overhanging were too threatening to venture out with the Blessed Sacrament. Father Deneckere had been watching the weather intently, and after a time his absence was noticed. Those in charge sought him everywhere, and at last went to his room where they found him deeply engaged in prayer. Soon after the clouds parted, the sun shone forth, and the Procession went on in its usual splendor to a happy ending. Though the skeptic mock his intentions, he must admire his faith. Many feared him for the moment, but memory has nothing but love and respect for him now. Noble priest, dear Father! But for thee we would never have had a taste of that Pierian Spring of which thou didst drink so deeply ; and better not, perhaps, for regret is the more poignant over wasted opportunities ; over what might be and is not, or could be and cannot. Still far from us be ingratitude. The happiest days of our life, and the saddest, are those filled with the memory of this saintly teacher's virtues. R. I. P.

Nearly all of the older priests at Conewago were born beyond the seas ; of their native homes and childhood days, whether in some quiet mountain place, by lake or river, or quaint historic town, little is known, for their lips were ever sealed by the virtues they practiced. Many a time, perhaps, cherished memories came over them that swayed every generous impulse of the heart, like the soft south-wind that brings new life to the fields in springtime, but they died away again as the distant peal of thunder, leaving no trace of the mighty forces disturbed. About 1870, two small boys, sons of Gen. Ewing, who represented this government in some capacity in France, spent a few days at Conewago. Father Deneckere, in company with a few of his school boys, took them down to see the Blue Spring one beautiful afternoon in October. He asked them many questions in French of what they had seen and heard in Paris, which they simply answered in the affirmative or negative, for their youthful minds were captivated with the attractions around them, and they ran now here, now there, climbing a tree or searching for something to throw in the water ; the venerable priest's thoughts must have been carried back many, many years ago, to scenes remembered in his own dear Belgium, for tears stole down from his bright, flashing eyes, and he turned away from their joyful capers to hide his own sad emotions.

With scrupulous correctness Father Deneckere regarded all holy things, and paid the highest reverence and veneration to the sacredness of religion in the performance of all the ceremonies of the Church. It was nothing unusual to find him in the church before the Blessed Sacrament at night when about to retire, and regularly at five o'clock in the morning at the altar saying his Mass. Well can we apply to him the words of the great LAMARTINE, and thus show the exalted thoughts and devotions of his inmost soul, for we have no language at our command to picture the grandness of the inner life of this beloved Father and pure and noble priest :

"Hail! sacred tabernacles, where thou, O Lord, dost descend at the voice of a mortal! Hail, mysterious altar, where faith comes to receive its immortal food. When the last hour of the day has groaned in thy solemn towers; when its last beam fades and dies away in the dome; when the widow holding her child by the hand has wept on the pavement, and retraced her steps like a silent ghost; when the sigh of the distant organ seems lulled to rest with the day to awaken again with the morning; when the nave is deserted, and the Levite attentive to the lamps of the holy place, with a slow step hardly crosses it again—this is the hour when I come to glide under the obscure vault, and to seek, while nature sleeps, Him who aye watches! Ye columns, who veil the sacred asylums where my eyes dare not penetrate, at the feet of thy immoveable trunks I come to sigh. Cast over me your deep shades, render the darkness more obscure, and the silence more profound! Forests of porphyry and marble, the air which the soul breathes under thy arches is full of mystery and of peace! Let love and anxious cares seek shade and solitude under the green shelter of groves, to soothe their secret wounds! O darkness of the sanctuary, the eye of religion prefers thee to the wood which the breeze disturbs. Nothing changes thy foliage, thy still shade is the image of motionless eternity! Eternal pillars, where are the hands that formed thee? Quarries, answer, where are they? Dust, the sport of winds, our hands which carved the stone, turn to dust before it, and man is not jealous! He dies, but his holy thought animates the cold stone, and rises to heaven with thee. Forums, palaces, crumble to ashes, time casts them away with scorn; the foot of the traveller who tramples upon them lays bare their ruins; but as soon as the block of stone leaves the side of the quarry, and is carved for Thy temple, O Lord, it is thine; Thy shadow imprints upon our works the sublime seal of Thine own immortality? Lord, I used to love to pour out my soul upon the summit of mountains, in the night of deserts, beneath rocks where roared the voice of mighty seas, in presence of heaven, and of the globes of flame whose pale fires sprinkle the fields of air; me thought that my soul oppressed before immensity, enlarged itself within me, and on the winds and floods, or on the scattered fire, from thought to thought, would spring to lose itself in Thee; I sought to mount but thou vouchsafest to descend! Thou art near to hear us. Now I love the obscurity! Inhabited alone by Thee and by death, one hears from afar the flood of time which roars upon this border of eternity! It seems as if our voice, which only is lost in the air, concentrated in these walls by this narrow space, resounds better to our soul, and that the holy echo of thy sonorous vault, bears along with it the sigh which seeks Thee in its ascent to heaven, more fervent before it can evaporate. How can it signify in what words the soul exhales itself before its author? Is there a tongue equal to the ecstacy of the heart? Whatever my lips may articulate, this pressed blood which circulates, this bosom which breathes in Thee, this heart which beats and expands, these bathed eyes, this silence, all speak, all pray in me. So swell the waves at the rising of the king of day, so revolve the stars, mute with reverence and love, and Thou comprehendest their silent hymn. Ah, Lord, in like manner, comprehend me. Hear what I pronounce not; Silence is the highest voice of a heart that is overpowered with Thy glory!"

Or, with the celebrated LAVATER, on finding himself in a Catholic Church, exclaim:

"He doth not know Thee, O Jesus Christ, who dishonoreth even Thy shadow? I honor all things, where I find the intention of honoring Thee, I will love them because of Thee. I will love them provided I find the least thing which makes me remember Thee! What then do I behold here? What do I hear in this place? Does nothing under these majestic vaults speak to me of Thee? This cross, this golden image, is it not made for Thy honor? The censer which waves round the priest, the gloria sung in the choirs, the peaceful light of the perpetual lamp, these lighted tapers,— all is done for Thee. Why is the Host elevated, if it be not to honor Thee. O Jesus Christ, who art dead for love of us? because it is no more, and Thou art it, the believing church bends the knee. It is in thy house alone that these children, early instructed, make the sign of the cross, that their tongues sing thy praise, and that they strike their breasts thrice with their little hands. It is for love of Thee, O Jesus Christ, that one kisses the spot which bears Thy adorable blood; for Thee, the child who serves, sounds the little bell and does all that he does. The riches collected from distant countries, the magnificence of chasubles, all that has relation to Thee. Why are the walls and the high altar of marble clothed with verdant tapestry on the day of the Blessed Sacrament? For whom do they make a road of flowers? For whom are these banners embroidered? When the Ave Maria sounds, is it not for Thee? Matins, vespers, prime, and nones, are they not consecrated to Thee? These bells within a thousand towers, purchased with the gold of whole cities, do they not bear Thy image cast in the very mould? Is it not for Thee that they send forth their solemn tone? It is under Thy protection, O Jesus Christ, that every man places himself who loves solitude, chastity, and poverty. Without Thee, the orders of St. Benedict and St. Bernard would not have been founded. The cloister, the tonsure, the breviary, and the chaplet, render testimony of Thee, O delightful rapture, Jesus Christ, for Thy disciples to trace the marks of Thy finger where the eyes of the world see them not! O joy ineffable for souls devoted to Thee, to behold in caves, and on rocks, in every crucifix placed upon hills, and on the high-ways, thy seal and that of thy love! Who wilt not rejoice in the honors of which Thou art the object and the soul? Who will not shed tears in hearing the words, 'Jesus Christ be praised?' O the hypocrite who knoweth that name and answereth not with joy, amen. Who saith not with an intense transport, Jesus be blessed for eternity, eternity.

J. B. EMIG, S. J.

This venerable and distinguished Father was born July 26th, 1808, at Bensheime, Grand Duchy of Hesse Darmstadt, Diocese of Magunties. He arrived at Baltimore July 27th, 1832, after a voyage of sixty-three days. He entered the Society Sept. 24th, 1832, at White Marsh, Prince George County, Md., and completed his studies at Frederick; was ordained priest March 12th,

1889. His labors have been very great and useful, and as a missionary priest he is unsurpassed, his sermons being all deep and logical, as well as most impressive. He considers that he was miraculously directed to Conewago; having been uncertain of his whereabouts, and imagining he was near Mt. St. Mary's. For several years he taught in the St. Louis University, Louisville, and other western places, and came East about the year 1852. The greater part of the time then he spent at Frederick, preparing young men for the priesthood, and also doing missionary work in the surrounding States. He was sent to Hanover in 1877, and has now completed there a magnificent church, costing over $20,000, all paid for. At present he is raising subscriptions to frescoe the church, which will cost about $1400. In Sept., 1882, he celebrated his Golden Jubilee at Hanover with a High Mass, and received many marks of the respect and esteem in which he is held by the congregation. His health has been declining for a number of years, and he is a great sufferer all the time, but bears all patiently and with perfect resignation. He has his room at Mr. S. Althoff's, where he boards, but sleeps in the sacristy of the church. We hope he will be spared yet many years.

J. B. COTTING, S. J.

We have no dates in the religious life of Father Cotting. He was born about the same year Father Enders was; they studied and were at the Novitiate together. He was a native of Switzerland, and came to America about the year 1845. He was a faithful laborer on the Conewago missions. Father Cotting was an active missionary, and was noted for his many jokes and great sprightliness, but his influence was unbounded. At one time when in St. Louis, he was trying to get his German congregation to buy a graveyard, but they did not seem inclined to furnish the money. You will not purchase a grave yard, said he; but remember what I tell you: When the day of Judgment comes you will be buried among the Yankees and the Irish. You know their tricks. They will jump up and steal your bones, and you will have none with which to appear at judgment. This argument was so convincing that they gave in immediately, and the purchase was made.

About the time he attended the York Congregation, the Hanover Junction Railroad was made, and anyone who traveled that road will remember the long waiting at the Junction. Father Cotting used to say that he could go to York with his horse quicker than the cars could go, and he really did succeed on one occasion in getting ahead of them. The Irish laborers were devoted to him, and presented him with a fine carriage.

He labored several years at Conewago, and after that in Prince George Co., Md., and is still stationed in that State. His life, like those of his companions living and dead, is filled with good deeds, and usefulness in the Society. His labors everywhere were crowned with success. The old people at Conewago and Paradise, recall with great pleasure their recollections of the days of dear Father Cotting.

At one time when he was attending the South Mountain Church, a German complained to him that he never gave them German sermons. Come to my room, said he. The man went, and looking the door, Father Cotting made him sit down and preached to him over an hour in German. Now, said he, never complain any more about my sermons. He was stationed for a number of years in the lower counties of Maryland. He was riding out one day and passed the house of a Protestant minister, who was feeding his hogs. "Why, Father Cotting," said the minister, "you seem to have a great deal of time to ride about ; how does it happen ?" "Oh !" said Father Cotting, "you see, your reverence, I have no children to support and no hogs to feed." He was always traveling for the salvation of souls, and God crowned his labors with great success.

JOSEPH ENDERS, S. J.

Rev. Joseph Enders. S. J., died at the Novitiate, Frederick, Md., Sept. 10th, 1884, and was buried there Sept. 12th ; aged 77 years, 9 months and 23 days.

What does this simple notice not contain ? A life-time of years spent in the practice of every Christian virtue, and a life so full of good and exemplary works that it seems a pity to bury it in the humble and scanty records of so great a Society as that of Jesus, in which there is little individuality in life and less in death. It knows when a member entered the Society and when he departed this life, outside of that it is as silent as the grave. Its members have their being together in life and share each other's merits in death ; the highest is the lowest and the lowest is the highest—JESUITS.— Since they are so humble as to forget self and live for others, how dare we of the world disregard their wishes and their humility, and speak of what they live to forget—themselves. But we are to remember our prelates who have spoken to us the word of God, considering well the end of their conversation and imitating their faith ; and how can we do this better than by removing the veil of humility which in life hid their greatest virtues from the sight of men, that seeing and admiring the good they have done we may be moved to overcome our wordly attachment and draw closer to those heavenly desires which the inspired Word tells us are most necessary to the end for which we were created.

Father Enders was born in Bavaria, Germany, Nov. 17th, 1806. His parents were farmers, and pious people who taught him from the cradle the practice of his holy religion. At an early age he expressed his desire to become a priest, and his father took him to the nearest town to begin his studies. At the age of twenty-five he was ordained a secular priest in the diocese of Munich. Later he felt drawn to the Society of Jesus, and entered that order in a novitate of Switzerland, Sept. 28th, 1836. He came to this country soon after, and was sent to Conewago, Adams County, Pa., of which community he became Superior in 1847. From 1862 to 1869, he was Superior at Leonardtown, St. Mary's County, Md. He was returned to Conewago in 1871 as Superior. July 1st, 1884, Father P. Forhan took his place. He was then getting old and feeble and suffering from a painful ulcer at his leg.— Though the body was weak the will was strong, and he took the change very hard,—complaining that now he was no longer of any use. He continued to say Mass and very often forgot that he was no longer Superior. In the win-

CATHOLIC LOCAL HISTORY. 157

ter of 1884, he was removed to Frederick where his declining days could be made more easy. Saturday, Aug. 16th, 1884, the writer visited him there. He seemed in good health and spirits, having said his Mass that morning.— He asked all about Conewago, expressed a desire to see it once more, but thought the end was near, for which he was ready and waiting.

Father Enders, with Fathers Emig and Cotting still living, was the last of the missionary priests who labored at Conewago. Fathers Greaton, Wappeler, Manners, Frambach, Pellentz, and others, were the pioneer missionaries of Southern Pennsylvania. They began the settlement and put up the primitive churches. Fathers De Barth, Lekeu and others, followed from 1800, and kept the growing Church together; they began the improvements demanded by a growing age. Fathers Enders and Deneckere came before 1850, and attended the missions that are now surrounded by populous towns and have resident pastors. We have already seen how much Conewago is indebted to the labors of Father Enders. For fifty years he lived only for those in his charge. Year in and year out with him was a continual round of works of mercy and charity. Day or night, rain or shine, sick or well, DUTY was to him an imperative command. Rest he never knew, and never thought of his own wants. All were his friends, and he was a friend to everyone. Kind, humble, patient, warm-hearted, hospitable and hard-working,—in life and in death resigned to the will of God.

REV. ADOLPHUS LEWIS DE BARTH (Walbach) was at Conewago off and on from 1800 to 1828. He became manager of the estate in 1811, for those who held the title on the part of the Society, and was at that time a resident of Adams County, according to the Letter of Attorney from Rev. Francis Neale, on file in the Recorder's office of said county. Father De B. was the son of Count De Barth and Maria Louisa de Rohme; born at Munster, Upper Rhine, Nov. 1st, 1764; ordained at Strasburg in 1790; driven from France by the Revolution, he came with his father to America; assigned to missionary duty by Bishop Carroll, he labored at Bohemia Manor, Lancaster, and Conewago; was Vicar General to Bishop Egan, and after his death Administrator of the Diocese, and himself twice declined the Bishopric.— He was the brother of Col. John De Barth Walbach, U. S. A. Father De B. is remembered by some of the old citizens of Conewago, as a very earnest, faithful priest, and a cultured man. He was very severe and strict. Many little incidents are related of him, by which he is remembered. Some friends at Littlestown once gave a dinner to the Fathers, to which the young gentry of Conewago were invited. The learned Father White, then a student, was spending some time at Conewago for the benefit of his health.— He joined the company. When Father De Barth saw the young student and Miss Sallie Lilly coming riding together, he was very much displeased, and after dinner they ordered their horses and returned to the Chapel. After that he would not allow him to ride out with young ladies. In former times the Fathers frequently dined out, but seldom within our recollection.

The names of two distinguished priests are met with at Conewago, who deserve a short notice, for few are acquainted with their history; they are, Rev. Virgil Barber, in 1836, and Father Samuel Barber, about 1845. Daniel Barber, a Congregationalist minister in New England, became a Catholic in

1816. Virgil Barber, his son, also a Protestant minister, entered the Church with his father. He was born May 9th, 1782 ; went to Rome in 1817, was ordained there, labored in Pennsylvania and Maryland, became Professor of Hebrew in Georgetown College, where he died March 27th, 1847. Mrs. Virgil Barber and their four daughters became Sisters, and the son, Samuel, joined the Society of Jesus.

REV. JOSEPH HERONT was born in Lyons, France, Nov. 2d, 1755. He came to America in 1794, and purchased " Herontford," near Pigeon Hills, afterwards the "Seminary Farm." Aug. 1st, 1812, he was ordained. and admitted to the Order of St. Sulpice : he was for a short time occupied on the missions of lower Maryland ; was Treasurer of St. Mary's College, Baltimore ; and in Nov., 1817, went to the Island of Martinique, where he died April 8th, 1818. He was not related to Rev. John Tessier, President of St. Mary's, but bequeathed the farm to him as Superior when he prepared to enter that Order. Rev. Louis Regis Deluol, connected with the "Seminary Farm" as President of St. Mary's, was a priest in France several years before he came to this country. He returned to France near about 1850, and died in Paris, Oct. 15th, 1858.

Father Matthias Manners, (Sittensberger,) the first resident pastor at Conewago, about 1750, was born Sept. 29th, 1719, in the Diocese of Augsburg, Germany ; labored in Maryland and Pennsylvania ; died at Bohemia, June 17th, 1775.

Father Bernard Diderick, from Belgium, a Walloon, is referred to in Father Lambing's Researches. He was at Conewago in the early part of Father Pellentz's pastorate, and we have alluded to him as Fr. "Detrick."

BARON DE BEELEN.—This was a man of some distinction in his time, and as he is buried at Conewago, we give a short sketch " When Joseph II. attempted to open the river Scheldt, he designed to establish commerce between Belgium and the United States, and to promote this end he sent the Baron de Beelen Bertholff to reside in Philadelphia, not as an accredited minister, but as an observer and correspondent." When the Continental Congress adjourned its sessions to York, the Baron also removed there, and made that his home pretty much until his death. Local tradition says he lived there in great style. The Conewago Jesuits were well acquainted with the family. His son, Anthony, lived in Pittsburg, (see Lambing). He had another son who died East, and a death record at Conewago of a Francis Beelen may be the same. Old people inform us that he married a daughter of Wm. Jenkins, of Abbottstown, against which his parents were much opposed. The Fathers assisted the widow and kept trace of her. She lived a while in Baltimore. An old teamster of Father De Barth, still living, says he was sent to see her by that Father. The Baron and his wife are buried at Conewago. When the new part was built in 1850, it covered their graves, and the marble slab was laid in the floor, in the aisle near the Blessed Virgin's altar. It reads : " In memory of Frederick E. F. Brn. de Beelen Bertholf, who departed this life the 5th April, 1805, aged 76 years. Joanna Maria Thresia, his wife, who departed this life the 11th Sept., 1804, aged 72 yrs. May they rest in peace." It is said that a contagious disease prevailed when the Baron died. The man who brought his body from York, left the coffin standing in front of the church and hurried away. There it stood all day, everyone in dread of the disease. Towards evening Father De Barth sent over to the Lilly farm for help, and two colored men came and assisted him in the last sad duty in the burial of the once distinguished man.

THE WINCHESTER CHURCH.

For the following sketch of the Winchester Church, we are indebted to Father O'Reilley ; and to Mr. Wm. McSherry, Jr., for the Gettysburg Church history. Both were received too late for insertion among the other churches.

The early history of the Catholic Church in Winchester is almost entirely unknown. Perhaps the only certain fact about it is, that it was one of the oldest churches in the Valley. From an old gentleman, John Heist, a Protestant, it has been learned that in 1794, when he settled in Winchester, the Catholic Church was in appearance the oldest in town, and public opinion conceded the claim of its antiquity. Of those instrumental in its building, little is known. The ground was given by Mr. McGuire, an Irish gentleman, the ancestor of a family famous in Virginia as physicians and surgeons. Its present representatives are Dr. Wm. McGuire, of Winchester, and Dr. Hunter McGuire, of Richmond. The latter was Stonewall Jackson's physician, and the Surgeon-General of the Confederate Army. The old church, a stone building of moderate dimensions, was almost entirely built through the liberality of a wealthy Frenchman. Most of the pioneer Catholics slumber in nameless graves in the old cemetery. A moss-clad tomb is inscribed to the memory of a daughter of John Holker, Esq., 1794, late Consul-General of France, and Agent of the Royal Marine. This may have been the wealthy Frenchman to whose christian liberality tradition ascribes the old stone church. The first priest of whom tradition speaks, is Father Dubois, who visited this place from Conewago, Pa., about 1790. After him came Fathers Cahill and Whelan, the latter the first priest known to visit Winchester regularly. There were few Catholics here in the early part of this century. A marble headstone in the old graveyard reads, "In memory of Patrick Denver, a native of County Down, Ireland, who departed this life March 31st, 1831, in the 85th year of his age." This is the grandfather of Gen. James Denver, prominently mentioned as the Democratic candidate for President in 1884. Denver, Colorado, and more than a score of other cities and towns in the West have been named in his honor. About 1840, came upon the scene the grand and venerable old pillars of the present congregation, who have manfully withstood the storms and shocks of most half a century, for its sake, and who like true sons of St. Patrick, which they boast to be, never wavered in the faith—the only inheritance they brought from their own Isle of Saints. These hoary veterans of the faith are, John Fagan, Michael Hasset, M. Lynch, and Denis Sheehan. Of these, John Fagan alone lived in town. For four long years they had not the happiness of being present at the Holy Sacrifice. At last, in 1844, their dear Saviour had compassion on their loneliness and sorrow, and sent them Rev. John O'Brien, then stationed at Harper's Ferry, who visited Winchester once in three months, and offered the Holy Sacrifice for the half dozen Catholics present. It was not until 1847, that things began to change for the better. In that year turnpikes were being built, on which many Irishmen and Catholics worked. A priest from Harper's Ferry now came regularly once a month, and continued to do so until the outbreak of the Civil War in 1861. Fr. O'Brien was succeeded by Father Plunket, a most popular and eloquent priest, whose memory is still honored by all who knew him, Protestant and Catholic alike, not only here but throughout the Shenandoah Valley. After him came Fathers Talty and Costello. In 1861, came that thrice unhappy event, the war. The little church and hopeful congregation at Winchester did not escape its ravages. They were scattered, and the dear little church they loved so well was left in ruins. Among the most fearless of Stonewall's and Mosby's followers were numbered Winchester Catholics. The dashing bravery of a Russell or a Reardon is to-day a password in the Valley After the war they returned to find no temple in which to worship. In the years of bloody strife that had passed, God seemed to have been forgotten and his temples to have lost their sacredness for men. A stable was made of the sweet little church upon the Hill. The ruins alone were left after the storm was over. Undaunted, however, were the few Catholics. Their own Soggarth Aroon still visited them and that was enough. With Michael Hasset and his good wife they well knew the priest and his people would always find a Caed Mille Failthe, and in his cosy little parlor month after month they assembled for divine service. Through the zeal of their young pastor, Rev. J. J. Kain, the congregation soon grew too large for the little parlor chapel, and larger rooms were provided. A future church was contemplated ; plans were then made for raising the funds, and successfully carried out through the great efforts of Father Kain, ably assisted by Mrs. Hasset and Routzhan. In 1870 the corner-stone of one of the largest churches in town was laid, and in the following year the little congregation of about a dozen families worshiped in its basement. Hard were the struggles to complete the work. To add to their troubles, in May, 1875, their beloved pastor was taken from them and consecrated Bishop of Wheeling. Father Van De Vyver succeeded, and the church was completed in 1878, and dedicated under the special patronage of the Sacred Heart of Jesus. On this joyful occasion the celebrant was no other than Bishop Kain, who had started the enterprise in 1868, and for six long years labored hard for its completion. The Catholic spirit was not yet satisfied. The congregation yearned for a resident pastor. Through all the weary years of labor and waiting, Winchester was only an out mission belonging to Harper's Ferry, long visited once a month, and that on a week day. Rev. J. Hagan became the first resident pastor in 1878. For him the congregation built a comfortable residence on the lot adjoining the church. A steeple was added, and placed in it one of the largest and sweetest toned bells in the Valley of Virginia. Father Hagan also founded a parochial school, which now flourishes with an average attendance of 45,—a number more than equal to all the Catholic souls in Winchester in 1865. Rev. Hagan was succeeded in June, 1882, by Rev. D. J. O'Connell, D. D., at present Rector of the American College, Rome. He remained pastor until Oct., 1888. when he was succeeded by Rev. J. B. O'Reilly. In that short period no pastor ever endeared himself so much to the congregation and people of Winchester. He purchased a most beautiful site for a new Catholic cemetery.— Finally, the little congregation of not more than a score in 1865, worshiping in a small private parlor, is now grown to over 300 souls. The Catholics have a handsome church, a school, a pastoral residence, and a resident pastor. All their property is paid for, and no debt hangs over them to encumber their future.

Let us add that Rev. Father O'Reilly, the present pastor, is a worthy successor of the faithful priests who have labored before him in the Valley.

THE GETTYSBURG CHURCH.

The early Catholics in and about Gettysburg were chiefly Germans. They were poor, few, and widely scattered ; but whether the sun shone or the rain fell, in the dust of summer and the snow of winter, they went, (many on foot) " to hear Mass on Sunday and Holydays of obligation." A few attended church at Emmettsburg, Maryland ; some at Littlestown, Pennsylvania ; others at St. Ignatius, in the Mountain ; but most at Conewago Chapel, in the valley. The first two named are about ten and the last two about twelve miles distant from the town. Rev. Matthew Lekeu, S. J., the Superior of the Jesuits at Conewago, and Rev. Michael Dougherty, S. J., one of his assistants, were the first to establish the congregation and build a Catholic church at Gettysburg. The task was a hard one ; but where God's glory or the salvation of souls is concerned the Jesuit knows no hardships. The good Catholics generously responded to their appeal, and even deprived themselves to contribute to the new edifice. Early in the year 1830, the matter assumed definite shape. Among the largest contributors were Peter Eline and Peter Martin, who each gave one hundred and fifty dollars, and Jacob Norbeck, who gave, as his subscription, a lot of ground (of about the same value) situated near the south end of West (now Washington) street, on which the church was erected. The following advertisement appeared in the county papers in reference to the building of the church.—" NOTICE. —The subscribers having been appointed Agents by Rev. Mat. Lakieu to receive proposals from the date hereof until the first of May next for the building of a Roman Catholic Church in the borough of Gettysburg, of the following dimensions, viz : The church to be 40 feet in length and 30 feet in breadth, outside, with a semi-circular or semi-decagon Sanctuary at the East (it should read West) gable end of the Church of 15 (afterwards printed 7½) feet radius inside. A steeple to be raised in front, one-half thereof within the church, of 12 feet square, and to be 65 feet in height. The foundations of the church, sanctuary, and steeple to be composed of sufficient rough stone work, and the body of the same to be of sufficient brick work ; the side walls of the church to be 22 feet from the floor, and the walls of the sanctuary of the same height. The roof of the church, sanctuary, and steeple to be covered with pine shingles. The roof of the steeple to be a polygon roof : and that of the sanctuary to correspond with the shape. The contractor will have to find all the material, hands, etc., necessary for the erection of said building, a plan whereof has been deposited with the subscribers, agreeably to which the said church will have to be built. The altar, pulpit, and ornamental work will not be included in said proposals, as they will be added after the erection of the church. It will be required that the contractor finish the church agreeably to the plan, during the ensuing summer. Persons desirous of contracting for the building of said church, will please apply to Samuel Lilly and Joseph Sneeringer, Sen., near Conewago Church. April 5, 1830." The contract was given to a Mr. Barkley, who did the carpenter work ; and under his direction Ephraim Hanaway did the mason work, and James Bohn the plastering. The corner-stone was laid on Wednesday, the 11th day of August, 1830. There was no Bishop present. Two sermons were delivered in the old Court House, one by Rev. Paul C.

Kohlman, a Jesuit. The building was almost completed, when on Thursday, the 19th day of May, 1831, it was struck by lightning, "the conductor not being completed." "A plasterer (Jonathan Gilbert) at work in the steeple, was prostrated, and remained senseless for some time, but recovered. The fluid passed down the cupola, then passed off at right angles to a saw on a post, split the post, and passed down the wall of the steeple to the front door, making a groove." The church was dedicated on Sunday, Oct. 2, 1831, by Rt. Rev. Frs. P. Kenrick, Bishop of Philadelphia. The music was furnished by the choir from Emmettsburg, Maryland. The text of the sermon was, "Make unto yourselves friends of the Mammon of iniquity." The church was called St. Francis Xavier's. It cost about $1800. To the description as already given, (in the proposal) it may be added that the ceiling was caved, and there was a gallery over the door. The church contained twenty pews with one center aisle. Among the original members were Jacob Norbeck, Peter Eline, Peter Martin, Michael Gallagher, a lawyer, Dr. C. N. Burluchy, George Richter, Nicholas Codori, George Codori, Mrs. Elizabeth Allen, the McLoughlins, McAleers, Lazarus Shorb, Nicholas Eckenrode, Daniel Sherkey, Mrs. Thompson and but a few others. Rev. Michael Dougherty, S. J., was the first pastor, Lewis Norbeck and Daniel Shirkey were the first altar-boys. The lot given by Mr. Norbeck was also used as a grave-yard. The first burial authenticated, was that of Mrs. Elizabeth Allen, who died November 10, 1831. Among the early marriages after the church was built are Margaret Eisenman to Michael Zhea, by Father Dougherty, in September, 1834, and John Hamilton to Laurah A. Eline, by the same pastor, April 28, 1837. Mr. Hamilton was one of the first converts. The congregation increased rapidly under the guidance of good Father Dougherty. Among the members of 1840 are to be added to the original ones the Doersoms, Warners, M. Zhea, John Martin, John Carver, Smiths, Hemlers, John Ertter and some others. A bell weighing about 400 pounds was procured for the church in 1842 or 3. Father Dougherty closed his long and successful pastorate in the latter year. About this time there was Mass about every two weeks, before this it was only once a month. Rev. F. Kendler (from Conewago, but not a Jesuit.) came here about the 6th day of June, 1843. He was followed by Rev. Joseph Dietz, S. J., who was in charge from about the 27th day of August, 1843, until March 11, 1848. Father Dietz made a sacristy in the church, prior to that the priest robed behind the altar. He also organized a choir, before his time the whole congregation sang in German. Mr. Weigle was the leader; the music was all vocal. He also had a picture of the Crucifixion placed above the altar. Father George Villiger, S. J., the next attendant, came about March 16, 1848, and left in Oct. of the same year. About the 27th of Dec., 1848, Rev. J. B. Cattani, S. J., assumed charge and remained until about the 10th of Nov., 1849. He was succeeded about Dec. 8th, 1849, by Rev. James B. Cotting (he was from Conewago, but did not sign S. J. to his name.) The following were the pew holders, Jan. 1, 1851: Jacob Norbeck, John Norbeck, Jacob Case, Andrew Stock, Francis Booty, John Hamilton, John Carver, John Martin, Nicholas Codori, George Codori, John Weikle, Valentine Warner, Lazarus Shorb, Joseph Smith, Nicholas Hoffman, Jacob Kuhn, George Jacobs, James Wagamon, Joseph Shillen, Anthony Codori and Philip Krixer. A pew was reserved for the poor. In the first years the pews were free, but in 1851 the pew rents amounted to $145.56. The congregation from 1840 increased so rapidly that the church soon became too small. Father Cotting took upon himself the burden of providing a new place of devotion. He was a most zealous worker, and being popular with all classes, was a most successful canvasser for contributions. Catholics and Protestants alike generously responded to his appeal, and among the contributors was Rev. S. S. Smucker, D. D., the President of the Lutheran Theological Seminary at Gettysburg. On the 22d day of Dec., 1851, the following notice appeared in the local papers; "To CHURCH BUILDERS.—Sealed proposals will be received by Nicholas Codori in Gettysburg, until Saturday, the 10th day of January next, for building a Catholic Church in Gottysburg. Plans and specifications for the church can be seen at any time by persons wishing to build by calling on Nicholas Codori, one of the committee, in Gettysburg. By order of Rev. J. Cotting. Nicholas Codori. John Martin, Joseph Smith, Jacob Case, committee. N. B.—Rev. James B. Cotting yet continues the officiating clergyman, and by his liberality and good conduct the congregation is in a prosperous condition." The contract was awarded in Jan., 1851, to George and Henry Chritzman. The contract price was $3800, but many extras were added. They gave out the mason work to Henry Kuhn, and the plastering to James Bohn. The old church was torn down in March, 1852, and on Friday the 26th, while the South wall was being prepared for removal, it fell on Henry Hollinger and Charles Buckmaster (colored), two of the workmen, and killed them. The bricks were used in the new church, having become the property of the contractors. In about April, 1852, a lot 75 by 180 feet, situated on West High street, on which the church was built, was purchased for $750 from Ferdinand E. Vandersloot: the deed seems to have been made to St. Joseph's College, of Philadelphia, Pa., in trust for the Catholic congregation worshiping in St. Francis Xavier's Church in Gettysburg, Adams County, Pa. The corner-stone of the new church was laid on Sunday, June 20th, 1852, by Rt. Rev. John Neumann, Bishop of Philadelphia. About a year later, (Sunday, July 31, 1853), the same prelate (who had laid the corner-stone,) dedicated the church to the service of the Living God. The following is a description of the Church as it appeared about the time of its dedication: The building is of brick, 48 feet wide, 90 feet long, and about 40 feet high. It has a Roman cupola of about 60 feet. It contains a fine sanctuary, accompanied on either side by a sacristy or confessional. The height of the inside walls is about 26 feet, and the ceiling is plain or level. It contained 64 pews and room for more. There is a center and two side aisles. A broad gallery used by the choir extends over the entrance from wall to wall. It has also a fine pipe organ. There was a large oil painting representing the raising of a dead man to life by St. Francis Xavier, (painted by Francis Stecker,) placed back of the altar. There were alcoves above the sacristy, from which the sermons were sometimes preached. The old bell was transferred to the new cupola. The first marriage after the completion of the new church was that of Charles McFadden to Laurah Amanda McIntire, by Father Cotting. August 1. 1853. Among the first baptisms was Anna R., daughter of Daniel and Elizabeth Lee, August 8, 1853, also by Father Cotting. This faithful pastor did not remain to enjoy the fruits of his successful labor, but in obedience to the call of his Superior, left August 29, 1858, for other fields of usefulness, followed by the prayers of his devoted and grateful flock. He was succeeded September the 11, 1858, by the learned and eloquent Father

F. X. Deneckere, S. J., who greatly improved the interior of the church and established a Library and also a Rosary Society. This holy priest was the last regular Jesuit pastor, and about the time he left, (November 2, 1858,) the Jesuit Fathers gave over the congregation and church property into the care and control of Rt. Rev. James F. Wood, Bishop of Philadelphia. A new charge was now formed out of St. Ignatius Church in Buchanan Valley, Immaculate Conception, of Fairfield, and St. Francis Xavier's, of Gettysburg, with but one pastor residing in the latter place. About Nov. 14, 1858, Rev. Basil A. Shorb was appointed the first secular pastor. He remained until about the 24 of Feb., 1860. He was followed by Rev L. J. Miller, who was in charge from about March 14, 1860, to August 15, of the same year. The Rev. F. P. Mulgreu was stationed here from Sep. 16 to Dec. 27, 1860. Then came Rev. Michael F. Martin. who was here a short time. The next pastor was Rev. A. M. McGinnis, who was in charge from July 16, 1861, to about Oct. 27, 1863. In common with the other churches of the town, St. Francis Xavier's was used as a hospital during the Battle of Gettysburg. It was first occupied as such before noon of July 1, 1863, and was used for this purpose for several weeks. While the church was so occupied, Mass was said in a room at the house of Nicholas Codori. Father Joseph A. Boll assumed charge of the congregation Jan. 4, 1864. He at once repaired the damage done the church during the battle. In June following his coming, he had the church frescoed and ornamented with shadow statuary painting, representing the twelve apostles. The work was done by Mr. George Seiling, of Reading, Pa., and was finished in the following Sep. Mr. Philip Doersom had purchased the Crucifixion, (painted by Mr. Gephart, of York,) which hung in the old church, from Father Deneckere. He had it newly framed and the painting repaired. Father Boll desired to purchase it, but Mr. Doersom declined to sell ; but consented to its being placed in rear of the altar, if a proper recess were frescoed for it. This was done, and the words "Copiosa Apud Eum Redemptio" forming a suitable arch were painted above it. The picture is still there, but owned by Mr. Deersom. The large painting was removed to a side wall of the sanctuary and is still there. About the same time an elegant walnut pulpit, designed by Mr. Seiling, but made in Gettysburg, was placed in the church. During August of 1865, the last cent due by the church was paid. Gas was first used in the church in 1871. In the latter part of the same year a lot was purchased almost opposite the church and the building of a parsonage was commenced thereon Dec. 1, 1871, and completed Oct. 5, 1872. It is a fine large brick dwelling, and cost, completed and furnished, over $7000. It was mainly paid for by monthly contributions, lasting four years. In the spring of 1873, the Mountain Church was detached from the Gettysburg charge, and since Mass is celebrated the first three Sundays at the latter place, and the fourth Sunday at Fairfield, other church days being divided. The parochial school house was commenced in June and finished in August, 1877. It is a roomy frame building furnished in modern style, and is located in rear of the parsonage. The first school session began Sep. 1, 1877. Father Boll took charge personally and taught the classes. His assistant was Miss Kate Marley, of Columbia, Pa. The following year he continued to teach, being assisted by Misses Mary Kummerant and Emily L. Martin, of Gettysburg. The school continued under the same control until Feb. 1880, when Mr. Martin F. Power took charge of all the classes, the pastor still being the nominal head, but no longer teaching, excepting Christian Doctrine. It was a success from the beginning, and still continues so. Its course is high, full and practical. There are about 90 pupils. In Dec., 1877, the old bell was exchanged for a new one weighing 1288 pounds. On the 8th of the same month—the feast of the Immaculate Conception—its sweet notes rang forth the Angel's Salutation of 4000 years ago—being the first time the Angelus was regularly rung in Gettysburg. In the fall of 1880, Fathers Bouch and Trimple—two Redemptorists—gave a mission which resulted in much good. They also erected a mission cross, which is attached to the inside wall of the church near the Confessional. In the summer of 1881, Father Boll replaced the old church windows by beautiful burnt memorial ones, which are historical and of superior workmanship. They were made by F. Hoeckel, of Baltimore, and cost about $1000. Father Boll having obtained a nine months' leave to travel in Europe and Palestine in the fall of 1881, Rev. Henry Belt was appointed to take his place. He remained in charge until the following summer. His gentle and dignified manner at once won him the affection and respect of the congregation. Father Boll resumed charge after his return from abroad. He had only returned a few weeks when he was appointed pastor at Lebanon, Pa. Rev. John J. Shanahan was then appointed pastor. He was only here a few months, long enough to arouse a new spirit of devotion among the people, and by his eloquence and learning fill their hearts with increased love of God. There were many links that bound Father Boll to the earliest charge he filled, and at the first opportunity he returned to the scene of his early labors, in Dec., 1882. Jan. 3, 1885, the last debt due by the congregation was paid. St. Francis Xavier's Catholic Beneficial Society was organized Jan. 4, 1885, with about 85 members. It has about 50 now. The Library was re-organized in April of the same year, and has about 600 (hundred) books and 40 members. There were 5 acres, 29 perches of land bought June 4, 1885, and laid out for a cemetery. Ex-Sheriff Jacob Klunk, Esq., was the first buried, on September 8, 1885. The cemetery was blessed by Rt. Rev. J. F. Shanahan, Bishop of Harrisburg, Sunday, September 13, 1885. The school children, society, and congregation went in procession from the church to the grounds before High Mass. The congregation numbers about 600. The title to the church property is in the Bishop of Harrisburg in trust. It is worth about $18,000. The congregation do not owe a cent of debt. They have the finest parsonage, the best bell, and the handsomest church in the town. Among the present members are found some of the wealthiest and best citizens of the county. The liberality of the past generation has descended to the present, and as the generous contributor looks about him and sees what he has helped to accomplish for the church, he recalls the words of the Psalmist: "I have loved, Oh Lord, the beauty of Thy House and the place where Thy glory dwelleth." WM. McSHERRY, JR.

Gettysburg, Oct. 12, 1885.

GATHERING UP THE SCRAPS.

A. M. D. G. ET B. M. V. H.

We gather up the fragments that remain, "LEST THEY BE LOST."' They may seem trifling to some ; others can appreciate their importance, to whom such scraps of our early church history that is lost and forgotten would indeed be valuable. So with these : they will grow in interest. They might be put in better shape, and come in more consecutive order, but time will not allow. The object we have most in mind is their PRESERVATION.

Rev. James Stillinger, a priest in Western Pennsylvania, (see LAMBING'S Hist. of Western Pa., p. 402), died Sept. 18, 1878. His father was born in York Co., Pa. Fr. S. worked as a printer in Chambersburg and Gettysburg, when a boy ; entered St. Mary's College through Father Dubois, and became a priest in 1830. Lambing mentions a priest at Conewago in 1789, named John B. Causey, who did missionary work in Western Pennsylvania. He came from Philadelphia to Conewago and from there was called to attend the death-bed of Father Browers, in Westmoreland Co., Pa. This Father, among other bequests, willed some personal property " for the use of the Poor Roman Catholic Irish, that does or shall live at the Chappel, on Conewagga." There is no record of what became of Father Causey, (see LAMBING, p. 364.) Rev. Francis Fromm came from Germany in 1789, and from Conewago he went to the Western Pa. Missions. Father Pellentz visited these missions from Conewago. Rev. Peter Heilbron was among the early priests in Western Pa. He died at Carlisle about 1816. Father Brosius, while at Conewago, also visited McGuire's settlement, in Cambria Co., and after him came Father Gallitzin. Rev. Jas. Bradley, a priest in Blair Co., was ordained at Conewago, Sept. 20th, 1839, by Bishop Kenrick. Father O'Brien, one of the first priests in Pittsburg, spent a short time at Conewago about 1820, when his health compelled his retirement from active labor in the ministry.

Rev. A. A. Lambing's father was baptized at Conewago April 12th, 1807, and became one of the pioneer Catholics of Western Pennsylvania. Father Lambing is widely known for his valuable and extensive research in Catholic history, and also as a learned writer on Catholic subjects. His labors in the interest of Catholic local history have been very successful. The most laudable effort of his life is the establishment of a publication devoted to the early history of the Catholic Church in this country. Catholics should encourage it, and make it permanent,

Fragments of names and dates, gathered from the old account books at Conewago : Among those employed as laborers when the priests yet farmed the land, we find the following : John Strasbaugh, blacksmith : Henry Small, Alex. Robinson, Peter Majors, George Nace, Julian Plunket, Mary Koch, Cath. Chambers, Mary O'Neil, Susan and Mary Will, Eliz. Dellone, Mary Major, Cath. Baker, Mar. Strasbaugh ; Peter O'Neil, who entered the house on Monday, July 23d, 1827 ; Madalene Shaffer. John Adams. 1833, Aug. 23d, to Rev. Mr. Curley, of Georgetown, for expenses to return to college. May 19th, Father Vespre on stage to Georgetown. 1834, paid to Rev.

Mr. Divin on account of the Masses discharged for Father Provincial. 1835, March 20, to Trappist Brother, of Nova Scotia, for Father Docherty. July 13, for the voyage of Father Helias; when he arrived. Father C. Paul Kohlman was recalled to Georgetown. The sketch of Conewago heretofore alluded to, thought to have been written about 1880, is of a later date, as the following scrap, which belongs to it, clearly shows: "Father Barber arrived here to make his retreat, and will probably stay with us. Father Helias received orders of our Father Provincial to go to Missouri; he started the 6th of Aug., 1835, with the stage of Littlestown." Father Helias died in Missouri in 1874, at an old age. He came from Europe with Father De Smet and his companions, for missionary work in the West, and was one of the first priests west of St. Louis. 1850, Rev. Wirzfeld collected for Waynesburg. The collection for Episcopate fund of that year sent by Brother Lancaster. 1851, collection for "Milwauki" by Rev. Latzman. 1852, Rev. Moore visitor at Conewago. 1845, collection by Father Dietz for Rev. Wacthlen. 1852, loan to Fr. Early, sent by Bro. Redman to St. John's. 1858, Nov., boarded Bro. Logan; at Conewago for his health. 1854, Feb. 6th, boarded Fr. Kreighton; most likely there for his health. Thomas Will entered our house April 1st, 1830; was to be furnished with "cloth of our own manufactory." 1844, names of Brothers Quinlan and Cavanaugh. About this time, a painter named Gephart, was at Conewago; painted picture of Miss Sally Lilly's father, one of Mr. McSherry's father, and Mr. Bange's father; also, picture of St. Ignatius, long on B. V. altar, and picture of St. Francis Regis; a little painting for Nippero's Valley; and a painting to be sent to Gettysburg, "which shall remain in my possession until that congregation pays $30." Clotilda Stigers mended priests' vestments and attended altar. Sister Ann. Superior at McSherrystown. There is a list of young ladies who attended the school at that time, as follows: Mary E. Adelsperger; Adeline, Catharine and Susanna Kenney; Louisa Maria Shorb, Harriet Linco Walmsley, Catharine Baker, Alphonsia Walsh, Catharine Stephens, Margaret Colgan, Anna Mary Linn, Catharine Sneeringer; book for M. Euphrosina. It is gratifying to see that the young ladies of that time, from about 1834 to 1840, had real solid christian names, and no fancy prefixes like young ladies now have. 1844, Thos. Lilly Proc. Prov., settled accounts of Fr. Lekeu. Names of Steinbacher, Dietz and Kendler, the latter no Jesuit. 1845. Revs. Dietz, Kendler and Philip Sacchi. April 8th of that year, P. J. Verhaegen, S. J., signed as Visitor. There is mention of a Mother Boilvin among the first Sisters at McSherrystown. Dec. 30th, 1845, "Madame" Boilvin gave $20 to Mr. Kendler at his departure for Milwaukee. 1847, May 18th, Father Verhaegen, Visitor. 1850, Oct. 17, Ignatius Brocard, Visitor. Sept. 16, 1865, Angelus M. Paresce, Visitor.

Rev. J. B. Causey, or Cause, came to Conewago from Philadelphia, between 1787 and 1789.

Nov. 10th, 1845, letter from Francis Patrick Kenrick, Bishop of Phila., to Rev. N. Steinbacher, Superior of Conewago, in regard to Sisters leaving McSherrystown. He submits the matter to the judgment of the Sisters, who, notwithstanding the great sacrifice to them, incline to remove on account of the difficulty of access to McSherrystown. 1860, Father Manns attended Paradise. Petition from Paradise congregation to Superior for permission to have court grant a road from the Berlin Turnpike to the church, through farms of A. W. Storm, Joseph Clunk and church. Road was made, and comes out immediately in front of church.

When the Hanover and Baltimore Turnpike was built, $1000 stock was entered in the name of Charles Neal, 1811, Superior of the Maryland Missions. The Conewago priests from time to time drew the dividends, which at first were a fair per cent., and towards later years did not amount to much and the matter was entirely lost sight of for some years. Father Bellwalder was about the last to draw a dividend. Father Emig, of St. Joseph's, Hanover, took up the matter and writes to Father Enders, Superior, March 27th, 1882, as follows : Says he attended to the business as good as if a lawyer had been employed. Wants nothing for it but a habit, "mine is wearing out;" health has been very bad, coughing day and night, with pains in the head.

The following names and dates are gleaned from the letters of the Superiors of the Society :

1858, Oct. 20th, shall be obliged to diminish priests at Conewago—Father Reiter probably be taken.

To Father Cattani, Superior at Conewago, Feb. 23d, 1858 : We have lost Brother Marshall, in his 51st year in God's holy service in the Society.

1852, Brother Mattingly sent to replace Bro. Doyle. Father Manns recalled to Frederick in 1853, to make a year of Third Probation. Father Domperio succeeded Father Cattani as Superior for a short time, between 1865 and '66. Father N. Steinbacher died suddenly at St. Mary's, Boston, Feb. 14th, 1862. Father Roger Dietz died in 1860. He was "a man of prayer." In Oct., 1861, Father Sheerin was called to Baltimore from Conewago. Jan., 1863, Father Barrister sent to Conewago, to rest a while from the great labors and exertions, both of body and of mind, which he has endured for the past two years. He took Fr. Deneckere's place, who went for a short time to Boston to assist Father Reiter. Feb. 24th, 1863, Father Domperio sent to Conewago from Balto. In Jan., 1862, Mr. J. Shorb, architect, was sent from Balto. to superintend building at Conewago : the plans were soon after changed, and he was recalled. 1841, Thomas F. Mulledy, S. J., on a visit to Nice, appointed Father McElroy his attorney.

There is a scrap of a letter of introduction from a Conewago priest for a Protestant gentleman about to start for Rome, to Padre Trasset. No date or name ; says it is his seventh year on this continent; came in company with Fathers Rey and Dietz, the former gone to receive his reward, the latter "with us at Conewago." Anthony Rey was Socius Prov. in 1845.

John H. Nipper writes to Father Steinbacher from Frederick, April 6, 1845 ; sends respects to Bro. Quinlan ; says Father Sacchi is well, and he and Bro. McFadden send respects to the Fathers.

Release, Feb. 28, 1816, Lewis DeBarth and successors. By will of John Anselm, dec'd, of Hanover, he ordered 200 pounds to be given to Rev. DeB., for which he was to pay to Eve Anselm 6 per cent. interest ; she having married James Dullehide, of Berwick Twp., they gave release.

Father Deneckere writing from Frederick, 1858, says Latin class there is not superior to the few boys of the same category at Conewago. Bishop Neumann, 1859, paid Mother Magdalene $50 a year for each of the orphan girls at McSherrystown. April 23d, 1863, Bishop Wood acknowledges receipt of $286.15, from Rev. J. B. Cattani, collection for poor Ireland, "with our little share added." Florence J. Sullivan, S. J., Santa Clara College Cal.; baptized at Littlestown by Father DeHarth, 1828; his father was Timothy, and his mother Joanna O'Neill; Archbishop of San Francisco unwilling to confer orders unless certificate of baptism be produced. He was a Novice at Frederick about a year, when his health failed.

Father Villiger writes in 1858: Father Deneckere gave liberal subscription toward establishing a free school for girls with the Sisters, and for boys at Conewago: of which Father Enders was President and German; Deneckere Prefect and Latin; Bro. Redmond, Disciplinarian and English: Mr. Gross, History and Mathematics. He says, Father Dougherty attends Littlestown; myself and "Billy," Paradise and Millerstown. "Tom," poor thing, was run blind by Fr. Wigget, at St. Thomas'. The priests always had good horses, and valued them highly. Father George Villiger, who died at Conewago, was called "Little Father Villiger," and Fr. Burchard Villiger, now at St Joseph's, Phila., "Big Father V.," because they were the opposite in stature. These trivial items, seemingly of little account, are given with the best intentions: to many they will recall vivid recollections; and outside of their priestly character, they show the kind heart and cheerful spirit in the every-day life of the missionary. Father Enders attended Millerstown four years without any compensation, and gave $50 to silence some claims. In 1858, Father Enders writes from Leonardtown to Fr. Cattani at Conewago, for small picture of the Nativity, by Overbach, and St. Stanislaus by Stecher; desires to get copies for St. Joseph's, which was built chiefly through the exertions of Fr. Cotting. St. Joseph's, Phila., Jan. 13, 1860. —Father Ryder died yesterday morning at 10¼, after six days' severe illness. We are only two for work now. Father Barbelin and myself. Thos. Lilly, S. J. His remains were taken to Georgetown. Father Stonestreet alludes to the apportionment of the funds from German benefactors, between German missions of Boston and Richmond: and in 1855, by "Rev. Mr. Muller's express order, I sent a crumb to Conewago."

Feast of St. Mark, April 25, 1858, Father General constituted Rev. Burchard Villiger Provincial of Maryland, to succeed Chas. H. Stonestreet, who writes: "In this, my last official communication to the ever dear Province of Maryland, I cannot forbear to mention for encouragement and edification, that while Provincial I have never been disobeyed; and, moreover, have been always humbled personally, but aided officially, by the superior virtues of my brethren in Christ." He died suddenly of heart disease at Holy Cross College, Worcester, Mass., July 4, 1885, aged 72. He was a native of Maryland, stationed at Washington, Georgetown and Frederick. 1860, Fathers Enders, Deneckere and Cotting were at Newtown, St. Mary's Co., Md. Loyola College, Ap. 9, 1862.—The Bishop of Boston left here to-day with Father Early for Phila. Father Emig, from St. Louis, has been attached to our Province, and is now at St. Mary's, Boston. C. C. Lancaster, S. J., to J. B. Cattani, S. J. Phila., Dec. 30, 1859.—Rev. Father Sopranis will visit you (Conewago), Jan. 4. Father Ciccaterri and myself (C. C. L.) will accompany him.

April 11, 1858.—Thomas Lyndon, Pastor of Chambersburg, to Father Enders, Superior of Conewago, for priest to hear German confessions during Pascal season. Loyola, July 25, 1862, Fr. W. F. Clark sends by Fr. Vassi,

&c., to J. B. Cattani, Sup. at Conewago. July 18, 1858, Fr. Clark sends Bro. Riordan to Conewago for his health. Mother Ignatius, of St. Joseph's, McSherrystown, has in her possession a chair, which once belonged to Fr. Gallitzin. It was purchased of an aged lady, who in her childhood was a protege of that saintly man. It is said to have been the most pretending article of the kind in his household, and was even used by the Bishop when administering Confirmation.

William Arter did the plastering of the Conewago Chapel when first built. He was a peculiar man and did some very foolish things. At one time he kept a tavern at Hanover, and was well known.

Among the pewholders in 1820, were : Edw. Reily, Elizabeth Steigers, Nicholas Ginter, Margaret Storm, Samuel Lilly, Samuel Brady, Martin Clunk, John Dellone, Denis Carnahan, Michael Dellone, John Cook, Henry Lilly, Francis Marshall, Ignatius O'Bold, Michael Gallaher, John Smith, Adam Smith, Jacob Will, John Shenefelder, John Strasbaugh. The descendants of a few of these yet occupy the same pews, or at least the corresponding location, as new pews were put in by Fr. Enders.

Father Villiger, writing from Paradise in 1855 : Buried John Dellone last Dec., and early in the spring old Mrs. Noel from the Pigeon Hills. Old Mr. Alwine returned to his duties. Miss Cath. Strasbaugh, at Mr. Wise's, a convert, desires to become a religious. Aug. 9, 1856.—Fr. Stonestreet appoints J. B. Cattani Sup. of the church at Boston, of which we have charge for the Bishop, to succeed Rev. Ryder (also spelled Reiter, but no doubt the same) ; Father Lachat to take Fr. R.'s place. To have nothing to do with anything but spiritual matters. 1834, June 25, Joseph Wehrner, son of Benedict W., of Phila., born July 27, 1822, apprenticed to Mat. Lekeu, Rector and manager at Conewago, until he is 17. 1855.—Paradise Church robbed of its remonstrance, chalice and ciborium. Blessed Sacrament not there. Fr. Villiger, pastor. Michael Noel and old Mrs. Brieghner gave him money to replace them. Jos. Kuhn, Frederick, Peter and Michael Dellone presented chandelier, worth $60. Peter Noel will pay the half for stations ; Pius Fink the other half. Father V. adds : If we can we will make Paradise look like a paradise. Writing to a friend at Frederick, Father Villiger says : Frederick and Peter Dellone send respects ; also Mr. Will and his amiable family. He is getting rich, notwithstanding his liberality ; and fat, in spite of his chewing so much tobacco. Father Moranville, one of the early priests of Baltimore, went with Mrs. Harper, daughter of Charles Carroll, of Carrollton, to Berkeley Springs for his health. Wrote Aug. 20, 1823, health not much improved. In 1784, Charles Sewell, S. J., became first resident pastor of St. Peter's, Balto. He was a faithful and zealous priest, but no orator. He was at Conewago with Father Pellentz.

Near the church stands a large mission cross, erected in 1857, by the great missionary, Father Weininger. Father Maguire, and others, gave missions at Conewago. The galleries at Conewago were erected about Father Lekeu's time. They were removed by Father Domperio, on account of the opportunities they afforded for those inclined to distraction. The old bell at Conewago bears this inscription : " Andreas Vanden Cheyn, me fudit Lovanii Anno 1816 ; Ad Majorem Dei Gloriam, Dei Paroque Virginis Mariae." It is no doubt one of the many confiscated church and convent bells brought to this country in the revolutionary days of Europe. Some of them found their way to Protestant churches. One so in use at Gettysburg, has the inscription : "Maria de la Concepcion, per tvam immaculatam Dei Genetrix, Virgo defende nos ab hoste maligno, 1788." When the new steeple was finished at Conewago, the bell was pulled up into its place with ropes, by the boys then at Father Deneckere's school. Conewago is more or less connected with the mystery of Wizard Clip, in Virginia, but as we have nothing new to throw additional light on the affair, not much account will be given of it; Father Finotti has left full particulars in his Wizard Clip. Father Gallitzin wrote an account of it when at Conewago, after having given it a full investigation. His sketch was given out to read, and has never been heard of since. Some of the clipped clothes were brought to Conewago, and attracted so much notoriety that to avoid the importunities of the curious, Father Lekeu had them burned. Father Mulledy, when a scholastic at Conewago, saw them; so did Mr. Peter Smith, now dead, and others. Father Finotti was an Italian priest, with considerable patrimony, which he employed in his Catholic history researches. His collection of Catholic books and authors of America is a valuable work, and it is to be regretted that the second part was never finished. He had written a history of the church in Virginia, unfortunately destroyed by an accident. What a valuable addition it would be to our Catholic history ? what labors it cost ? what sad regrets to him who valued it more than gold or silver ? Father Finotti died from an accident, in California, about 1878—see sketch in his Wizard Clip. His library, a valuable collection of rare books and pamphlets, treating on Catholic local history,—the work of a life-time at a cost of nearly all he possessed,—was sold at public auction in New York in 1879, and scattered to the four winds of the earth. Though a stranger to this country, he sought under many difficulties to reclaim our early history, and by his interest and labors did a great deal to create a taste and a desire on the part of Catholics to have the early history of their church preserved. Let the name of FINOTTI stand among the first of our Catholic historians.

The novices of the Society of Jesus in Frederick taught the colored children the catechism and gave the colored people instructions in ante-bellum days. The Oblate Sisters of Providence, colored, were established in Baltimore in 1829, by Father Joubert, a priest from San Domingo. In slavery times, the colored people had their part in the churches through Maryland, where they attended services.

Bishop Kain, of Wheeling, opened the W. Va. Senate with prayer during legislative session of 1885; he also made the invocation when Gov. E. W. Wilson was inaugurated, March 4th of that year. Bishop Keane, of Richmond, was called upon to open the Virginia House of Delegates with prayer, March 17th, 1879; the first time within recollection that a Catholic prelate was so called upon in that State.

The consecration of Rev. J. J. Keane, Bishop of Richmond, took place in St. Peter's Cathedral, Richmond, Aug. 25th, 1878. Archbishop Gibbons was the celebrant; Rev. A. Van de Vyver, of Harper's Ferry, Deacon of the Mass; Archiepiscopal Cross-Bearer, Rev. J. J. Doherty, of Martinsburg; among the Bearers of Offerings, was Rev. Hugh J. McKeefry, then of Keyser; present as a Seminarian, Father Frioli, now of Keyser. Bishop Lynch, of Charleston, delivered the consecration sermon, from which the following is taken :

In the Diocese, over which he has been appointed to preside, he has had apostolic predecessors. Its first Bishop was Rt. Rev. Patrick Kelly. Learned, pious, mild and amiable, coming at his age, and coming from a professional chair, and finding what was, ecclesiastically speaking, a wilderness before him, with, I believe, only two priests in the entire State, he found himself unable to meet the hard physical work there required of a pioneer Bishop. Still he labored on until called to a more congenial field. He was transferred, in 1822, to the See of Waterford. For nineteen years he had no successor, and the church of Virginia was administered by the Archbishop of Baltimore.

"In 1841, Richard Vincent Whelan came as second Bishop, young, active, zealous, learned, with a large measure of that American tact which enables a man to look at difficulties undismayed, to rejoice at and overcome obstacles, to understand the needs and the circumstances surrounding him, and to undertake any work that may come before him. No wonder that in ten years the Church had so grown that the Diocese of Richmond might well be divided into two. Bishop Whelan took the new See of Wheeling, and his place in Richmond was filled by Right Rev. John McGill, your third Bishop. Of him what shall I say. I knew him too well, I honored him too highly, I loved him too dearly, to allow me to speak of him without emotion. You cannot forget him. Learned, eloquent, gifted with intellectual powers of the highest grade, he was respected by all,—while his earnest piety and the loveable, almost childlike simplicity and gentleness of his character, his directness in all things, and his boundless charity of heart could not but force all that knew him to love him. For twenty-two years he ruled the Diocese, and it prospered. He has passed away full of years, and his memory is still sweet among us. Of the fourth Bishop I am forbidden to speak. For he is present in that sanctuary. That he had so administered another office as to be chosen to fill the vacant chair of Bishop McGill, and that he so administered this Diocese of Richmond as after a few years to be chosen to occupy, as he does, the highest episcopal chair in the hierarchy of the United States. Long may he worthily preside over the venerable Metropolitan Church of Baltimore."

The old organ which was used in Old St. Joseph's Church, Phila., as early as 1748, came into the possession of the Catholic Church at Chambersburg, Pa., where it was used as late as 1875, and may be yet. It is said to be the first organ used in the U. S. It was used on several great occasions during the Revolutionary War, and no doubt is the same one alluded to by Kalm, the Swedish traveler.

In Nov., 1879, a new roof was put on Conewago Chapel, the old one having been on since 1848.

In March, 1878, the contract was awarded to Pius Smith, dec'd, for building the new brick house on the farm, below the Chapel. This contractor did a great deal of work for the Jesuits at their College, Woodstock.

May 26, 1878, Mrs. Joanna Sullivan, mother of Father Sullivan, was buried this week at Conewago, aged about 86 years. Peter Shanefelter, pensioner of the war of 1812, died May 27, 1878, aged 86. He was of the same family as was Father Shanefelter, of Goshenhoppen and the eastern part of Pa., in the beginning of this century.

Father DeBarth, an Alsacian by birth, was the second son of Count Joseph DeBarth, of a noble family for many generations Catholic. His brother, the late General E. Walbach, was John DeBarth Baron de Walbach, and when expatriated from France retained the name of Walbach. This explains the difference of names of the two brothers.

In 1803, Rev. Michael Egan, O. S. A., attended Lancaster from Conewago, where he had been assistant to Father DeBarth. He became the first Bishop of Philadelphia, consecrated Oct. 28th, 1810. He died in 1814, and was succeeded in 1820 by Bishop Conwell. In this interim Father DeBarth acted as administrator of the Diocese.

The name of Rev. John Blox appears on the Register at Conewago about 1840 or '50. He was an assistant at St. Joseph's, Philadelphia, in 1845.

Father Rey was killed in Mexico in the war of 1846. He went there with Father McElroy as volunteer chaplains of the U. S. Army.

Father Vespre died March 26th, 1860.

In March, 1862, Father Lilly died at Philadelphia.

In Father DeBarth's time, the extensive bottom lands along the creeks were well cultivated and yielded the best crops. After him they were left grow wild until reclaimed by Father Enders. In old times, as high as thirty and forty mowers were at work, coming together from different parts of the parish and giving their labor gratuitously. It was customary in those days to set out drink for the hands, though drunkenness was not as common then as now. In this respect Father DeBarth was very strict. A man, becoming drunk while thus working one day, quit his work and fell asleep. When Father DeBarth saw him, he commanded the men to haul him up to the house and placed in one of the pig pens, saying that as he made himself like unto a swine, he should keep like company.

Corpus Christi, 1876, Bishop Shanahan present at Procession. In Catholic countries on this day, the streets of the towns and the public roads are strewn with flowers and evergreens, as the Blessed Sacrament is carried along in Procession—a devotion intended to draw the blessings of God upon the growing harvests and the budding fruits of the earth,—a blessing in which the Valley of the Conewago has always liberally shared. This pious practice was instituted at Conewago by F. X. Deneckere. S. J., when he first came, and continued until late years, when it had to be discontinued on account of the thousands of people it annually attracted and the public show they made out of it by their irreverence. Father Deneckere spared no labor in making it grand and inspiring. The altars were arranged at a distance from the church and one in the church-yard. They rivaled in beauty and adornment the altars of many a church. The Blessed Sacrament was carried under a splendid canopy; acolytes preceded and children strewed the road with flowers; choristers dressed in white, young men and women bearing banners, emblems and statues, followed, and thousands of people came after, reciting the rosary. At each altar, the Benediction would be given, while the organ played, the choirs sang, bells were rung, and where the incense arose little children scattered flowers with their innocent hands; not unfrequently bands played and volleys were fired. Among the most beautiful of the altars was that of Miss Sally Lilly, erected near her house, every year that the Procession was held Poor Father Deneckere! it gave him more pleasure to thus render honor and glory to the Blessed Sacrament, than to have participated in the grandest demonstrations of men.

July 4th, 1876, High Mass in commemoration of the 100th anniversary of American Independence. By permission of Father Enders, the American flag waved from the steeple of the church. The priests were never found wanting in loyalty and patriotism, as far as right with their sacred calling, and consistent. At the death of a President, or for any other national calamity, the bells of Catholic Churches toll in sympathy, and from Catholic altars a sacrifice is offered in mediation or atonement.

Aug., 1876, Father Coppens, S. J., gave a mission in Hanover.

1877, Dec. 23d, Mass said on B. V. altar, on account of work on marble altar. Father Brady, Provincial, said Mass and spoke. 1877, June 3d, fiftieth anniversary of Pius Ninth's episcopate and 81st of his Pontificate; many Communions,—plenary indulgence.

New Year's morning, 1878, first Mass said on marble altar by the venerable Superior, Father Enders.

1878, April 27th, masons commenced work on the new brick house at the Chapel; old stone building torn away; was doubtless erected by Father Pellentz.

1878, May 5th, Father Deneckere preached on the Month of Mary, a beautiful and touching sermon—his streaming locks of silver gray flowed gracefully on his shoulders: and though his hands trembled, his voice was strong and clear, as he extolled the praises of the Mother of God, exhorted his hearers to be faithful and obedient children and follow in the footsteps of her Divine Son. Well do I remember the holy severity, edifying life and faithful teachings of this venerable Jesuit. 1878, Decoration Day. Maj. Jenkins Post G. A. R., of Hanover, decorated graves in Conewago Cemetery; Father Deneckere made address—a beautiful comparison between the christian warrior and the soldier of the world; favorably impressed all present. 1878, June 9th, Father Brady, Provincial, preached. June 23d, Father Haugh, of Frederick, delivered sermon on the Real Presence. July 4th, Lewis Will died, at an advanced age. He farmed Paradise Church a number of years; his brother and his father, Charley and Jacob, lived on the Conewago farm for many years, from about 1830. Before them, the land was farmed by the Superiors, who had men hired to do the work, especially teamstering. John Weaver became tenant after the Wills, and remained fifteen years; James Devine is now on the farm almost that long, if not longer. This is the oldest farm-house on the Chapel land, which originally comprised a section, or 640 acres. The old barn was blown down in 1825, and rebuilt. The second house and barn were built forty years ago, along the McSherrystown road; John Small, first tenant, remained until 1876; his sons, John and Ignatius, succeeded; in 1881, Ignatius took the farm, and soon after married a daughter of James Devine. Good farmers are never removed. When the third farm-house and barn were built along the Hanover road, about five years ago, John, son of James Devine, became the farmer. 1878, July, the marble altar was taken down; foundations gave way, owing to intense cold weather when first erected. July 10th, Frederick Dellone died and was buried at Paradise; was near 80, and a good Catholic to the church for a life-time. His father was Michael, and his grand-father Nicholas, who came to the Abbottstown settlement from France, returned and came again. 1878, collections for relief of Yellow Fever sufferers. Sept. 23d, Nicholas Fleigle died, aged over 80. Mr. O'Neill relates that when he lived at the church about fifty years ago, a man and woman were observed one day praying before the church, with extended arms. Father Lekeu learned that they were fulfilling a vow made during a storm at sea, where they lost a child. He assisted them to settle near Conewago; they were good Catholics and industrious people, and their children's children are now scattered through the parish. The early pastors of Conewago interested themselves in getting poor emigrants to settle in the Valley, and in some instances put up temporary shelter in the church-yard until homes could be secured for them. Oct., 1878, statues placed in the vacant niches in the walls. Oct. 18th, Bishop Shanahan confirmed 101 boys, 96 girls. Gave good instruction to parents and children; warned them against evil literature scattered broadcast now-a-days. He gave Communion. Oct. 20th, Father McGurk preached. Nov. 20th. Father Emig preached funeral sermon of Miss Annie O'Bold. Dec. 8th, Father Casey preached his first sermon at Conewago. Mat. Dolan died this day. Feast of Blessed Virgin; he was one of Father Deneckere's school-boys. Father Jamieson preached at funeral of Mrs. Stormbaugh in Jan., 1877.

DEATH OF FATHER DENECKERE.—Epiphany, 1879, Rev. F. X. Deneckere very sick at Littlestown; Father Enders went up to see him. Saturday, Jan. 4th, 1879 was a piercing cold day,—raining, blowing and freezing. Father Enders, Superior, did not want Father Deneckere to go, but he drove to Littlestown, and was nearly frozen when he got there. He lost his way or was confused and benumbed by the icy rain and cold; and stopping to ask the road, would not allow those who directed him to go along and drive, saying it was too cold for them to be out. He would not remain with any of his congregation at Littlestown, but went to the church where he had his sleeping apartment in one of the sacristies. There he was found sick and was properly cared for. Father Enders arrived the next day and administered the Sacraments. He died Wednesday, Jan. 8th, 1879. His remains were put in a neat coffin and placed before the altar. Thursday afternoon he was taken to Conewago, and interred in a vault under the altar, Friday morning at 9 o'clock, during a High Mass of Requiem. Father Casey said the Mass, and Father Enders made a few remarks. He said it was not customary for one of a family to proclaim the good deeds of another. As there was a large congregation present, he could not help but say a few words. Many years ago he and Father Deneckere were appointed on the Maryland missions, where they labored together; sometimes in the saddle day and night, attending sick calls and other duties of the missions. They were, with another Father, (Cotting,) removed to Conewago, where they had five missions to attend,—Conewago, York, Littlestown, Paradise and Gettysburg. God prospered their labors, and since that many new congregations have sprung up around them. They had been sent to other fields several times, but as often returned to "patch up" the old structure; and now as their days are being numbered, they have no other desire but to find rest near the altar where they served. [Poor Father, even that consolation was denied him, for he died and was buried at Frederick.] Lastly, he would fulfill the dying request of the late beloved Father, namely, to beg for him of the congregation and all with whom he came in contact during his life, pardon for any offence he may have given them, and to ask all to pray for him. Father Deneckere was a devoted teacher, and though advised by his Superior to give up his school on account of his increasing age and infirmities, he would not, but gave lessons yet to one poor boy even up to his death. He loved his school next to his sacred calling. saying that if he gained one addition to the priesthood, all his labors would be fully repaid. Eternal rest give unto him, O Lord, and let perpetual light shine upon him. May he rest in peace, Amen. Rev. F. X. Deneckere was a brother of Rev. Hippolytte Deneckere, who was six or eight years his junior. Rev. F. X. Deneckere was a student all his life, and while he taught his boys at Conewago, he himself took lessons in German from Father Enders, to perfect himself more in that language. Besides French, his mother tongue, he spoke English and Latin as well, and was a good Greek scholar. His name from the French is properly spelled " De Necker," but we have followed his own way of writing it " Deneckere."

1879, Jan. 25th, Rev. Geo. Villiger came to Conewago to take Father Deneckere's place. May 25th, Fathers Casey and Emig gave the Jubilee.

Procession on Corpus Christi ; large crowds. not the best order ; Superior preached of the want of respect and reverence for holy things.

Dec. 18th, Sister Amelia (McSherry,) buried at St. Joseph's Convent, McSherrystown. 1880, Feb., collections for famine sufferers in Ireland ; Sisters collected aid, seeds, &c., and sent to friends in need. No procession this year ; Father Dufour preached on Corpus Christi. Decoration Day, May 30th, Rev. Dufour made address in Conewago Cemetery, and Ed. S. Reily at Mt. Olivet, Hanover. July 18th, Father Flanigan went to Bonneauville, Rev. Shanahan, its pastor, being absent on a visit to Ireland. Father Enders announced that Sisters intended building a larger chapel ; old chapel was too small and unhealthy.

Aug. 1st, Father Archambault preached his first sermon at Conewago ; is to succeed Father Casey at Oxford and Paradise. He went to finish his studies ; was an energetic young priest ; had the churches in his charge repainted and improved.

Aug., 1880, letter from Father Dufour. from Louisiana. to a friend ; requests prayers for several converts that they may remain steadfast in the faith.

Oct. 17th, Father Gutti, of Philadelphia, said early Mass

Christmas, seven Masses, over 1000 Communicants. Library remodeled, catalogued and put in order. Have a very large library, many rare and valuable works. The Little Chapel is used for a library. There used to be nothing but a small passage connect the church with the priests' house. Father Enders, about 1870, had it enlarged and a beautiful altar erected therein, where he said Mass in winter, and had his confessional in the room adjoining,—a room long occupied by Father DeBarth, while the front room adjoining was used by Father Lekeu. Father Manns' confessional is under the north gallery steps ; Father Deneckere's was the first in the south wing, and the one nearest the Sanctuary was used by Father Enders and different priests. For twenty-five years, Father Manns has never been away from his confessional on church days, and oftentimes is found there, praying, when there is no one about. He is a great confessor. The room adjoining the parlor was occupied by Father Enders as Superior. The house was plainly furnished under him. His room had nothing but the necessary furniture, a folding cot, erected in a boarded up doorway, was opened out and arrangranged for him by Brother Donohue in the evening, and in the morning closed up again. Under Father Foran, the house has been remodeled and refurnished. Father Deneckere's room was above the parlor. Those who were in it once will never forget the various collection of invention, science, toys, mechanism, &c., which he had in use, some for one purpose, and some for another, and at which he spent the very few leisure moments at his command. The Bishop's room was diagonally across from his. The rooms fronting south were occupied, one by Father Manns, the rest by other priests and students, as they came. The saintly Brother Donohue occupied the attic. He was a faithful servant. About 1884, he was sent to Frederick, his health failing. In another attic room was stored the "old library." It was a valuable collection of books, probably brought together by the priests and accumulated in one way or another. There are thousands of books out of use and print now, old Bibles, and treatises on theology, philosophy, and various commentaries by the old scholars and masters. They are in all languages; some printed as early as the sixteenth century.

In the spring of 1885, the small (old) window glass in the church was taken out and modern glass put in, some stained. Aug. 29th, 1885, the work of enlarging the priests' house nearly completed. The building is now three-story all around, with a French roof, and a large porch fronting the churchyard.

During vacation at the Convent in McSherrystown this summer, the old day-school houses were torn down and new ones erected. Sister Patrick, who has charge of the boys' school, collected the funds herself to build the new school house, and assisted in the work of building with her own hands. She is an energetic Irish Sister, a great favorite as a teacher with the boys.

Will of Charles Hughes, made Feb. 7th, 1881, witnessed by C. Paulus Kohlman, S. J., and Andrew McManus. Wills to Father "Lague" (Lekeu) " all due him " and his weaver's loom. He lived in one of the small houses below the hill at the Chapel. His father's name was Patrick; he died near Abbottstown, and was carried to Conewago by his sons. Charles Hughes had a weaver shop near Bonaughtown; there Peter Smith, (dec'd, at the age of 86.) learned his trade.

To all people, to whom these presents shall or may come: I., Francis I. Neale, of Georgetown, Dist. Col., send Greeting. Whereas, I, the said Francis I. Neale, by the last will and testament of Rev. Robert Molyneaux, became heir to an estate in Conewago Twp., Adams Co., Pa., lately held by the Rev. James Pellentz, and now in occupation by Rev. Lewis DeBarth, &c., filed in the Register's office for the city and county of Phila., &c., I do hereby constitute, &c., Rev. Lewis DeBarth, of Adams Co., Pa., my lawful attorney, &c. Signed June 21st, 1811. R. McIllhenney, John Larentz, James McSherry, Franz Marshall, witnesses.

Francis Neale, of Charles Co., Md., appointed Rev. Matthew Lekeu his attorney for the Conewago property, signed in the City of Washington, July 24th, 1828; acknowledged before Geo. Naylor, J. P.; attested by Wm. Brent, clerk of Circuit Court; Certified by W. Cranch, Chief Judge Circuit Court; and by "H. Clay."

The following tradition comes down to us through good and intelligent people of Conewago: One of the ancestors of the Marshalls, Jacob or Joseph, was a close man and self-willed. He had one son a priest, and one or two were Brothers. His daughter desired to become a religious, but the father would not consent; all her entreaties were in vain. She was a young girl, very good in every way, and had never been away from home. After fruitless prayers and entreaties, she left her father's house one night, and made her way in the direction of Westminster. Dense forests then covered most parts of the country, and she was soon lost, not knowing which way to go. Recommending herself to the care of the Blessed Virgin she continued her journey, when a young man came riding along on a snow white horse, and asked her where she was going. She told him her story, and he assisted her to mount the horse with him, nothing uncommon in those days. After riding all day, he halted his horse before an humble-looking house, and told her they were at the Sisterhood she wished to enter, and she was kindly received by the good nuns. The young man rode off, no one knew whither. Even if the young man was only a traveler passing the way, she had reason to thank God for her guidance and protection.

Years ago, Conewago was called the Chapel of the Blue Spring, but the name was never very generally accepted. A young student at Dickinson, named Barnitz, from Hanover, wrote a romantic story about 1849, entitled The Recluse of the Conewago, in which he uses the expression "Blue Spring Chapel." The Blue Spring is a strong stream of water, issuing from the limestone rocks in the church bottom, below the Chapel, and flowing into the Conewago. The water has a bluish cast, and hundreds of feet of rope let down failed to reach any bottom. There are large fish in it. It seems to be more or less affected by the actions of the tide, and has never been known to go dry. The students had a boat on it, and it has always been something of an attraction. Such caves, springs or sink holes are common in limestone countries.

From a diary kept by one of the Fathers at Conewago, from Feb., 1844, to Oct., 1846, we glean some interesting notes. The writer evidently was a German, and was either Father Steinbacher, or Dietz.

In the month of February, 1844, Father Nicholas Steinbacher, in his 47th year, the 24th of his priesthood, and the 12th of his admission to the Society, was transferred from Goshenhoppen to Conewago, by the Provincial, Father J. Ryder. The resident priests at Conewago were, Fathers Philip Anthony Sacchi, Roger Joseph Dietz and Rev. F. X. Kendeler, a secular priest. That was the time Father Thomas Lilly was sent there to adjust the "old accounts" of Father Lekeu, who had been an easy manager, having allowed long standing accounts without settlement. The first Provincial of the Society for the Province of Maryland was Rev. Wm. McSherry, S. J., and prior to that there were no Visitors to examine the accounts and to keep business matters straight as they now do. At that time much of the Society's business management in other places was not so systematically conducted as it is now. No blame is attached to the Superiorship of Father Lekeu, except that he was too easy in conducting business. He is remembered as a kind and generous priest, who tried to make all around him happy. Conewago gained more through his labors and the liberality of his friends in France, than the Society lost by his want of financial ability. He was removed to White Marsh, where his health suffered. His Superiors said he might re-

CATHOLIC LOCAL HISTORY. 179

turn to France, where he died.

1844, May 18--Rev. Kyle came here from Phila., after the burning of St. Augustine's; remained eight days. July 4, Madame Murphy died at McSherrystown; she is the fourth nun dying there since its commencement. Aug. 5, Rev. Fathers Rey and Tuffer, Messrs. Earley, McGuire, McSherry, Lynch, Gillespie and Kreighton, Scholastics, arrived to spend vacation. They held services at the adjoining churches. Father Tiffer (or Tuffer) preached his first sermon at Paradise. Sept. 11, Bishop Kenrick arrived to give confirmation at our churches. Father Steinbacher used to be gone two weeks, attending the Mountain Church and doing missionary work in Nipper's (also written Nippero's) Valley, probably somewhere along the South Mountains. The other Fathers attended McSherrystown, Littlestown, Gettysburg, Paradise and the home church; all preached English and German; sometimes Father Steinbacher would preach English and German at one Mass at Conewago. Oct. 9th, there was a long letter from Father De Smet, from Lima; he is in excellent health; gives a very interesting account of his travels, and particularly when they discovered that he was a Jesuit; since they had not seen one since the Suppression of the Society. Oct. 17, Revs. Curry and McCloskey called here on their way to McSherrystown; will say Mass there in the morning. Oct. 22d, Mass was said for the repose of the soul of Father DeBarth, by Father Steinbacher. 28d, Father Ryder, Provincial, arrived. Will leave for Phila. on the 25th, where he is to preach a charity sermon, for the building of a small church near the ruins of St. Augustine's. Dec. 25, Father Steinbacher said Mass at midnight at McSherrystown. 28th, He received a letter from Father Fenwick, announcing the death of Father Young at Alexandria. 1845, Jan. 1st, Wm. Detrick, a school teacher, became a convert under Fr. Steinbacher. Jan. 9th, John Smith buried, Father Steinbacher played the organ. 15th, The Provincial, Fr. Verhagen, ordered Fr. Sacchi to Frederick to take the place of Fr. Vespre, who goes to Phila. Father S. left Feb. 7th with the stage to Balto., where he takes the cars to Frederick. Feb. 17th, Samuel Barber, S. J., arrived here in place of Fr. Sacchi. April 10, Fathers Provincial and Rey arrived, will go to Phila. April 24, sixteen men put up scaffolding to paint the church. 28, Messrs. Monachesi and Uberti here from Phila. to paint. April 30, Father Steinbacher left for Reading to lay the corner-stone of a new church. May 1st, an altar decorated in the school room, where Mass will be said during May, as the painting of the church prevents its celebration there. May 29th, Father Zocchi, from Taneytown, paid us a visit and took dinner. June 11, the painters finished and scaffolding taken down. 14, John Nippers and Bartholomee, Novices, arrived here from Frederick for a cow, which Father Steinbacher presented to the Novitiate. 28th, Brother Macarius, of the Trappist order, from Mount Mallory, County Waterford, Ireland, arrived here, he got $1000 in two weeks at Phila.; he got about $70 at Conewago, $16 from the Boarders and $2.50 from the Mother. July 7, Rev. Galligher, from Brownsville, came to collect for his church. 14, Rev. O'Hara, of Chambersburg, stopped with us a few days. 27, Rev. Myers, from Washington, said Mass and preached. Oct. 9, Rev. Kendler left for Milwaukee; Father Lynch came in his place. (He left for the College at Worcester, Nov. 24th.) Dec. 2, Father Provincial by order of the Father General, ordered solemn fast for suffering Jesuits in Europe. (Father Gibbons' name now mentioned.) Dec. 12, 1845, Father Dietz went to Taneytown to give last Sacraments to Father Zocchi. He died on the 19th, and Father D. sang the High Mass at his funeral on the 20th. 1846, Jan. 15, Rev. McCaffry and McClosky paid us an agreeable visit. Feb. 28, 1846, Father Dietz took his departure; ordered by the Provincial to Bohemia. (Gave the diary to Fr. Gibbons.) They were all sorry when he left, except Brother Quinlan who was laughing. March 15, Father Verhagen, Prov., said Mass and preached. 16, Fr. Tuffer " arrived here to take charge of the congregation." (He might have been Superior between Frs. Steinbacher and Enders.) April 2, Brother Patrick Carroll arrived from Georgetown. 4th, Bro. Quinlan left for Alexandria. May 24, Father " Vandevil " preached at Conewago, after the lapse of 21 years since his last sermon at the Chapel. June 10, " got an account of the death of Brother Quinlan, by letter from Father Coombs." 11, Father Samuel Mulledy preached a very eloquent sermon. July 12, Brother Marshall arrived from Georgetown. 14, Rev. Mr. " Curry," from the College, paid us a visit. Aug. 2d, Rev. Mr. " Vero " preached panegyric of St. Ignatius. There is mention of a Brother Leary at Conewago at this time. Aug. 20th, Messrs. McGuigan and O'Callahan, scholastics, left here for Frederick. (This must have been the Father O'Callahan who was fatally injured on a veassel during a storm.) Aug. 24th, Messrs. Duddy and Gillespie arrived from the College; Rev. Messrs. Jenkins and Griffin, from the Seminary, paid us a visit. "It is learned that old Father Barber has arrived safe at Georgetown College."

There are many little details in the every-day life at Conewago, that would be interesting to many of our readers, but space forbids. Father Dietz's strong voice is playfully referred to. It is said he could easily be heard down at the Church yard gate, while reciting the Introibo at the foot of the altar. When Edward Reily, Sr., died, Father Dietz came to the house and walked with the funeral to the church as the corpse was carried there.

Sunday, Nov. 22d, 1885.—Spent a few days at Conewago. Last Sunday the mission cross erected by the great missionary, Weininger, about 35 years ago, was removed from the north side of the church to the rear of the graveyard, and raised there, after having been reincased with boards. It is the intention to remove the priests from under the altar, and bury them around the cross. Many a prayer was said at the foot of the old mission cross. It was erected in 1857.

Father Finnegan, a very old priest, has been at Conewago since 1870. He was a Maryland priest, born in Ireland, and ordained by Bishop Marechal in 1826. His mind was affected for some years, and now he is quite childish. There was some question about the validity of his ordination. He was a learned priest, and during the month of May, we remember while at school, he would sing the office of the Blessed Virgin every morning in his room. Every Sunday morning he would feel his way into the Sanctuary, a venerable looking little man with flowing white hair, and receive Communion. He seldom spoke to anyone. When the school boys did him any little service in his room, they would some times take advantage of the occasion to ask assistance in their lessons, which he would kindly answer in a very few words, but say nothing more. Poor Brother Donohue took great pleasure in assisting the boys with their lessons, for which he received many a severe scolding from Father Deneckere. Father Di Maria, another aged priest, spent a few years at Conewago about that time, and found great pleasure in taking part with the school boys in their play. He was a delightful old Father, smoking his long meerschaum pipe, and always looking for some fun. He put the weather-vane on the stable, which we believe is still there. He was fond of snow birds as a delicacy, and on the coldest day he might be seen with an old musket looking for these birds, and if he had hit all he shot at, few would have been left. Mrs. Strausbaugh, a very old German woman, lived below the hill at that time, and every day came up to the church to pray. Father Di Maria thought he would have some fun with her one day, and began telling her some wonderful story he had made up for the purpose. She listened earnestly, then walked off, saying, "Es kent sei, ovver ich glaube net,"—It might be, but I don't believe it. The joke was turned, and the Fathers enjoyed themselves at his expense.

In looking over the old records, not much additional matter was found to note. Many of the names of the forefathers of the families now living in the valley, appear in baptismal, marriage and death records. Their publication would be interesting to the generations now living at Conewago, and those to come. To prepare and publish them would necessitate great labor and expense. Nicholas Will died Jan. 1st, 1808, doubtless the great-grandfather of the present Wills; so with the Overbaughs, Smalls, Lillys, Storms, Shorbs, and hundreds of the early settlers, on the different missions attended from Conewago. Lorenz Gubernator has the title of organist after his death record. He must have conducted some kind of a choir in old times. John L. Gubernator played the organ in Father Lekeu's time. Father Steinbacher changed organists, and Anthony Smith took his place Then John S. Brady had charge of the choir for many years. Father Forhan had a new choir organized, with David Smith as organist,—a son, we believe, of the old organist.

A few more names of priests were found on the records, as sponsors: Rev. John N. Mertz in 1803, 4 and 5; Rev. N. Zocchi in 1804; Rev. Carr in 1808; Rev. D. Carolus Nagot in 1818; Rey. A. Marshall in 1817.

The first baptismal record by Father Enders is on Sept. 26th, 1847; and that of Father Manns in Sept., 1853. He was ordained at Frederick, June 17th, 1853. After a short stay at Conewago, he labored elsewhere until 1862,—since that at Conewago. He now attends the Sisters at McSherrystown. His spare moments are devoted to the translation of some religious works in German in the original, and has quite a collection of manuscript copy. One of the Sisters aids him in the English translation. Father Herman Richard attends Paradise and Oxford from Conewago. He is a very genial Father; born May 8th, 1834; entered the Society Oct. 1st, 1857.

Conewago, though not a classic land of artists and poets, has its charms, many of which are derived from its religion. "The palaces of Genoa and Venice, without their churches, would not compensate for their scorched and unhealthy marshes. The monotonous plain of Milan would be no delightful recollection without the thought of its Cathedral. The formal hills which border the pale and turbid Po at Turin, would inspire no interest if they were not crowned with that votive Church of the Superga. The low, sandy banks of the Arno would not arrest the pilgrim at Pisa, if there were not the soil of Calvary in the Campo Santo, the Cathedral, the Baptistery and the Campanile. The vale and hills of Florence, with their famed but disappointing stream, are unquestionably surpassed in natural beauty by the English valleys of the Severn or the Wye; but art, inspired by the Catholic religion, has raised that dome and tower in the Tuscan plain, and crowned the hills which encircle it with those beautiful convents which Michael Angelo used to regard with rapture. How hideous would be the range of the Appenines, if it were not for Camaldoli and Alvernia ! Who would be attached to Sienna, if it were not for its cathedral and Gothic towers ! and what pilgrim from the North would be attracted to Ancona by the scenery of that level shore of the Adriatic, if it were not for the hope of arriving at the house of our Blessed Lady." Though fair and fertile the Valley of the Conewago, it is surpassed in extent by that of the Cumberland, and in abrupt and everchanging scenery by the valleys of the Potomac and the Shenandoah ; but the Church of the Sacred Heart fills the mind of the Catholic with thoughts of the early missionaries, and his own pioneer forefathers of the faith in days of Colonial hardships and persecutions ; it touches his heart by the dearest memories there cherished for time ; and raising it to heavenly desires, carries him back over the pathway of the Catholic Church to the fountain-head of all that we have in this world or hope for in the next.

Though the fields may be green and the harvests rich ;—though man be in the enjoyment of all the comforts and pleasures of life, health and wealth ; there are times when his soul complains and will not be satisfied. "Without an altar, not the shade of the lofty groves, not the soft meadows, not the stream descending from the rocks, and clearer than crystal, winding through the plain, can satisfy the soul of man. Left in the presence of nature alone. it faints and becomes like earth without the dew of heaven ; it is oppressed by the contemplation of that vast immensity ; it loses its tranquility and its joy. Man in himself can find no rest or peace ; and how should he find repose in the works of nature, when these themselves are forever restless ? The fire mounts in a perpetual course, always flickering and impatient ; the air is agitated with conflicting winds, and susceptible of the least impulse ; the water hurries on, and knows no peace ; and even this ponderous and solid earth, with its rocks and mountains, endures an unceasing process of disintegration, and is ever on the change."

"Even to the mere poetic soul, what a delightful accompaniment to the silent hymn of nature, is that chiming of angelus bells which rises at evening and at noon, and at the sweet hour of prime, from all sides of a Catholic valley ?—bells that may well be termed of the angel ; that are not rung, as in other lands, by base hands, through love of sordid gain, to celebrate some occasion of sensual joy, temporal and vain, soon to change to mourning as vain ; but by pious hands, through the devout intention of inspiring men with thoughts of prayer."

After all our efforts to arrange some kind of a history of Conewago, many things yet remain that might be worthy of preservation. Some account could be given of the many humble and holy lives that were passed unseen by the hurrying crowds of the world, but what cares the world for such ? Cold and ungrateful are even our best friends ; those who were nearest and dearest to the Fathers in life, it grieves us to say, are found most indifferent to their memories after they have passed away. At most, it will only be a few years until others take our places. Life is too short and busy to have much thought except for the present. Why then any further record ?

The birds sing the same among the trees this year as they did in the long ago. The seasons bring the same joys and pleasures as of old. Some rejoice to-day, while others mourn. The bells ring as sweetly and toll as sorrowfully though centuries have elapsed and generations disappeared. The sound of song or the organ's peal may die out to some while first reaching the ears of others. Eloquent sermons, ceremonies most grand and imposing,—everything that pleases the eye or touches the heart, shall be heard until time is no more. The Church inspires man with the same lofty desires as she did in the days of the great Masters at the Cradle of Arts, and Literature may still find the Rise and Decline of Nations among the rich memories and everlasting beauties of an Ara Coeli. What matters it whether nations are unborn or buried ; one is the same as the other ; life is death and death is life, and though to-day be full of memories, to-morrow all will be oblivion. Why rehearse all that is dear to me in the Book of Memory ? Why turn its pages, and search for faded scraps and treasured relics ; why look for the corners of bright leaves turned down, and drop tears over pages that are dark and stained with remorse ? Has the vulgar crowd nothing more to mock at ;— nothing less sacred for its amusement than the memories of the past ? Shall my farewells amuse them, while the hoary ferryman plys his oar ? Fate inexorable ! Destiny eternal ! Never has man evaded thee, and mortal never will. "Unhappy guest at the banquet of life, I appear for one day and die ! I die, and on my grave no one will scatter flowers. Farewell, fields that I love ! and thou, sweet verdure ! and thou, smiling solitude of woods ! Sky, beauteous canopy for man ! admirable Nature ! for the last time, farewell !"

> "Not always full of leaf, nor ever Spring ;
> Not endless night, nor yet eternal day :
> The saddest birds, a season find to sing ;
> The roughest storm, a calm may soon allay.
> Thus with succeeding terms, God tempereth all,
> That man may hope to rise, yet *fear* to fall."

THE OLD CONEWAGO CHURCH.

ENLARGEMENT OF CONEWAGO CHURCH IN 1850.—From some memoranda of an official report of Father Enders, Superior, made Feb. 29th, 1852, we glean some facts in regard to the enlargement of the Conewago Church in 1850. So many changes are constantly taking place in everything, that the surroundings of Conewago only this short time ago seem strange to us. This was the more forcibly called to our mind when a few weeks ago we overheard several middle-aged people before the Church at Conewago, recalling to each other the changes that had taken place since they as boys had attended catechism there ; few of their companions remained ; tho old Fathers were all gone, and marked changes on every hand impressed them with the flight of time.

In considering the enlargement of the church, one source of regret was the necessity of removing part of the walls of the old church and destroying some of the artistic decorations that had shortly before been executed. But the need of more room and accommodations was felt, and it was the will of the Bishop, Superior and the greater part of the congregation, that the old church be enlarged instead of building and maintaining a new church in some other part of the parish. The enlargement was effected by taking down the sanctuary and replacing it with transepts, making the building cross-form and the church fully as large again. As the old part of the church was painted in the very best style, there was no alternative but have the new part painted in harmony with the old. The title of the church is of the Sacred Heart ; this was to guide in the choice of the objects represented. "It was our good fortune to find an artist who was fully equal to the task, having carried off the first premium in the historical art of painting in one of the best European Academies." The three wonders of divine love in the Redemption, *i. e.*, the Incarnation, Death of the Saviour, and the Institution of the Blessed Sacrament, form the principal subjects of the painting, to which correspond His coming from Heaven, His return to the Father, the Adoration of the Holy of Holies by Angels, in the ceiling ; the representation of the Blessed Trinity forming the center-piece, in a blind cupola of about 20 feet diameter, bordered with stucco leaves in gilt and bronze. In the Blessed Trinity the Son is represented in the bosom of the Father, receiving the Sceptre of Supreme Dominion, with the left hand, holding at the same time the cross, whilst the right hand is raised to bless ; the heart being visible ; the Holy Ghost appears in the form of a dove. This is a most imposing composition, carried out with all the splendor that color is capable of imparting. In the left side against the wall is the Nativity, the Infant lying in the manger, the Blessed Virgin on her knees, whilst St. Joseph is prostrate in an act of adoration ; an Angel hovers on high, whilst the background presents a landscape, covered by the darkness of night ; close by the crib where lies the new-born babe on a pallet of straw, is a stall for cattle, which reach over towards the child, as if to impart warmth by their breath on the tiny body of the Creator of all Nature, now exposed to the cold and dampness of the manger at Bethlehem. Above this in the ceiling of the transept, is represented the Saviour, who was the expectation of the nations, descending from Heaven, and as it were taking leave of His Father, returning with one hand the Crown of Glory, whilst the other hand is receiving from the Father the cross with the crown of thorns. Two Archangels are supporting the holy group, holding a scroll with an inscription. In the other transept against the wall, is the the Death of the Saviour, with which corresponds His Ascension into Heaven above in the ceiling, His entering into glory in contrast with the act of His deepest humiliation. Christ on the Cross, having already expired, is masterly carried out in design and in its anatomical dispositions. At the right side are standing the Blessed Virgin with an expression of immense sorrow, and St. John also overwhelmed with grief, close by in readiness to support her. At the foot of the cross is Mary Magdalene on her knees, drying up with her veil the blood that flowed from the holy Victim.

The master-piece was reserved for the Sanctuary,—The Last Supper and the Adoration of the Blessed Sacrament. The Sanctuary forms a half circle, presenting a surface of some sixty feet in breadth. Little less than half of that space is taken up with the picture proper, the rest in decoration of the grandest style. The artist chose the moment when Christ consecrated the bread, holding it with the left hand, whilst the right is raised to bless it, and the eyes to Heaven. The twelve Apostles are around the table in the most reverential attitude, and with expressions of the deepest interest and devotion. Above in the ceiling is the Adoration of the Blessed Sacrament, which is surrounded by myriads of angels, intoning in full chorus the *Tantum Ergo, Sacramentum*, accompanied by music on various instruments. The richest decorations surround these scenes; vines encircle the whole Sanctuary, over gilt columns with arches, where clusters of grapes are ranged, and the root or main stem of the vine proceeds from a chalice in the hands of a figure of our Saviour. Stars are shining in the blue sky background of the painting in the ceiling, and the full moon rises in the east on a background of the shades of night in the Last Supper. All these paintings are done on the plastering of the walls. The same artist painted the death of St. Francis, on canvas, which is now over his altar, and the Fourteen Stations, of four by six feet, which adorn the walls. "If the latter bear marks of hurry, the former is elaborate, and succeeded perhaps best of all." "All the paintings, which bear the stamp of originality, and genius, are of brilliant colors and present a most imposing view; and whilst they are attracting numbers of the curious, they fail not to contribute to the edification and instruction of the faithful."

After the completion of the improvements, the church was first used for the celebration of the half-centennial Jubilee, which was held in most of the congregations with a retreat,—at Conewago, March 16th to 23d, 1851. Two Fathers of the Tertianship conducted the exercises at Gettysburg and Littlestown. The next event was the solemn consecration of the Church. Aug. 15th. While the ceremonies were going on inside the church, one of the Fathers preached in German to the assembled crowd outside. Sunday following the solemn benediction of the graveyard took place, which in consequence of the enlargement of the church, had to be extended. It has been several times since enlarged, and now almost reaches the public road passing back of the church. Many changes were made in the outbuildings, stables, fences, and gardens, at that time. The priests' house was enlarged, so as to throw the kitchen farther away from the church. A large cistern was dug near the new kitchen; the old carriage house was turned into a bake and wash house; the stables were removed farther down; the gardens and yards enlarged and fenced in, and a high stone wall built between the garden and the graveyard, separated before by a "slight plank fence."

Among the letters of the Fathers, there are few that add anything to the history of Conewago. There is some correspondence between Father Enders and Rosalie Stecker, Innsbruck, Austria, about some paintings. Francis Stecker painted the Conewago Church, and executed several paintings preserved there. What relation between them, we cannot say. There is a letter from Thaddeus Brzozowski, St. Petersburg, to Father Adam Britt, June 20th, 1809. One from Ehl, Ehrenbreitstein, Prussia, to Fr. N. Steinbacher, (of whom the writer was a former student,) Aug. 10, 1887. Circular letter from Pope Pius VII., (Savona,) Aug. 25th, 1809, to Cardinal Caprara, Archbishop of Milan, about the state of religion. Encyclical letter issued at Dublin, 1810, III Kalends of March, by the General Assembly of Bishops of Ireland, in reference to the state of the Church.

July 31st, 1859, corner-stone of the Church at Bonaughtown, (Bonneauville,) Adams Co., Pa., was blessed by Fr. John Baptist Cattani, S. J.; the sermon by Father Hitzelberger, S. J.

Where private letters of the Fathers throw any light on Catholic history, or give any reference to Conewago, we have taken the liberty of using them, from the great desire to do what we can for the Conewago history. If we have done well, it is reward enough, if not so well, we hope it may be pardoned us. MACH. XV. 39.

Bishop John Timon, when deacon, was resting a while at St. Mary's settlement, Arkansas. One day he turned up missing. No one could give an account of him. Father Odin, Father Ball and others, became alarmed. It was in the days of bears and wolves. A grand search was instituted. Towards evening the Rev. John Timon was discovered at a small cabin several miles distant, sleeves rolled up, axe in hand, and beads of sweat on his brow. It seems that he had heard of the poor and lonely old widow who had lived there, with no one to chop her winter's wood. Having stolen away, unawares, from his companions, he was finishing his first cord when the hunting party came upon him with horns and rifles. They did not exactly take up a subscription for the widow. Each one gave a turn till the woodpile disappeared.

When Rev. Samuel Mulledy was at the point of death, he begged re-admission to the Society of Jesus from Rev. A. M. Paresce, Provincial, which was granted. Though in the agony of death, he was so moved by the joy and happiness it gave him, that he sprang out of his bed and on bended knees pronounced the Formula of the Society, in the presence of Father Joseph Loyzance, Rector of St. Francis Xavier College, New York. He died a most saintly death on the night of the 8th of Jan., 1866, assisted in his last moments by one of the Fathers of the Society.

Father John Barrister, S. J., writes to a friend at Conewago, from Loyola, (Balto.) Oct. 31st, 1859, sending his respects to Fathers Dougherty and Manns, and to Brothers Redmond and Donohue. He says Father Sopranis, the Roman Visitor, arrived, accompanied by the brother of Fr. Ciocaterri, S. J., acting as his Secretary; went straight to Georgetown. "Father Tom. Mulledy saw them, who reports that the old gentleman, notwithstanding his age, is in excellent health and spirits, and extremely glad to see his American friends once more. His accounts from Italy are very gloomy. Our Fathers in the Pontifical States are in daily expectation of an outbreak, especially in Rome; they all hold themselves in readiness for another expulsion. Napoleon begins to quarrel with the Pope, because the latter will not come over to his views; he intends to withdraw his troops from Rome, which, of course, will be the signal for a revolution in central Italy, and then, Pio Nono, farewell." He says Father Dougherty was the patron and admirer of the nephew of the great Uncle. He says, "Father Enders was here some time ago; the fracture of his collar bone has been cured," though the use of his left arm is not quite restored. "Father Deneckere went to see his sister in Philadelphia, not long ago, who, he writes, is declining fast with consumption."

The bell on Christ Church, (Protestant,) Gettysburg, Pa., has the following inscription in Latin, "Mary of the Conception, by thine Immaculate Conception, Virgin Mother of God, defend us from the malignant foe." There is a Portugese inscription, giving the date of its manufacture as 1788. It was a confiscated convent bell from Portugal. One of the *christian* ministers of the Lutheran College at Gettysburg, talks about its having been "superstitiously baptized," and having "many a day rung out the matins or vespers for lazy monks or cloistered nuns." We are very glad that the bell is not otherwise *deformed*. It is a grand and lasting testimonial to the Immaculate Conception.

The organ in the Paradise Church was purchased through the efforts of Fr. J. B. Cattani, while Superior of Conewago, at a cost of $500. He drew up the subscription papers, to which are attached the following names: Pius Fink, John Klunk, Mary Hoffman, Geo. and Michael Strubinger, Valentine Shulz, Francis J. Wilson, Joseph Weil, Mich. Hoffman, Daniel Miller. Sam. Hair, John Felty; Samuel, Michael, Catharine, Eliza, Levi, Cornelius, and Noah Bievenour; Frederick, Michael, Peter, Sarah, Rose and Mary Dellone; Caleb, Levi, and Aloysius Brieghner; Albert Storm; Peter, Michael, Joseph, Sarah A., and Caroline Noel; Francis Wise, Lewis Will, Anthony Shane, Cath. Strausbaugh, Klunk family, Jac. Sterner, Jacob Wise, Ed. L. Kuhn, Anne Little, Wm. Dahlhammer, Sebastian Wise, N. Long, Francis Mayer, John Elder, Mich. and Sam. Alwine, Magdelene and Ann Burger Briechner, Eliz. Chambers, Jane Car, Mar. and Mary A. Chambers, N. Welker, Martin Gephard, Lewis Weaver, Andrew and Eliz. Kuhn, Geo. and Moses Moore, J. F. Koehler, Jos. J. Kuhn, Geo. A. Goy.

Father Steinbacher contracted with Mr. Monachesi, of Phila., for the painting of Conewago Church, at $700, in the presence of Father Vespre, S. J. The work was done from April 23d to June 12th, 1845. He was allowed $100 more "in order to have a quite excellent altar piece." This was the Assumption of the Blessed Virgin, now on the B. V. Altar. The following are some of the names appearing on the subscription papers for repairing Conewago Church in 1844-5, Father Nicholas Steinbacher, Superior: Ignatius, Vincent and Catharine O'Bold; John Groft, Mary Strausbaugh, B. J. McManus, Teresia Swartz, Francis Little, Geo., Anne, Mary and Cath. Eline, Eliz. Adams, Barbara and Catharine Oaster, Eliz. Will, J. A. Eline, John and Thomas Little, J. W. Busbey, Anthony Strasbaugh, Edw. Nugent, Adam Foller, Cath. Miller, Samuel Stormbach, Thomas McKinney, Anna Stormbach, Lilly & Reily, Leonard Shaffer, Patrick Harkins, Francis Bauer, T. Owings, John McKinney, Sr., S. J. Owings, John Burkee, John and Mat. Ginter, Henry Horat, Eliz. Egan, Geo. Ginter, John, Peter and Cath. Krichton, J. S. Adams, Conrad Fink, the Klunks, the Adamses, Swartses, Leonards, Kuhns, John Oaster, Joseph Coopsor, Josephine Kelly, Matilda McClain, Charles L. and John L. Gubernator, the Wills, Conrads, Littles, Jacob Dellone, Busbeys, the Smiths, Renauts, Hildts, Wises, Althoffs, Peter Neiderer, John Marshall, Wm. Detrick, Joseph Sneeringer, and others. This seems to be the McSherrystown, Hanover and Brushtown list, and is the only one found among the old papers.

Thos. A. Fitzgerald writes to Father Reiter at Conewago, from Fairfield, Adams Co., Pa., Aug. 31st, 1858 : says congregation is very anxious that one of the Conewago Fathers attend their church, and they will make every effort to pay off the debt and make up something for the pastor ; speaks very kindly of Father Villiger, who attended them previously ; gives names of families of the congregation : Jesse P. Topper, Adam Sanders, Samuel Cole, Casper Meyers, Gregory Topper, B. Kebel, James, Anthony and Peter Sanders, Peter Dick, Michael Lauver, Joseph and James Bowling, Mrs. Butt, Alex. Weaver, Michael Cole, Michael Finnegan, Mrs. Peters, Daniel Beisecker, with whom priest stayed ; Mrs. Butler, Zacharias, Andrew, Charles and widow of John Sanders, Andrew, Barney and Samuel Bigham, Mrs. Beisecker, Mrs. Finnifrock.

P. J. Verhaegen, S. J., writes to Fr. N. Steinbacher at Conewago, under date of Phila., May 31st, 1845 : asks for more information about the *war-like spirit* manifesting itself at Paradise, if not under inviolable secrecy ; says he entertained the Chief of the Chippeway Nation at the College, Georgetown, last Friday, and had an hour's conversation with him in French ; had a letter from Rev. Fr. Verreyde, Jesuit Superior of the Indian Missions : Chief told him that the Indians " got completely bewildered by the contradictory doctrine preached to them by the Protestant ministers, and that they wanted Catholic Blackgowns to instruct them."

Henry Eckenrode, of Mountpleasant Twp., Adams Co., Pa., bequeathed to Father Enders the " principal of his property," to be equally divided between the Conewago and the Paradise Churches.

Will of Maximilian Rantzau, S. J., made Jan. 15th, 1824, at St. Inigoe's Manor, in favor of Rev. J. W. Beschter, Rector of St. John's, Baltimore : Witness : Joseph Carbery, Enoch Combs. Father R. had a sister in Europe, to whom Fr. Beschter wrote through Mr. Springger, of New York, that she could keep what property " is to come yet," or send it on, at her option. Father Rantzau died at Frederick, Aug. 7th, 1827, at 8 o'clock A. M., after having preached the Sunday before the panegyric of St. Ignatius ; he was attacked by palsy or appoplexy. He was born " in Germany, at Alberstre, near Munster, in Westphalia," Dec. 23d, 1769.

There is a notice of the death in Paradise Twp., York Co., Pa., of Mrs. Catharine Wise, aged 80 years, 11 months and 4 days ; and two days after, her husband, Sebastian Wise, died, aged 85 years; 4 months. Several verses to their memory are added. From the artistic pen flourishes following, we are sure it is in the hand writing of Rev. Ferdinand Helias, S. J., but no name nor year appear.

Novitiate, Frederick, Aug, 15th, 1862, Patrick H. Lower, S. S. J., in the name of the Scholastics who spent their vacation at Conewago, thanks the Superior for the " kindness, generosity and more than fatherly care over us during three happy weeks we spent at Conewago." They returned to Frederick in hacks; stopping at Taneytown for dinner. where they found that Father O'Neill was not at home. They send respects to Frs. Dougherty, Manns and Deneckere, and Bros. Redmond, Donohue, and Doyle. James A. Ward, S. J., adds: "They were full of their visit and continually mention in their conversations some of the many kindnesses they received. I was glad to perceive how much they appreciated the good order of your house and the piety of your devoted congregation. I trust that it will remain ever a bright spot in their memories, and be a new reason for them to bless the good God who called them to His service."

There is a letter from Rev. J. Barrister, S. J., St. Mary's, Alexandria, July 17th, 1863, to one of the Conewago Fathers, which for the local information it contains we publish nearly entire. It is a long time since the great event he speaks of, and many changes have taken place. Fath. B. was at Conewago a short time, where he is remembered. The letter is in a pleasant vein of humor, and shows the genial disposition of the Father. From this distance we can look back upon the war without fear or favor. There is but one sentiment now, North or South. Except at Gettysburg, the North had little experience of the ravages of war, in comparison with the South, which is only now rightly beginning to recover from its effects. Conewago was not molested. There was a rumor about the time of the battle that troops were coming to destroy the church. Preparations were made, home companies organized, and whatever could be done for its defense and protection, but no hostile soldiers came. The people fed the passing troops of whichever side, and after the battle at Gettysburg, hastened to the field with provisions and clothing for needy friend or foe. The Southern soldiers behaved well and fought bravely. Those were days of terrible fear and danger. Remembering now at what great peril was the safety of our country, we shudder to think how much indifference existed in the North, and are surprised at the great sacrifices made in the South, where men, women and children threw all they had into the cause. The bitterest remembrances North or South are not from any acts of the true soldier, but from the contemptible treachery of traitors at home, who perhaps in times of peace fed from the table of those whose lives and property they placed at stake when the enemy came. In their zeal for the cause, we might give extremes by Catholics North and South. In one of the Southern churches, when the priest came on the altar to say Mass one morning, he was surprised to see a small Union flag at one of the front pews, where sat a strong and aged Union man. The priest refused to ascend the altar until the flag had been removed. Doubtless he would have done the same had it been a Confederate emblem. In the South the women were the hardest to reconstruct. To this day we know an intelligent lady, and a good friend and Catholic, who has left the word Federal (States) erased and Confederate in its place, in the prayers for the people and the government, in her prayer book. In the North it is related of several priests, who refused to give the Sacraments to those who took up arms against the Union.

To return to Father Barrister's letter: "I suppose you have had quite exciting times in Conewago on the occasion of Lee's visit. Did any of his pious followers come up the hill to worship in your beautiful chapel? If so, woe to the two "Bills," they must long have swum the Potomac with other horseflesh, as prisoners of war, never to be paroled. Lee's recrossing over into Virginia is now a fixed fact; it took the world by surprise, much more than his landing in Maryland and penetrating into Pa. This is already the second attempt and failure to make conquests for the slave power. I trust it will be the last. Providence, it would seem, does not wish that slavery should be saddled again on any free State in which it has been abolished. * * * * Many troops must have passed through Adams County during the past two weeks. Are their tracks anywhere visible, except on your miry roads? * * * * Poor Brother Redmond and his chickens! To what a fright they must have been put when the Rebels came to take the eggs, and then the Federals came, who, because they were weak and faint with marching, were sure to take the whole roost for broil and soup. The reason I speak of Bro. R.'s henroost, in connection with such grave events, is because to-day is a Friday and Bro. Cassiday gives us eggs, which invariably makes me think of Conewago eggs." [Priests from the cities always enjoyed the fresh country produce at Conewago.] "Father Kroes has been away from here most of the time; his health is, however, no better. * * * * About Alexandria everything bears the impress of the war. Most of the churches and public buildings are still used for hospital purposes, as also the homes of rich Secessionists who left for the South. All the farms for 16 or 20 miles are lying waste; as all the fences are gone, the poor people of the town and country, who formerly perhaps could hardly feed a goat, now can keep as many cows in summer as they can pay for, and find plenty of pasture on the farms of the rich Virginians who have skedaddled to Dixie. * * * * Many destroyed and broke up their furniture, to prevent it from falling into the hands of their supposed persecutors; others sold it to the Jews for a trifle to raise a few dollars for traveling expenses. * * * * When they returned to their homes, they had perhaps not a straw mattress to lie on. How the Almighty now punishes American pride by the very thing which once made these people so boastful and haughty, I mean their 'Glorious Union and Heavenborn Constitution.' O tempora, O mores! There was a time when the haughty Virginian looked down upon the poor Irishman or the humble mechanic from his arched window with an air of contempt. Now an Irish soldier or a Massachusetts cobbler with a shoulder strap, sits on his lofty porch of Corinthian columns, smoking his pipe or chewing his tobacco. How capriciously the wheel of fortune can turn ups and downs in a little time. Please remember me to Aunt Sally, Mrs. Reily, the Lillys and Jenkinses, and give my special love to Fathers Manns and Dougherty, and him who drew his first breath either on the top or at the bottom of the classic hills whereon the Eternal City rests her foundations. * * * * Nor do I forget your worthy cook, Br. Redmond, and Brother Donohue, Grand Almoner and Privy Counsellor to the Patriarch of Gettysburg and the Mountains."

A clipping from the *Herald*, Hanover, dated Blue Spring Chapel, June 29th, 1885, gives an account of a tornado that passed over the Conewago Valley June 27th of that year. The houses and barns of Mark Little, Joseph Sneeringer, Jacob Little, Peter Kraft, Samuel Forsyth, Edw. Reily, Joseph Schilling, were more or less injured and destroyed. Fences, trees and small buildings were scattered and blown down by the storm. In the same paper, under date of Jan. 26, 1837, is an account of an unusual meteoric display in the Valley; under date of Ap. 19, 1837, there is a notice of the burning of the

CATHOLIC LOCAL HISTORY. 191

large property of Samuel Lilly, near the Conewago Church, now occupied by John L. Jenkins.

BIRTHS FROM THE CONEWAGO REGISTERS.—1793, Feb. 19, Salome, daughter of J. and Cath. Shury ; sponsors, Maria Fink and "Rev. P. Erntzen." 1794, Jan. 25, Jos. A., son of Wm. and ———— Schlusser, sponsor, F. X. Brosius. 1794, Feb. 8, John Timon, son of Henry and Cath.; John " Cunes " and Christina Wolf. 1794, born Feb. 12, bap. on 19th, John, son of Jacob and Helen Timon ; spons., John " Coon " and Christina Wolf. This was Bishop Timon. There were a number of John Kuhns, and we have not been able to learn who was his god-father, or god-mother, further than the names. Some think Christina Wolf was a servant girl on the church farm. The Wolfs are and were Protestants. There is some connection between these two last baptism entries, as will be seen. 1796, May 2, Wm. Shorb, son of Jacob and Christina ; spons., Stanislaus Cerfoumont, S. J , and Margaret Sneeringer. 1796, Oct. 5, James, son of John and Cath. Shorb ; Spons., S. Cerfoumont and Maria Coopser. 1796, Nov. 25, bap. Jan., 1797, Anna Cath. daughter of Peter and Cath. Lambing ; spons., Robert and Mar. Owings. This was a relative of Rev. A. A. Lambing's father. 1798, Nov. 25. Mary, daughter of Jacob and Helen " Timmons " ; spons. F. X. Brosius and Maria Kuhn. This must have been a sister of Bishop Timon. The name was spelled "Timmons," and the two were originally of one family. We have frequently heard it said that the first Timmonses of Conewago were related to the Timons. 1795, May 25, John Phil., son of Phil. and Ger. Weber ; spons. J. Schumacker : signature, " R. Fran. Xaverius Brosius." 1800, Oct. 24th, bap. Nov. 3d, Stanislaus Xav., son of John and Mary Eckenrode ; spons. F. X. Brosius and Mar. Marshall. 1796, April 25, signature of " R. Jacobus Pellentz." 1800. Oct. 22d, Sarah, daughter of Anna (Coopser) and Samuel Lilly ; spons. Henry Lilly annd Sarah Owings. This is the present aged Miss Sally Lilly, well known at Conewago, and also in the Society for her kind hospitality to visiting priests. 1803, April 28, Sarah Cath., daughter of John and Maria Fink ; spons. F. X. Brosius and Cath. Martin. Father Brosius was the companion of Father Gallitzin.

DEATHS.—1802, March 6th, Thomas Dorditch, alias Bush, nearly 70 years old, natus natione Ungarus. He may have been an exile or a refugee. 1800, Dec. 3d, Nicholaus Delow, aged 84, born in France. His posterity remains to the fourth and fifth generation. 1799, Oct. 15th, James Small, aged 58. 1806, Francis, an aged colored man. 1790, March 25, Paul ————, a widower, aged 77, who served as sacristan. 1798, May 22d, Jasper Michel Felder, "Sacristanus noster," aged 58, " natus prope Bruschsal in Germania. Oremus." 1798, July 20th, Joseph Herman, a good man, humble and patient, confined to his bed for five years, aged nearly 70. There are a number of old tombstones in the graveyard, but many of the oldest are so worn by time as not to be discipherable, while others are lost. When the new part of the church was built, many of the old tombstones were stood outside along the church, and few remain after half a century. We append a few : Mary Ann Weisen (Wise), " gebohrne Hitzelbergerin," born Jan. 4th, 1775, died 1781. Anna Mar. Kleinin (Little), born Feb. 1st, 1723, died April 30, 1796. Thomas Adams, b. July 15, 1735, d. Dec. 5, 1776. Mary Regina Breighner, b. Aug. 26, 1785, d. Sept. 18, 1787. John Faller, b. Nov. 21, 1717, d. Dec. 4, 1784

John Storm, b. Jan. 21, 1725, d. Jan. 1, 1805. Anna Margaret, wife of Robert Owings, died April 12, 1802. John Kuhn died in 1826, aged 78, and his wife, Theresa, in 1821. This *may have been* the god-father of Bishop Timon. Anna Cath. Ehrweinin, b. ap. 30, 1725, d. March 15, 1799. Abolonia Ehrman, born in 1763, died in 1801. Julianna Sneeringer, b. Aug. 1st, 1742, d. Oct. 9, 1813. Catharine Becker, b. Ap. 6, 1746, d. July 7, 1790. Christian Dabber, b. Dec. ——, 1715, d. July 13, 1789. Anna Mar. Eckenrode (": Eckenroden"), b. Aug. 1st, 1709, d. Dec. 6, 1790. Samuel Lilly, born in 1699, when William III was on the throne of England ; died June 8, 1758.

Besides other valuable information of Conewago already obtained, we are indebted to MRS. JANE JENKINS for the following interesting notes of its history :

Father Boarman never lived at Conewago, but visited it once a month from Maryland. Father Divin died at York or Carlisle about 1830 ; was no Jesuit. [The priest who labored at York from 1822 to 1836, was Rev. Patrick J. Dwen or Dween. From the fact that the name on the Conewago records as early as 1820, is always spelled "Divin," we are of the opinion that they are not the same, but different priests. If the name "Divin" does not appear in the records of the Society of Jesus, then they are one and the same.] Father Wm. Marshall was at Conewago in 1817 ; he went to sea, died on board and was buried in the ocean. When the church was enlarged by Father Enders, there was a desire to build instead a new church in Hanover. Lilly's mill was built by Henry Lilly, about 75 years ago. He was the father of Revs. Thos. and Samuel Lilly, S. J. ; the former labored for many years in the lower counties of Maryland ; died in Phila. about 1863, aged 53 ; Samuel only lived a year after ordination ; was Vice President Loyola College, Balto., when he died, aged 85 ; he was a holy man and gifted, writing fluently prose or verse. Father Lekeu came about 1820 ; he was greatly beloved for his sweetness and charity, but was no financier, and after his removal the management of the property was put into the hands of laymen ; he came of a wealthy and aristocratic family, who sent him many valuable things—vestments embroidered on velvet, altar service inlaid with precious metals and stones ; from Conewago he was sent to Whitemarsh, where he became unhappy on account of the influence of the climate on his health, and the great change in his habits, and he returned home to die among his friends.

There were two Fathers Mulledy, Thomas and Samuel. Father Tom was Provincial and freed all the slaves in the communities of the Jesuits ; he was a Virginian, rather rough and ready, but a man of great character and powerfully built. Father De Barth was no Jesuit, but lived among them many years. Father Tuffer was pastor after Father Steinbacher, and was succeeded by Father Enders. [In the diary of Father Steinbacher and on the books, he says he "hands over" the money and affairs to Father Gibbons.] Father Cattani was a Bavarian ; came to America during the troubles in Europe in '48 ; he was not always a Jesuit, only after his mother's death, whom he cared for while a secular ; he was all zeal and holiness and his charity for the poor was boundless. Father Dom Pieri or Domperi, an Italian, succeeded Father Cattani at his death Aug. 30, 1865, he had a great dread of horses and his heart longed for the gentle donkey of his native land ; he was removed to Boston, where he still has charge of an Italian congregation, who idolize him. Father B. Villiger succeeded him: he was Provincial at one time, and his management in spiritual and temporal matters was very successful; he was a fluent speaker and greatly beloved. He was removed to the Gesu, Phila.; he was a Swiss, ordained in this country, and from his wonderful mastery of the English language no one would imagine him a foreigner. Father Cotting was, I believe, a Swiss, and was in the Novitiate with Fathers Enders and Cattani, being about their age. Father Bellwalder succeeded Fr. Villiger; he was a German and did not suit for a large English congregation; he is now at Buffalo, in a German College. Father Charlin was pastor for a few months; he was a Frenchman, and a saintly man; removed to Boston where he still remains. Father Di Maria was at Conewago for his health, in 1870, about a year; he went to Philadelphia and died at St. Joseph's hospital. Father Jamison went to Troy, N. Y., from here, and afterwards to Boston where he still remains. Father Casey left Conewago for Frederick to make his tertianship: was at Washington after that. Father Quinn went from here to Europe to make his tertianship; his relatives live there; he returned in 1884 and is now at Troy. Father Brocard was the first Provincial I remember; he was a Belgian; Fathers Stonestreet and Villiger followed; Father Paresce, an Italian, was the next; he was a holy man and well liked. Father Keller, of the Western Province, was Provincial two terms; so was Father Brady, who was a great favorite, now President of Worcester College. Father Fulton the present Provincial, is a Virginian, an able man, and seems to be succeeding admirably.

Father Finnegan was an Irishman but became a Jesuit in the U. S. He labored at St. Inigoes, but his mind giving away he was no longer allowed to perform his priestly offices. He remained there as a pensioner until the house was burned in 1870, when he was sent to Conewago where he still remains. He had great talents and was a fine scholar and preacher. He is now in his 85th year, and is blind. There was a Fr. Timothy Kelley here about Fr. Steinbacher's time; he was an Irishman; also Brother Quinlan, who taught a small school. Brother Gahan, an old Irishman was cook for years, also Bro. Redmond, an excellent scholar; there was a Bro. Doyle, a painter, about 1858 or '60, who gave the interior of the church some touches. Bro. Maurice Cavanaugh was also one of the cooks; he was original and warm-hearted, and thought the Germans had not a single virtue. The greater number of Brothers who were here might be called "institutions"; they all remained so long. The present Brothers are, Donovan, McGonigle and Hamilton, all worthy representatives of their native land.

The Sisters of Charity were the first who had a school at McSherrystown. The Ladies of the Sacred Heart came about 1840; Madam Gallitzin, niece of the great Father, was the General of the order. They imagined the climate was unhealthy and left; the house remained vacant for about four years, when some members of the order returned. Their school was successful until Madam Verhulst, a Belgian, was sent as Superior, who did not believe in American customs, especially of having fires in winter. The house was again vacant, when in 1854, the Sisters of St. Joseph took possession and have been very successful. Many have been received into the Order from among the Catholics of the Valley. Two daughters of Samuel Sneeringer entered about 1858; Matilda, a daughter of Bernard Noel, Sister

Lucy ; Mary Fleshman, Sister Berohman ; Miss Creighton, of McSherrystown, entered about fifteen years ago, Sister Stanislaus, teacher of drawing and painting ; a lady of remarkable talents. Samuel Sneeringer has two daughters at Chestnut Hill, Sister St. Ephrem and Sister Raphael, both teachers of music. Miss Poist, of McSherrystown, is a useful member at Lebanon. Miss Busby, daughter of J. Busby, is in religion Sister St. John ; she has two Sisters at Chestnut Hill. Salome Noel, sister of the Jesuits Fabian and Michael, is a member of St. Joseph's, also Anna Brady. Joseph Sneeringer had a daughter, Kate, who joined the Sacred Heart, and died many years ago. Madames Gubernator, Sullivan and Bumgardner, were all from these parts, also Madam Donaho, an orphan, who was raised by the Lilly family. Madam Bowles was a daughter of Mrs Sullivan, a poor widow, whose children were raised by strangers ; there was a Jesuit among them, now in California, a most talented man now over sixty. Madam Bowles was a widow, very talented, and the nuns educated her ; she was afterwards Superior at Eden Hall until her death. Sister Willet, daughter of George W., is a religious of the Sacred Heart. Sister Tuttle, an orphan raised by Miss Sally Lilly, belongs to the S. H.; she entered at Eden Hall. Norrisdale, in 1855, where she still resides, aged about 50. Ann Smith, daughter of the late Joseph Smith, near Irishtown, is at Chestnut Hill as Sr. Bridget, aged about fifty, twenty-five in religion. Miss Noel, of Paradise, entered many years ago ; Madie Noel, of New Oxford, and Miss Koehler, of Abbottstown, have been lately received at St. Joseph's. Two sisters of David C. Smith died in that Order, Helen and Verlinda. Matthias Martin, dec'd, of Irishtown, had a daughter who entered at McSherrystown about 12 years ago, Sister Agnes ; she died about two years ago, aged 34. He had two daughters Sisters of Charity ; one died young, Caroline ; the other, Agnes, is still living, and has been a member for thirty years. Two of the Dellones, and Miss Shorb, of Littlestown, became Sisters of Charity years ago ; the latter, Sr. Ann Alexis, was widely known as one of the most useful and zealous members of her order ; she died a few years ago in St Louis, at an advanced age, beloved by all who knew her. Sister M. Clare. of Frederick, is a sister of the Fathers Lilly ; she joined the Visitation Order at the age of eighteen, and is now fifty-four. Her life has been spent in teaching the higher branches, and she is a beautiful penswoman, and always teaches one of the first classes in writing. There is one, though of the colored race, must not be forgotten, she was taken from the county almshouse by Mrs. Valinda Jenkins, who raised her with a mother's care ; Susan Jones was her name ; she showed remarkable piety in her childhood and youth, and no weather ever kept her from Mass or Holy Communion. At length her pious wishes were crowned with success and she became an Oblate Sister at Baltimore, where she lived a most holy life and died Jan. 17th,1868, the very day on which her good and beloved Mistress breathed her last. May they both rest in peace. Mr. Joseph Clunk, of McSherrystown, has two daughters of St. Joseph,—Mary entered about 1870, Sister Antoinette ; Alphonse entered about 1880. Annie Kuhn, daughter of Edw. J., and granddaughter of the late Judge Kuhn, is a Sister of Charity at St. Louis. She entered at McSherrystown in 1877, at the age of sixteen. Rosa. daughter of J. E. Smith, entered at McSherrystown several years ago ; she has an aunt there,—Sister De Sales. Annie McSherry, of White Hall, became a Sister at Chestnut Hill. There may be others, whose names have escaped memory, or who joined the orders years ago.

Wm. Gubernator, a German, was the first organist at Conewago. He was self-taught. His son, John L., succeeded and held the office many years, through Father Lekeu's time. He was a fine musician, and had a deep, sonorus voice. Miss Baumgardner, who taught school, had charge a while ; she joined the S. H. about 1849. Prof. Bolster and family acted in that capacity for a short time, and also one of the elder Smiths. John Brady succeeded, having taken lessons in Baltimore ; he served faithfully for thirty-two years. D. C. Smith has charge at present ; he is also a good musician and a fine singer.

Rev. Patrick Duddy was at Conewago for two years, about 1865, rather as an invalid though he did considerable duty. He was born in Ireland about 1820, and was for a long time a prefect and teacher at Georgetown College. He has been stationed at St. Joseph's. Phila., since, and is still in delicate health. Father McNierny was there about the same time ; he was born in Washington about 1824 ; ordained about 1862 ; he afterwards left the Society, but died an edifying death about 1870. Fathers Lynch and Gibbons were at Conewago about the time of Fathers Steinbacher and Tuffer, 1844 to 1846. Father Gibbons died young, at White Marsh ; he was born about 1820. Father Lynch died recently ; he was born in Ireland about 1814. Father Dom Pieri, I think was born in Trent and educated in Rome ; and place the date of his birth at about 1820. Father Charlin, who succeeded him for two months at Conewago, was a Frenchman, born about 1814 or '16. Father Cattani was a Bavarian, but his father was an Italian. Fathers Enders, Cattani and George Villiger were educated together at the same College ; and if Father Enders had been buried at Conewago where he desired to be, and which had such great claims as a fit resting place for him. all three would have lived together in death as they did in life, though I am sure their souls are happy in Heaven. As the dates are given only from memory, they may not be exactly correct.

Fathers Thomas and Samuel Lilly were born in the red brick house along Lilly's dam, standing yet. They were sons of Henry Lilly, who was a son of John, and he a son of Samuel, who came from Bristol about 1730. He was a fuller in England ; the Lillys carried on a woolen mill for many years along the Conewago. Several of them represented York County in the General Assembly before 1800.

In Conclusion.—There are yet many things connected with the growth of the Catholic Church, that we should like to notice, but more time and labor have already been given than can well be spared. The Councils form an interesting part of the history of the Church in America, and so her various institutions of religion and learning, but we are compelled to forego further mention. The history of Conewago dates back to the time when there were only a few priests and a few Catholic churches in America ; now there are thousands, and millions of the faithful. One hundred years ago we found no colleges ; now the great project of founding a Catholic University has taken definite shape and Washington has been selected as its site. During the Council in Baltimore, in Nov., 1884, a pious and wealthy Catholic lady presented several hundred thousand dollars for the purpose, and the Bishops and priests are making every effort to has an on the great desire of the Church in America. Will this country ever have a Catholic daily paper ? The Catholic press is stronger and more prosperous than ever before. Rome has showered favors on the Church in our country, by bestowing blessings on her, and honors and titles on her most worthy clergy. Leo XIII. is a watchful Vicar of Christ, and the needs of the Church and the care of the faithful find in him a noble guardian,—a worthy successor of the saintly Pontiff, Pius IX., who truly bore many crosses from Heaven that the light might come after him, and some day they will be numbered among the saints by the church militant. The American Church is now without a Cardinal, but Catholics are looking hopefully and expectantly towards Rome, from New York, from Baltimore and from the West. They who next bear this high rank will be eminently deserving, and there is none more so than the Primate of the Church in America who presided at the late Council, Archbishop Gibbons of Baltimore. As yet the Church in the East commands attention by reason of age, strength and wealth ; but already the church in the West is making itself heard and felt, and the day will come when the East will pay tribute to the West in ecclesiastical affairs as well as in matters of politics, trade and finance. Catholics have everywhere their schools, and the question now agitated, of greatest interest to them, is their being compelled to support the public schools where they send no children. This can only be accomplished by supporting men and measures, and not blindly following any party as has been too much the case heretofore. The Catholic Church as an institution in this country has succeeded so prudently and wisely thus far, that it occupies a most desirable vantage ground in American history, past and present, and has a most hopeful future. Never has it been found wanting in true religion, education, science and patriotism. While skepticism and infidelity are now proclaiming themselves boldly in the public places, and millions are following the worldliness and tendency of the age to unrestraint in mind and morals, threatening ultimate chaos to all profession of faith in revealed truth and the teaching of ages, the Catholic Church stands firm as the Rock on which she is built.

Many are led away, alas ! by the false glamor of a progress as deceptive as it is base and hollow. This age " lives too fast," without the fear of God before it or a thought of what is to come hereafter. In many things the Church is led away by the worldliness of the age, and is bound to share eventually in its results. At all times and under all circumstances, God has raised up some one for its safety and protection, and the gates of hell shall never prevail against the Church that He has promised to be with forever. Never was there greater necessity for the watchfulness of the Catholic Church than now. May she not be found sleeping when the bridegroom cometh !

The Church has every reason to rejoice, while at the same time there are causes of regret in the spiritual and natural order of things. Even now she is mourning for the loss of her highest prelate and first Cardinal, John McCloskey. He was born in Brooklyn, N. Y., March 20th, 1810, and was baptized by Father A. Kohlman, S. J., the first pastor of Old St. Peter's, in New York. Cardinal McCloskey was educated at Mt. St. Mary's, and ordained by Father Dubois Jan. 22d, 1884 ; consecrated Bishop March 10th, 1844 ; succeeded Archbishop Hughes in 1864, and created a Cardinal Priest in 1875. The history of his life is the history of the Catholic Church in New York. He was loved, honored and respected by all. When created a Cardinal, it surprised the American world and gave rise to much speculation as to the intentions of the Catholic Church, but when he died not a voice was raised except to praise and bless him. His life was full of great works and good deeds, that will live after him to the glory of God. He died on Saturday, Oct. 10th, 1885, at 12-50 A. M. He was buried beneath the altar of the magnificent Cathedral in New York, Oct. 15th. Thousands attended the funeral ceremonies, and many priests and Bishops were present. Archbishop Corrigan celebrated Pontifical Mass. Archbishop Gibbons preached the sermon.

The last moments of the late Cardinal were happy and peaceful. It was midnight Friday night when the dying Cardinal opened his eyes, and a smile came upon his white lips. The strong, saintly spirit seemed to shine for a moment in the thin features, and then the eyes closed again. Slower and slower the white raiment of the couch rose and fell. One wasted hand held a silver crucifix and the other pressed it to his bosom. There was deep peace upon the still face, and the snowy locks were brushed back upon the pillow.— Worn with watching and nursing, Dr. Keyes sat near his patient and looked into the venerable countenance with great tenderness.— Archbishop Corrigan stood at the foot of the bed, robed in black cassock with purple sash. His head was bowed and his lips moved. Mgr. Farley gazed upon the dying man with moistened eyes, and the Rev. Dr. McDonnell, tall, clear-eyed and sorrowful, stood beside Mgr. Preston. Soon the doctor

CARDINAL JOHN M'CLOSKEY.

OLD ST. PETER'S.

We close this sketch with an engraving from an old print of the first Catholic church in New York city. It was here the cardinal was baptized, and he was the last living priest to remember the old building. It was completed on Nov. 4, 1775, and will shortly celebrate its 100th anniversary. On its site stands the present St. Peter's, in the rear of the Astor house. Thousands upon thousands of emigrants landing on our shores have sought out this church to return thanks to Providence for their safe passage raised his hand and whispered that it would all be over. Then the Cardinal's nieces entered the room. They were clad in black. As the ladies approached the deathbed several pale nuns stole softly in at the door, and four priests from the Vicar General's house came in after them. All the watchers knelt. The weary eyes opened for the last time. At the feet of the dying man was a small table, whereon, between two burning tapers upheld by golden angels, was a glittering crucifix, and in the center of it two pieces of the true cross of Christ. At the left was another bright taper, and beside it lay the scarlet cap of the Cardinal. From the walls pictures of St. John, the Cardinal's patron saint, and of the Virgin Mary looked down in the dim light. At the side of the bed was Father Dubresse murmuring prayers for the dying. The priest's eyes dwelt lovingly upon those of his superior when they opened. There was a soft sound of crying as the ladies approached the death couch. Again the strong soul and fine intellect dwelt in the face, and again the eyes closed. The light sparkled on the little silver crucifix, and shone in the well-worn Bishop's ring upon the white hand. Still Father Dubresse prayed for the gentle spiritual shepherd. The low trembling voice vibrated all through the room. Then the light seemed to die upon the white walls as the Cardinal met his last sorrow. The dying face writhed with pain, the weak hand clasped the crucifix still closer, and the sobbing of the ladies was heard as they knelt. Now the white raiment of the couch hardly moved at all. The loving priest had ceased his prayers. A strong sigh broke from the lips of the dying man, and then there came into his face the smile of one who has reached home after a day of labor. No one said it. The doctor did not move from his place. The broken hearted women and the meek-eyed priests still knelt. But there came into the room a hush, and the watchers knew that the Cardinal's throne was vacant.

Corrections and Additions.

In the hurry and confusion of a printing office, wherein most of the labor on this book was done, many typographical errors have crept in, and on the same account its grammatical construction is often faulty and commonplace, much in the line of newspaper work. The facts and dates have received more particular attention, and are as nearly correct as possible under the circumstances interposed by time and life's fitful tide. The really intelligent reader will understand all this and more. For the rest we care not. The mite we have to offer will never be noticed by the great builders of the Church's history. If it affords an humble soul any little satisfaction, our greatest expectations are more than realized ; and from such, a fervent prayer in our behalf will be a greater reward than is deserved.

The encouragement and assistance given us by many good priests and pious persons, will ever be kindly remembered. To Father Thomas C. Middleton, O. S. A., of Villanova, we are especially indebted ; also to Father John A. Morgan, S. J., of Woodstock, now of St. Joseph's, Philadelphia ; and to Martin I. J. Griffin, Esq., the Catholic historian of Old St. Joseph's. May their labors in the great work before the Church in America be successful ; and their reward, promised to every faithful servant by the good Master of us all, full beyond measure. Our obligations are gratefully acknowledged to the *Catholic Publication Society*, of New York, Laurence Kehoe, Esq., Manager ; and to the *Catholic Mirror* Publishing Co., of Baltimore, for courtesies extended.

Such corrections and additions are here made as seem most necessary, leaving the rest to the reader's intelligent judgment and kind forbearance.

Page 41.—The Franciscan Missionaries sent to Maryland were, Father Massey, 1672 ; Polycarp Whicksted, 1674 ; Basil Hobart, 1675 ; Henry Francisco, 1675 ; Edward Golding, Henry Carew, Superior of the Missions, 1677., *Oliver's Collections*, p. 541.

Page 43.—"Josiah Creighton" is a *traditional* name. Father Greaton's name was *Joseph*, and Old St. Joseph's, Phila., was built by him and named after him.

Page 45.—Some claim Fr. Henry Neale died at St. Inigoes. Conewago was *always* subject to the Maryland Missions to which it belonged.

Page 47.—Reference to Gov. Gordon, who died in Phila., in 1736: Mr. Griffin thinks Gov. *Morris* is meant. (See Pa. Archives and *Rupp's* History of Lancaster Co.) Fr. Wapeler, also spelt Wappelar, was in America eight years, and the date of his purchase in Lancaster may have been earlier than 1740.

Page 50.—Two last lines and first two lines of first paragraph refer to each other.

St. Thomas Manor not always the residence of Superiors ; ceased to be so fifty years ago.

John Baptist De Ritter, S. J., was second pastor of Goshenhoppen, 1765 to 1785 ; visited Haycock, Reading, Makunzie, Cedar Creek, Sharp Mountain ; was at Allentown in 1774: died Feb. 3d, 1787.

Page 52.—Father Pellentz made Conewago *his home* from 1758 *until his death* in 1800.

Page 53.—Father Carroll at Conewago: Mr. Griffin makes the date 1785.

Page 55.—Erection of Conewago church *begun*: From a scrap of a report to the Society by Father Enders, we see that preparations were made as early as 1785, as great labor was involved by the dressing of the stone and hauling them from near East Berlin.

Page 57.—Father Molyneaux, (so spelled by Father Neale, to whom the title of the Conewago property descended ; spelled *neux* in Soc. rec.,) was *Superior* of the Jesuits ; died Dec. 9th, 1808 ; was President of Georgetown College, where he is buried. In his diary there is the following entry : May 15th, 1775, would speak to Mr. Cauffman about signing over lands in Pigeon Hills to Mr. Lewis. Father Lewis succeeded him as Superior ; but we do not know what land was meant, except that it was a tract about two miles from Abbottstown. It *may have* been the "Seminary" land, and that Joseph Heront came into possession of it through his acquaintance with Father Molyneaux, as they were both exiles from France.

Page 58.—Father Brosius founded a school at *Mount* Airy, where not so.

Page 60.—Herr Schmett, (Mr. Smith,) Father Gallitzin : James McSherry, member of the Penn. Legislature from Adams Co., in 1811, introduced the resolution authorizing Father Smith to assume his right name of Gallitzin.

Page 62.—Father *Roloff* was pastor of the Holy Trinity (German) church, Philadelphia, in 1826.

Page 63.—Fr. James *Cummiskey*, a secular priest, pastor of Old St. Joseph's, Phila., in 1824-5, was a brother of Eugene Cummiskey, Catholic publisher about forty years ago, and uncle of the late Eugene C., also a publisher.

1850, Sunday; Sept. 26th, at Conewago, by Bishop Kenrick, Rev. James Bradley ordained priest; Thomas Gegan, Thos. R. Butler, F. X. Gartland, Edward Sourin, sub-deacons; 368 confirmed at 9 A. M.

Page 63.—Father Beschter was stationed at Frederick in 1816-18, with Father Maleve; was Rector of St. John's, Balto., in 1824; was at Georgetown College in 1829. Father Randanne came to this country in 1817; was Professor of Latin at St. Mary's College, Balto., died at St. Charles College, Howard Co., Md., in 1864. Father Alexius Elder was born in Oct., 1791; died in Jan., 1871.

Page 68.—The Pope who suppressed the Jesuits against his will, was Clement XIV.

Page 65.—For reference to Frs. Britt and Byrne see Laity's Directory of 1822, not now in our reach; may be White Marsh, *England*, but we think Russia is correct.

Page 68.—Dween and Divin are no doubt the same; he attended the York church and was at Carlisle as late as 1840.

Page 69.—*Zacchi* should be Sacchi, and *Kendler* Kendeler. *Hatting* we can find no trace of and think it a mistake for Cotting, as Father Cotting built the York church and not *Hatting* as we have stated. Father Sacchi attended York from 1841 to 1843.

Page 69.—Rev. Nicholas Steinbacher, S. J., in May, 1842, blesses cornerstone of the Immaculate Conception Church, Nippenose Valley; in June, 1842, blesses corner-stone of St. John the Baptist Church, Pottsville; visits Danville from Nippenose Valley, where he goes four times a year; was at Lebanon in 1843. Father Steinbacher would be gone from Conewago two and three weeks, attending the Mountain Missions and those in "Nipper's" Valley, as he entered the name in his diary, 1844 to '46.

Page 70.—*Monaschei* should be Monachesi.

Page 74.—The statement that Father Enders built the old school houses is doubted, and believed to have been built by Father Lekeu. Father Enders put up the first iron fence before the church.

Page 75.—16th line—Bellair or Bell Air; 21st line—ante-*pendium*.

Page 81.—Sisters Anne and Agnes *first two* sisters.

Page 90.—15th line—School or *novitiate*. (Is "noviceship" in will.)

Page 103.—James J. *Gormley* pastor of Bonneauville.

Page 106.—The corner-stone of the Mountain Church said to have been blessed by Rev. Fenan, *S. J.* We have never heard of the name before, especially not of the Society of Jesus. It may have been Phelan, who attended Chambersburg before 1800. He was a "traveling priest," further we know not; his name is spelled Phelan, Failin, Feilin, and several other ways. He is mentioned by Finotti. *Who was he ?* He is mentioned as far west as the Ohio, and through Cumberland, Potomac and Shenandoah Valleys.

Page 109.—Father Zocchi was ordained in *Rome*, which he visited shortly after 1800. See Life of Mother Seton. There is a book of his preserved by some one at Westminster, wherein his ordination is recorded.

Page 116.—The Hagerstown Church :—The name Tieman should be Tieran or Tiernan. Frs. Cahill and Gallitzin from about 1818, 3d line from the bottom. Page 117.—Rev. James Redmond seems to have taken charge of the Hagerstown church during the summer of 1818, when the records begin. Corner-stone laid in 1826, not '25. The church was dedicated Oct. 5th, 1828, by Archbishop Whitfield, of Balto. Rev. J. Ryan was pastor, still remembered by some of the old members of the congregation as a man of great personal influence. He was sometimes called upon to quell disturbances along the Canal, and succeeded better in restoring order than a company of soldiers. He is buried in front of the church. See sketch of the dedication in U. S. Catholic Miscellany. Charleston, Oct. 18th, 1828. High Mass was sung by the Archbishop, assisted by Rev. J. McGerry and Rev. J. Purcell, of Mt. St. Mary's. Thirty-two persons were confirmed. Father Purcell preached an able sermon. Father Flaut was a saintly man. Father Moran, now in Princeton, N. J., labored zealously at Hagerstown during the war, and was liked by all. Page 120.—6th line, Sisters received $700. In July, 1885, the Sisters of St. Joseph left the Hagerstown Mission. The School Sisters of Notre Dame, Govanstown, Md., took their place. Aug. 10th, Sister Ignatia, Superior; Sisters Germain, Geralda and Sentfrida, arrived; about 120 pupils attend the school. A Fair was held in Sept., and $1400 realized towards paying the debt on the church. Father Manly, the present pastor, is laboring hard for the improvement of the church and the success of the congregation.

Page 124.—Armand, not the Marquis who died of fever in Phila., in 1798; Gen. Armand suffered death on the guillotine during the French Revolution.

Page 127.—Tryer is more correctly spelled *Treier*.

Page 129—Rev. Pierce *Maher*.

Page 133.—Father John Dubois landed at *Norfolk*, where not so; was founder of Mt. St. Mary's, and afterwards Bishop of New York.

Page 134.—Richard and Wm. McSherry were *twin brothers*.

Page 135.—In speaking with Misses Anna and Magdalene McSherry, who knew Father Whelan personally, we learn that he was a man of great merit in every way; sweet in his disposition; plain in his ways and self-denying to the last. He was born in Baltimore, educated at Liege; died in Baltimore; and buried at Wheeling, which is greatly indebted to his labors. Leaving his See of Richmond because his great peace-loving soul was ever willing to give others their own way, he went to Wheeling, where he became the father of the church and the first Bishop of-what will some day be a flourishing diocese. Labor with him overcame all difficulties; if he had a church to build he collected the money and worked at the building with his own hands; if he had missionary duties to perform, nothing could deter him; hundreds of miles to ride or walk were nothing to him; if the roads were impassable he took to the fields; if the creeks were high he took to the water and swam across. When yet a priest he built a small brick church at Berkeley Springs. While working at the building himself one day, some strangers looked on and inquired of him who the architect was; he answered that he was; they asked him who the contractor was; he replied himself; and who is the pastor said they; I am. While in Europe he had letters to influential persons, of whom he asked aid in his work. In Vienna he called on a rich nobleman, who had many such calls and was in consequence often compelled to limit his assistance to small sums. He gave Father Whelan $5, who expressed his thanks in so earnest and sincere a manner that the nobleman was moved to make inquiries as to the merits of the aid asked, and when Father Whelan returned to America the gentleman sent him a considerable sum. The life of Bishop Whelan was most edifying, and the example he leaves is truly that of a saint.

In speaking to these ladies we ascertained further that the Rev. Sylester Boarman, S. J., one of the early priests at Georgetown College, was a brother to the father of Commodore Boarman, whose daughters Misses Anna and Nora, are now living in Martinsburg; the family, like that of the McSherrys, is one of the oldest in Maryland and Virginia.

Page 138.—*No Sister* died in Martinsburg ; Sister Victoria's death took place only recently.

Page 143.—John Boler and August Thumel were ordained the Sunday before Christmas, 1885 ; the Sunday after Christmas there was a Grand High Mass at St. Joseph's, Martinsburg. Father Thumel. celebrant ; Father Rector of St. Alphonsus', Balto., deacon ; Father Boler, sub-deacon ; Father McKeefry, Pastor, Master of Ceremonies. Same Page.—Albert Carroll's remains were removed to Baltimore by the family.

Page 144.—CUMBERLAND CHURCH.—1879, Rev. F. S. Ryan appointed to take charge of a new parish at Washington. He was at St. Patrick's, Cumberland, for eight years ; at his departure received gifts from St. Patrick's Sunday-school, and silver altar service from pupils of Sisters of Charity ; was accompanied to the depot by Revs. O'Brien, of Lonaconing ; O'Connor, of Mt. Savage ; Schmidt, of Frostburg, and Fenie of Barton. Rev. Luigi Sartoris assistant at St. Patrick's. The monument erected by St. Patrick's congregation in memory of the late Rev. Edw. Brennan, for twenty-six years pastor of the church, was unveiled Dec. 9th, 1885, the first anniversary of his funeral. It is in St. Patrick's Cemetery ; of dark Quincey granite, 20 feet high, surmounted by a cross, and cost $800. Rev. Ed. Brennan was born April 18th, 1827, in Kilkenny, Ireland ; died at Cumberland, Md., Dec. 6th, 1884; was pastor of St. Patrick's from July 16th, 1858. The priests present at the unveiling ceremonies were, Fathers O'Connor, Clarksburg, W. Va.; Mattingly, Oakland, Md. ; Frioli, Keyser, W. Va. ; McDevitt and Wunder, pastors of St. Patrick's ; Schmidt, of Frostburg ; O'Connor, of Mt. Savage ; Manning, of Lonaconing ; Clark, of Barton ; Brennan, of Westernport; Wilson, of Harper's Ferry ; and Francis and Hermann, of St. Peter and Paul's Church, Cumberland.

Page 146.—First priest ordained in America, " Etienne " Badin ; Mr. F. X. Deckelmayer writes from Chambersburg, that he was well acquainted with Rev. Stephen Theodore Badin at Bardstown, Ky., from 1839 to 1843, where he heard him preach and say Mass. Father B. told him he was the first priest ordained in America, Father Gallitzin the second, and Father Floyd, an Englishman, the third. Father Badin was born in Orleans, France, July 17th, 1768 ; was ordained priest in the old Cathedral church. Baltimore, May 25th, 1793; he died April 21st, 1853, with Archbishop Purcell, in Cincinnati.

Page 148.—Last line. *I. H. S.*
Page 154.—Father Emig's birthplace is *Bensheim*, Diocese of Mentz.
Page 155.—16th line, *Althoff's*, where not so.
Page 163.—17th line, contract awarded Jan., 1852.
Pages 162 and 3.—" Laurah " Eline and " Laurah " McIntire should be *Sarah*.

Page 164.—12th line, *Mulgrew*. Lewis Kumerant, a native of Gettysburg, finished his studies at Mt. St. Mary's and became a priest about 1881 or 2.
Page 165.—7th line, *in anticipation* 4000 years ago.
Page 168.—Fr. Steinbacher *died*.
Page 169.—The Painter Overbach was doubtless *Overbeck*.
Page 170.—3d line from bottom, *Deiparacque*.
Page 173.—Michael Egan, O. S. F.; he was assistant to Father De Barth and attended Conewago occasionally from Lancaster, but did not reside at Conewago.
Page 180.—2d line of 2d paragraph, about 28 instead of 35 years.
Page 183.—19th line, *plies* his oar.

Philip Mayer was one of the builders of Conewago Church in 1787. He had a saw mill in the mountains and was killed there.

Many minor typographical errors have to be passed by unnoticed. Proper names are sometimes spelled differently, and names of persons are often hard to get correct. So many names and dates have made our work particularly difficult.

AN OLD CAUSE.—From the records of a suit pending in the Circuit Court of Berkeley Co., W. Va., Mr. D. C. Westenhaver, a young Catholic lawyer of Martinsburg, has prepared a sketch of an old legal case that throws some light on the early settlers of the Potomac Valley. James Quinn died in 1805, and directed in his will that he should be buried in the Catholic graveyard near Smithfield, or "Wizard Clip." Rev. Denis Cahill and Dr. Richard McSherry, both connected with the Livingston affair, were the executors. The estate consisted mainly of bonds, made by one Josippi Minghinni, for the payment of the purchase money yet due on a piece of land sold by Quinn to Minghinni; these were bequeathed to Fr. Cahill, J. Minghinni and the Misses McSherry living in Martinsburg. The only indebtedness was an open account due Luke Pentoney, of Martinsburg, but so complicated that Fr. Cahill considered a suit necessary to settle the amount due before paying the claim. Before its termination, Fr. C. left for Ireland in the Spring of 1806, assigning the bonds bequeathed to him to Luke Tiernan, member of the Catholic publishing company, of Michael Tiernan & Co., Baltimore. The claim of Luke Pentony was finally paid by Josippi Minghinni, the security of the executor, Father Cahill having in the meantime died in Europe in 1816. It is thought that one of the bonds willed to him had been left with some one to pay the claim, but no proof exists except that one of the bonds was never heard of. When the bonds assigned to Luke Tiernan became due, Josippi Minghinni declined to pay them, because he expected to be called upon as security of the assignor, Fr. Cahill, to pay the Pentoney claim yet in litigation. Tiernan consequently instituted suit upon these bonds in 1818; and it is to enforce the collection of the judgments then obtained, that the present suit of Tiernan vs. Minghinni was brought. These matters have continued in controversy in one form or another to this day, and the case has now gone to the Court of Appeals for the third time, a striking monument to the "law's delays," equaling in antiquity and interest Dickens' famous creation of "Jarndyce vs. Jarndyce," in the Bleak House. Three generations of litigants, a host af lawyers on one side and the other, many of whom have been men of national reputation, have passed away, but the cause still continues on the docket. The names of Catholics mentioned in this connection, the presence of Father Cahill in Martinsburg, and the existence of a graveyard known distinctly as "Catholic," prove that the pioneers of the church and the Church itself had found a home here much earlier than is generally believed by historians. It is also a fair inference that Mass was celebrated at certain intervals in Martinsburg before 1800, and not after that as the date of the first Mass is generally placed.

SUPERIORS OF THE MARYLAND JESUIT MISSIONS.

1633, Andrew White; 1636, Philip Fisher, *alias* Percy, *alias* Thomas Copley; 1639, John Brock; or Poulton; 1642, Philip Fisher, *alias* Percy; 1645, Bernard Hartwell. The Society was dispersed and its members fled into Virginia. 1646 to '51, Philip Fisher; 1654, Francis Fitzherbert. 1656, Society again dispersed. 1661, Henry Warren, *alias* Pelham; 1678, Michael Foster, *alias* Gulick; 1684, Francis Pennington; 1686, Thos. Harvey, *alias* Barton; 1690, Francis Pennington; 1696, Wm. Hunter, *alias* Weldon; 1701, Robert Brooks or Brooke; Peter Atwood. Thomas Mansell, *alias* Harding; 1725, George Thorold; 1735, Vincent Philips; 1736, Richard Molyneaux; 1740, Thomas Poulton, *alias* Brook, *alias* Underhill; 1747, George Hunter. In Oct. 1756, he returned to England; came back in July, 1757; Jacob Ashby, *alias* Middlehurst, Superior in the interim. He went to England in 1769, and in 1770, Ferdinand Farmer, true name Steinmeyer, Superior during his absence. 1771. John Lewis, until Bishop Carroll was appointed in 1783; Robert Molyneux, 1805; Charles Neale, 1808; John A. Grassi, 1812; Anthony Kohlman, 1817; Peter Kenney, 1819; Charles Neale, 1821; Francis Dzierozynski, 1823; Peter Kenney, 1830. In 1831 the Missions of Maryland were formed into a Province. Wm. McSherry first Provincial: his successors were: Thos. F. Mulledy, 1837; Francis Dzierozynski, 1840; James Ryder, 1843; Peter Verhaegen, 1845; Ignatius Brocard, 1848; Chas. H. Stonestreet, 1852; Burchard Villiger, 1858; Felix Sopranis, 1859; A. M. Paresce, 1861; Joseph E. Keller, 1869; Robert W. Brady, 1877; Pennsylvania always belonged to the Maryland Missions, and in 1879 New York was added, and in 1880 the title was changed to the Maryland-New-York Province, Robert Fulton Provincial since 1882. The Colleges of the Society have a long line of illustrious members who presided over them, commencing with Georgetown, 1791, with such names as Plunkett, Molyneaux. Dubourg, Neale, Matthews, Grassi, Fenwick, Kohlman, Dubuisson, Mulledy, McSherry, Ryder, Maguire, Early and others. So with Gonzaga College, started in 1821, at the head of which were Kohlman, Marshall, Keiley, Blox, Barber, Deneckere, Villiger, Stonestreet, Clarke, Wiget, Jenkins, Fulton, Murphy, McGurk. What material for Catholic history! The Novitiate of the Society was started at Georgetown in 1806; transferred to St. Inigoes, then to Whitemarsh, and after that to Frederick where it is still located. It has had at its head such Masters as Francis Neale, Peter Epinette, J. W. Beschter, A. Kohlman, Charles Vanquickenborne, Francis Dzierozynski, F. Grivel, Samuel Mulledy, Samuel Barber, A. M. Paresce, B. F. Wiget, J. A. Ward, Joseph O'Callahan, Felix Cicaterri, A. J. Tinsdall. The Society numbers many learned and saintly men. Its members were with the first discoverers; they braved every storm, gained every inch of ground by labor and perseverance, until now vast is there domain; in christian warfare, powerful as an army in battle array; their deeds would fill volumes upon volumes of history;

CATHOLIC LOCAL HISTORY. 205

they have preserved the faith by their labors, and embellished the Church by their lives and their learning. We have seen great things in our day; what the future will reveal we may not know.

Among the names of priests appearing on the marriage registers of Trinity Church, Georgetown, D. C., are the following:—

Father Neale, 1806-'18 ; J. Grassi, 1806-'18 ; T. Detheux, 1818-'25 ; Father Fenwick, 1815-'17 ; J. McElroy, 1821 ; G. Saunen, 1824 ; St. Dubuisson, 1825 ; J. Smith, 1825-29 ; M. Dougherty, 1825-27 ; (at Conewago after that ;) Van. Lommel, 1828-30 ; Th. Finigan, 1828, now at Conewago, bent under the weight of nearly ninety years, and has become as a little child ; F. M. Lucas, 1830 ; St. Dubisson, 1831 ; R. B. Hardy, 1833-4 ; F. M. Lucas, 1832-39 ; F. Barbelin, 1836 ; P. Leary, 1837 ; W. Grace, 1837 ; J. Curley, 1838 ; Ph. A. Sacchi, 1838-40, after that at Conewago ; P. P. Kroes, 1838-43 ; S. Fenwick, 1839; T. Ryder, 1840 ; P. B. O'Flannigan, 1841-52 ; Bishop Eccleston, 1842 ; J. X. Aiken, 1843 ; Anthony Rey, 1845 ; J. McElroy, 1846 ; J. Combs, 1847 ; J. Ralfe, 1847 ; C. Vincinanza, 1847 ; whose name appears in a diary at Conewago in 1846, where he stopped several times as a guest of the Fathers ; J. M. Finotti, a learned Italian, ordained at Georgetown ; priest, teacher and writer ; died at Denver, Col., (from the effects of a fall), Jan. 10th, 1878, after having received the last Sacraments from Father Matz, of Georgetown, Col. R.I.P. J. McGuigan, 1848 ; L. Vigilante, 1849 ; D. Lynch, 1849 ; J. A. Ward, 1850 ; J. A. Aiken, 1850-60 ; T. Arnellini, 1851 ; F. Wiget, 1851 ; D. Solari, 1852 ; James Ashwander, 1853-63 ; J. E. Pallhuber, 1853-68 ; Rt. Rev. J. McGill, 1855 ; John Early, various times ; L. Roccofort, 1861-68 ; A. L. Jamison, 1863-68 ; A. Charlier, 1863-67 ; A. Janalick, 1863 ; Chas. Stonestreet, 1864 ; F. N. Jubitosi, 1866 ; A. F. Ciampi, 1867-68 ; Charles Jenkins, 1868, L. H. Sache, 1868-70 ; J. Guida, 1869 ; B. A. McGuire, 1868 ; C. Stonestreet, 1870-74 ; C. Cicaterri, 1871 ; P. Duddy, 1873 ; E. Sourin, 1873 ; L. Roccofort, 1873-76 ; J. S. Sumner, 1873 ; G. B. Cleary, 1875 ; J. B. DeWolf, 1874. Others are : Fathers Epinette, Redmond, J. P. DeCloririere, J. Wallace, J. Contiume, F. Dzycroziusky.

Among the subscribers to "*The Catholic Christian Instructed,*" published at Baltimore in 1809, are the names of a number of Priests, but unfortunately the copy we possess has several pages torn out. The following names appear :

Boston.—Rev. T. A. Matignon, Rev. Mr. Chevreus.

Philadelphia.—Revs. Dr. Egan, Mr. Hurly, Mr. Harold.

Georgetown.—Rt. Rev. Leonard Neale, Bishop of Gortyna ; Rev. Francis Neale, Pastor of Holy Trinity Church.

Washington.—Rev. Wm. Mathews, Rector of St. Patrick's Church ; Rev. Notley Young.

St. Inigoes.—Revs. Francis Neale, Richard Clarke.

St. Mary's (Newtown.)—Revs. Igns. B. Brooke, Francis Maleve, M. Boulton.

St. Thomas, Charles Co.—Rev. Charles Neale, Mount Carmel ; Rev. John Henry Zachiah, Revs. Henry Pele, Charles Waters, John Fenwick, John Henry.

Kentucky. Stephen Theodore Badin, Bardstown ; Rev. Charles Nerinckx.

that in Father Gallitzin's time there was no Catholic priest from the Susquehanna to the Potomac, or from Baltimore to St. Louis as Scharff has it, must not be taken literally. From the beginning of 1700, when Southern and Western Pennsylvania, and the borders of Maryland and Western Virginia began to be settled, priests were to be found wherever there were Catholics,—here to day,— miles away to-morrow. We have endeavored in this work to follow the outline of their labors. In the Indian settlements on the Ohio and its tributaries, priests found their way with the French and Canadian expeditions long before the early missionaries traveled the circuit, and the See of Gallipolis was no fancied creation but a movement of Rome to carry the Gospel into the unexplored regions of America. (*See Lambing's Researches.*)

The mists of time have long since gathered over the pathways in the early history of the Catholic Church, which we have endeavored to trace. Names and places are almost forgotten, and the even ground we walk on to-day may conceal the graves of the past. Why then should the spirit of mortal be proud? The same fate is in store for all! What matters it how humble were the lives and lowly the occupations of the pious settlers who have gone before? All honor to them. They made more sacrifices for God and for us than we are making in our time. The arm that swung the axe belonged to a hero who could wield the sword. More honor to the men who handled the pick to clear the lands of this free country, than to the "heroes" who crushed Europe with tyranny and deluged the world with blood.

HIERARCHY OF THE UNITED STATES.

ARCHBISHOPS.

NAME.	SEE.	CONSECRATED.
Most Rev. Peter Richard Kenrick, D. D.	St. Louis, Mo.	1841. Nov. 30
William H. Elder, D. D.	Cincinnati, Ohio.	1857. May 3
Patrick A. Feehan, D. D.	Chicago, Ill.	1865. Nov. 1
John Joseph Williams, D. D.	Boston, Mass.	1866. Mar. 11
James Gibbons, D. D.	Baltimore, Md.	1868. Aug. 16
Michael Heiss, D. D.	Milwaukee, Wis.	1868. Sep. 6
J. B. Salpointe,	Santa Fe. N. M.	1869. June 20
Patrick John Ryan, D. D.	Philadelphia, Pa.	1872. April 14
W. H. Gross, D. D.	Portland Oregon.	1873. April 27
Michael A. Corrigan, D. D. Coadj.	New York, N. Y.	1873. May 4
F. X. Leary, D. D.	New Orleans.	1877. April 22
Patrick W. Riordan, D. D.	San Francisco, Cal	1883. Sept. 16

BISHOPS.

R't Rev. Dr. John Loughlin,	Brooklyn, N. Y.	1853. Oct. 30
L. De Goesbriand,	Burlington. Vt.	1853. Oct. 30
Thomas L. Grace,	St. Paul, Minn.	1859. July 24
John Hennessy,	Dubuque. Iowa.	1866. Sept. 30
Edward Fitzgerald,	Little Rock, Ark.	1867. Feb. 3
William G. McCloskey	Louisville, Ky.	1868. May 24
B. J. McQuaid,	Rochester, N. Y.	1868. July 12

William O'Hara,	Scranton, Pa.	1868	July 12
Tobias Mullen,	Erie, Pa.	1868	Aug 2
J. F. Shanahan,	Harrisburg, Pa.	1868	July 12
J. P. Machebeuf,	Denver, Col.	1868	Aug 16
Thomas A. Becker,	Wilmington, Del.	1868	Aug 16
John J. Hogan,	Kansas City, Mo.	1868	Sept 13
S. V. Ryan,	Buffalo, N. Y.	1868	Nov 8
P. J. Baltes,	Alton, Ill.	1870	Jan 23
C. H. Borgess,	Detroit, Mich.	1870	April 24
P. T. O'Reilly,	Springfield, Mass.	1870	Sept 25
L. M. Fink,	Leavenworth, Kan.	1871	June 11
Joseph Dwenger,	Fort Wayne, Ind.	1872	April 14
Richard Gilmour,	Cleveland, Ohio	1872	April 14
Francis McNeirny,	Albany, N. Y.	1872	April 21
T. F. Hendricken,	Providence, R. I.	1872	April 28
E. P. Wadhams,	Ogdensburg, N. Y.	1872	May 5
F. Mora,	Montery, Cal.	1873	Aug 3
John J. Kain,	Wheeling, W. Va.	1875	May 23
R. Seidenbush,	St. Cloud, Minn.	1875	May 30
J. A. Healy,	Portland, Me.	1875	June 2
F. X. Krautbauer,	Green Bay, Wis.	1875	June 29
John Ireland,	St. Paul, Minn.	1875	Dec 21
John Tuigg,	Pittsburg, Pa.	1876	Mar 19
James O'Connor,	Omaha, Neb.	1876	Aug 20
J. L. Spalding,	Peoria, Ill.	1877	May 1
John Moore,	St. Augustine, Fla.	1877	May 13
F. S. Chatard,	Vincennes, Ind.	1878	May 12
J. J. Keane,	Richmond, Va.	1878	Aug 25
L. S. McMahon,	Hartford, Conn.	1879	Aug 10
John Vertin,	Marquette, Mich	1879	Sept 14
Ægidius Junger,	Vancouver, Wash. T	1879	Oct 28
J. B. Brondel,	Helena, Mont	1879	Dec 14
Martin Marty,	Yankton, Dak	1880	Feb 1
J. A. Watterson,	Columbus, Ohio	1880	Aug 8
P. Manogue,	Virginia City, Nev	1881	Jan 16
F. Janssens,	Natchez, Miss	1881	May 1
J. C. Neraz,	San Antonio, Tex	1881	May 8
Kilian C. Flasch,	La Crosse, Wis	1881	Aug 24
W. M. Wigger,	Newark, N. J	1881	Oct 18
M. J. O'Farrel,	Trenton, N. J	1881	Nov 1
H. P. Northrop,	Charleston, S. C	1882	Jan 8
N. A. Gallagher,	Galveston, Tex	1882	April 30
H. J. Richter,	Grand Rapids, Mich	1883	April 22
J. Rademacher,	Nashville, Tenn	1883	June 24
D. M. Bradley,	Manchester, N. H	1884	June 11
H. Cosgrove,	Davenport, Iowa	1884	Sept 14
Isidore Robot,	Indian Territory		
A. J. Glorieux,	Boise City, Idaho	1885	April 19
C. P. Maes,	Covington, Ky	1885	July 18
R. Phelan,	Pittsburg, Pa	1885	Aug 2
J. O'Sullivan,	Mobile, Ala	1885	Sept 20
Vacant,	Savannah, Ga		

ADDENDA.—Page 158.—Fr. Delnol came to this country in Sept., 1817, left in Nov. 1840. Page 204.—Wm. McSherry, S. J., first Provincial, son of Richard McSherry ; born in Jefferson Co., W. Va. ; died Dec. 17th, 1889, at Georgetown. His father Richard with the twin brother Wm., came from Ireland and settled near Leetown, Va., which is near Smithfield, (Wizard Clip). Wm. had no children, and all the present McSherrys are descendants of Richard McS. and Anastasia Lilly. " Richard " is a family name, the late Dr. Richard McS. in Balto. leaving a son Richard, great grandchild of the elder Richard. Page 201.—Fr. Whelan partly educated at Mt. St. Mary's and with the Sulpicians in Paris. Page 202.—Rear Admiral Charles Boarman born in Charles Co., Md., Dec. 24th, 1797 ; occupied prominent positions as officer in U. S. Navy ; died Sept. 13th, 1879, at his home in Martinsburg. His father, Charles, was a Professor at Georgetown as early as 1797 ; died 1819 ; educated with his brother at Liege, in Belgium. Page 198.—Fr. Charlin should be *Charlier*. Page 100.—Fr. Phelan. &c.—Catholics of Ky. petitioned Fr. Carroll for a priest. He sent Rev. Mr. Whelan, an Irish Franciscan, residing with Jesuits at New Town, and " past the flower of his age ;" started with some emigrants in 1787 ; returned in 1789 ; this may be the "traveling priest" called Phelan, Fuilin, &c. There were living in Pa. and Md. in 1774. twenty-two priests. members of the Society of Jesus when it disbanded : Thos. Digges. Benedict Neale. John Lewis. Mathias Manners, Ferdinand Farmer, Joseph Moseley; James Frambach. James Pellentz. Lewis Roels. John B. De Ritter, John Boone. James Walton. Ignatius Mathews, Peter Morris, Lucas Geisler. Geo. Hunter, Robert Molyneux, John Bolton, Sylvester and John Boarman. Charles Sewall. Austin Jenkins. Sylvester Boarman was a native of Md., educated at St. Omer's. died at Newport, Charles Co., Md., Jan. 7th, 1811 ; his brother John died at Newtown, St. Mary's Co., in 1797. aged 54. Fr. Roels born in Belgium. 1732. died at St. Thomas Manor, Feb. 27, 1794. John Bolton born in Eng. 1742, came to Md. 1771. died Sept. 9, 1809. When Fr. Carroll was appointed Spiritual Superior of the Church of the Provinces in 1788. steps were taken to establish a form of government for the church, at a meeting known as the Whitemarsh Convention, held June 27th. 1783—present Revs. Carroll. Ashton, Sewall, Diderick, Boarman (Sylvester), Neale, Roels, Bolton.

John Lewis born 1721 in England, came to Md. 1750. succeeded George Hunter as Superior of the Missions before 1773, and was himself succeeded by John Carroll ; died at Bohemia 1788, March 24th. Charles Sewall born in St. Mary's Co. near St. Inigoes, 1744, educated at St. Omer's, became a Jesuit and returned to Md. in 1774. Bernard Diderick came to Md. in July, 1782 or 3 ; died at "Notley Hall." July 3d, 1793. Father Wapeler returned to Europe in 1748. Page 21.—" Digges' Choice." The Digges were an old Md. family. Edw. D. was an early settler of Va., son of Sir Dudley Digges, who lost his life in the service of Charles I. He left a son Wm. who settled in Md. and left an older and a younger son. ancestors of two branches of the family ; the latter were Catholics and the Conewago Digges are their descendants. There was a Rev. Thomas Digges, S. J. Ignatius D. was married to Mary Carroll, sister of Eleanor. Fr. Greaton born about 1680 ; entered Society July 5, 1708 ; became a priest Aug. 4th, 1719 ; was at St. Inigoes in 1721 and '24 ; died at Bohemia Sept. 19, 1753. Rev. Robert Molyneaux born in Lancashire, Eng.. June 24, 1738 ; entered So. 1757 ; arrived in Md. 1771. Page 205.—Rev. Camillus Vicinanza, S.J., long pastor at Leonardtown, Md., died Dec. 30, 1878, aged 64. Rev. Charles Duhamel, a venerable and edifying priest, early pastor of Hagerstown and surrounding missions, was banished from France to the Island of St. Croix, where he labored for the salvation of souls. The early priests who attended the Cumberland missions were, Revs. Cahill, Dubois, Zocchi, M. Ryan, Maleve and Redmond ; after 1820, Revs. T. Ryan, F. X. Marshall, H. Myers, B. S. Piot and L. Obermyer, up to 1841. Fr. Dubois also visited Hagerstown, Chambersburg, Martinsburg, Winchester, and other places, from Frederick, where he was stationed in 1794. Father Gildea, who attended the Martinsburg missions from 1830, was born in Baltimore, Feb. 2d, 1804; ordained March 25th, 1829. The bell on the old church at Martinsburg, (now at Berkeley Springs,) was among a lot of confiscated convent bells sent to this country from Spain ; it was cracked probably in the sacking of some building in the revolutions. Page 193.—Miss Catharine Hemler, of Adams Co., Pa., made her profession at Georgetown Visitation Convent, Feb. 26th, 1845.—Sister Mary Ann. The corner-stone of the Paradise Church (page 88) was laid June 18th, 1848. At Trinity Church, Washington, July 4th, 1843, ordained by Archbishop Eccleston, J. A. Ward, John E. Blox, C. H. Stonestreet, Francis Clarke, W. M. Logan. Rev. J. H. N. Joubert, who established the Oblate Sisters at Baltimore, was born Sept. 8th, 1777, France ; went to San Domingo in 1801, came to Balto. in 1804, died at St. Mary's Seminary, Balto., Nov. 5th, 1843.

NEWSPAPER CLIPPINGS.

The Golden Jubilee.—The feast of St. Joseph, April 15th, 1833, was celebrated by the Jesuits of the Maryland-New York Province, as the fiftieth anniversary under provincial rule; the same day having been the 250th anniversary of the landing of the first Jesuits in Maryland. Father Wm. F. Clarke was the orator at the celebration, at St. Ignatius's Church, Baltimore, from whose sermon we take the following:-

Particular importance and solemnity have been attached to the fiftieth anniversary from the time that God instituted the jubilee year of the Jews. Hence the title "golden" is given to the fiftieth anniversary of a birth, a marriage, an ordination, a consecration.

We, then, in celebrating with jubilee the fiftieth anniversary of the Jesuit Province of Maryland, are imitating the time-honored custom of every country and of every people. We celebrate more than the semi-centenary of the Province. By a happy coincidence this is the two hundred and fiftieth anniversary of the departure from England of the Jesuit Fathers, destined for the first Catholic Mission of Maryland, in the Dove and the Ark—fit names for the vessels that bore to an ignorance and superstition flooded land the olive branch of the peace of Christ and the little family of religious that was to people the new world with children of God. Two centuries and a-half ago Fathers Andrew White, John Altham and Timothy Hayes, of the Society of Jesus, landed on the Maryland shore of the Chesapeake Bay, erected a Catholic altar, on it offered the infinitely Precious Sacrifice that represents and perpetuates the Sacrifice of Calvary, planted the emblem of Christianity—the Cross of the Crucified Redeemer—preached the Gospel to the aborigines; by baptism closed the gates of hell and opened the gates of heaven to their chief, the Indian King of Piscataway, his queen, their children, and the principal men of the nation, and founded the mother of all the churches of the thirteen original States—the Church of Maryland.

Maryland is aptly called the cradle of Catholicity and the day-star of liberty in America. And whence was Maryland the day-star of liberty? Whence was the banner of freedom, which nearly everywhere else had been furled and laid upon the dusty shelf of history, unfolded here to woo the breeze and kiss the sunlight of heaven? It was at the suggestion and urgent recommendation of Jesuits. Mr. Thomas Kennedy, a Presbyterian gentleman, and member of the Assembly of Maryland, published a speech, in which he asserted that "a Jesuit was the author of the first bill for liberty of conscience in Maryland;" and this was conclusively shown by a distinguished lawyer, the gallant General Bradley T. Johnson, in a late lecture before the Historical Society of Maryland.

We do not forget, but we publish with joy, that previous, even a century previous to the commencement of the Maryland Mission, in the Spanish and French colonies, which since have become parts of the United States, Franciscans, Dominicans and Jesuits had moistened and sanctified the soil with their sweat, their tears, their blood, their mangled and fire-charred limbs. Where is the Jesuit whose eyes do not glisten and whose heart is not aglow at the remembrance of the cruel and glorious martyrdom of our brethren—Rasle, Brebeuf, Lallemant and Jogues, and others. This last-named had been tortured with fire and scourge four years before his martyrdom. His nails were torn out and his fingers gnawed to the bone; but he escaped, and Pope Innocent II. granting him a dispensation to say Mass, to grasp with the stumps of his mutilated fingers the Sacred Host and the chalice of precious blood divine, remarked that it was "but just that the martyr of Christ should drink the blood of Christ."

Nor do I forget, but—glorying in every conquest of our leader, Christ, and deeply interested in the history of the country in which we live and which we love, my own, my native land—I turn with admiration and bow profound to the first of all the missionaries in America, the children of St. Benedict, members of that grand old Order, which has given more martyrs, more Popes and more Bishops to the Church than any other. Yes, centuries before the birth of the canonized founder of the Society of Jesus, centuries before what is generally called the discovery of America by the pious and heroic Christopher Columbus, the Benedictines had built churches, offered the Divine Sacrifice, administered the sanctifying and saving Sacraments, made converts, lived saints, and some of them died martyrs, not only in Iceland and Greenland, but upon the shores of Mt. Hope Bay, within the limits of what is now the State of Rhode Island.

As Pennsylvania is not only indebted to Maryland for the faith, but forms and has always formed a part of the Jesuit Mission and Province of Maryland, may we not, should we not mention one of the churches of that State which celebrates to-day a fourfold jubilee, St. Joseph's, Philadelphia, which, in one sense, is the oldest church in what was the British colonies of America? There was a much older church in St. Mary's city, St. Mary's county, Maryland, and other much older churches in St. Mary's, Charles and Prince George's counties, of this State. But scarce a vestige of St. Mary's city remains, and now I believe there is no church standing on the exact site of any of those old churches.

St. Joseph's, Philadelphia, stands on the very site where our Father Joseph Greaton erected the Chapel of St. Joseph in 1733, one hundred and fifty years ago. The church that succeeded it, built also by Jesuit Fathers, after having been in the possession of other priests for nearly forty years, was restored to the Jesuits by Bishop Kenrick in April, 1833, exactly fifty years ago. In that church General Washington and his staff, and Chevalier de la Luzerne, Minister of France, with his suite, attended the High Mass and solemn Te Deum sung in thanksgiving for the crowning victory of the War of Independence, won by the combined forces of America and Catholic France at Yorktown, Virginia.

From the time of Father White and his companions, the Jesuits here were subject to the Provincial of England, until the suppression of the Society by Clement XIV., July 21, 1773. After the suppression the Fathers forming the Mission and laboring in Maryland, Pennsylvania, New Jersey and New York—but having residences only in Maryland and Pennsylvania—continued to cling fondly together, preserved their organization, and thus there has been a regular succession of Superiors from Father Andrew White to Robert Fulton, the present Provincial.

Frederick II, King of Prussia, and Catharine II. Empress of Russia—the one, as he calls himself, a heretic, the other, a schismatic—appreciating the learning and virtues of the Jesuits, especially as educators of youth, preserved in their dominions the Society of Jesus, which the infidel ministers of the so-called Catholic kings of France, Spain, Portugal and Naples, had doomed to destruction. Pius VI and Pius VII, the immediate successors of Clement XIV, approved of the action of Catharine and her successor, Paul I.

The Jesuits of Maryland petitioned to be aggregated to the Society in Russia; their request was granted, and, in 1805, Father Gruber, then General of the Society in that country, appointed Father Robert Molyneux Superior of the Maryland Mission.

On the 7th of August, 1814, Pope Pius VII went in solemn procession from the Quirinal Palace to the Gesu, the great church of the Society in Rome, accompanied by the College of Cardinals, and greeted everywhere by the countless multitudes who thronged the streets with shouts of "Long live the Holy Father!" "Long live the Society of Jesus!" The Bull for the re-establishment of the Society in the whole world was read amidst the manifestation of extraordinary joy in every countenance, tears of happy gratitude coursing meanwhile down the cheeks of the hoary-headed and age-bowed members of the old Society, who had assembled in the church they so much loved, to look upon the countenance of their benefactor, to listen to the voice of the Vicar of Christ, the successor of Peter, bidding the Society of Jesus to live again—live to love and to labor as it had loved and labored before; live that, in serried ranks, like an army in battle array, it might bear the name of Jesus in triumph, as it had often borne it before, over land and sea, from country to country, and be a witness to the Saviour even to the uttermost parts of the earth.—(Acts i, 8.)

The first Superior of the Maryland Mission, after this solemn and total restoration of the Society of Jesus, was Father Anthony Kohlman, famous in history as the central figure in the celebrated case known in the courts of this country as the Catholic question in America—the question, whether a Roman Catholic clergyman can, under any circumstances, be compelled to reveal the secrets of auricular confession; which was decided negatively, in the Court of General Sessions, in the city of New York, in the year 1843, the Hon. De-Witt Clinton, the mayor of New York and the presiding officer at the trial, delivering the judgment of the court: that the Rev. Anthony Kohlman, rector of St. Peter's Church, New York, had a right to decline answering the questions proposed to him by the police magistrate and the grand jury in regard to the restitution of property made by him as a minister of the Sacrament of Penance.

Catholicity in Maryland and the Jesuits were identified from the advent of the *Ark* and the *Dove* to the death of Archbishop Neale, in 1817. At Bohemia, the name of our farm and residence, in Cecil county, Maryland, in the only Catholic school in this country, John Carroll and Charles Carroll of Carrollton were prepared by our Fathers for the collegiate course which they made in Europe. Charles Carroll of Carrollton, true to the lessons of his Jesuit preceptors, signed the Declaration of American Independence, in July, 1776. John Carroll entered the Society's Novitiate at St. Omer's in 1753, was ordained in 1759, became a professed Father in 1771, returned to America in 1774, was made Vicar-Apostolic, with power to administer Confirmation, in 1784, and in 1790 was consecrated Bishop of Baltimore, the limits of his diocese being the boundaries of the United States. As the first missionary in this country was a Jesuit, so the first Bishop and Archbishop of this country was a Jesuit, and the second Archbishop of this country, Most Rev. Leonard Neale, was a Jesuit. Their signatures appear, with those of other Jesuits, on our books as trustees of our property in Maryland and Pennsylvania until the respective death of each. Hence the body incorporated by the Assembly of Maryland to administer the property of the Jesuits was entitled simply the "Roman Catholic Clergymen."

Archbishop Carroll wished to have for his coadjutor and successor, first, Father Molyneux and then Father Gressel, both Jesuits. Father Molyneux declined, and Father Gressel died at Philadelphia, a victim of charity, during the yellow fever in 1798. So Archbishop Neale offered the nomination of coadjutor and successor to several Jesuits, but all declined.

This city was indebted to the Jesuits for the faith, and the facilities of practicing and enjoying it until the close of Archbishop Neale's administration, and particularly so indebted after that period. Here, indeed, were the Sulpitians from 1791. But their labors were almost exclusively confined to the education of subjects for the sacred ministry, in which, thank God, they are still zealously and successfully occupied. Nearly 140 years ago, when this now beautiful city was a little village, too poor to support a resident priest, a Jesuit Father from White Marsh, in Prince George's county, visited it regularly, celebrated Mass and administered the Sacraments. In 1784 Father Charles Sewall was stationed here. Father John Carroll joined him in 1786. Father Francis Beeston was here from 1794 to 1805. Father Enoch Fenwick, who built the present cathedral, was rector of old St. Peter's, then the Cathedral, from 1808 to 1820, and Father J. Wm. Beschter was pastor, from 1821 to 1829, of old St. John's, which stood where now is St. Alphonsus's. But from 1829 to 1849 the Jesuit was unseen in Baltimore, save as a pilgrim, and might exclaim as did holy Job: "They that knew me, have forgotten me. They that dwelt in my house have counted me as a stranger." (Job xix, 14, 15.) In 1849 Archbishop Eccleston welcomed the Jesuits back to the scene of their labors, the old homestead of their Carroll and their Neale. I had the pleasure of opening my pastorate at St. Joseph's, in this city, informing our Very Rev. Father General of that Archbishop's uniform kindness to us, and the happiness of being, by commission of the General, the bearer of his compliments and thanks to the Archbishop. At the invitation of his successor, Most Rev. Francis Patrick Kenrick, our Fathers opened Loyola College, in Baltimore, September 15, 1852.

When the Mission of Maryland became a Province, July 8, 1833, Rev. William McSherry was appointed Provincial. Of him it is related that when he was an infant in his mother's arms, a mysterious voice from mid air bade her take special care of that child, for he would be of service to the Church of God. He admitted me to the Novitiate shortly after his accession to office, and consequently I was well acquainted with him and with his successors, and I know something of the history of the Province. But that history I do not propose to rehearse. I would merely and briefly call your attention to the wondrous change wrought not in the Province only, but in the Church in this country and in the country itself. Fifty years ago the Province of Maryland was confined to the States of Maryland and Pennsylvania and the District of Columbia. Now, besides Maryland, Pennsylvania and the District of Columbia, it includes New Jersey, New York, Rhode Island and Massachusetts. Then there were but six Catholic colleges in the United States; one-half of them were in the Diocese of Baltimore, and two of the six were Jesuit Colleges—the present Universities of Georgetown, District of Columbia, and St. Louis, Missouri.— Then our Province had but one college, now it has nine. Then we had but four city churches; now we have 17. In the Province then there were only 86 priests, now there are 311; then 17 scholastics or candidates for the sacred ministry, now 156; then 30 lay brothers, now 173; the total then being 85; the total now 540.

In 1833 the Jesuits, Augustinians and Dominicans, were the only religious Orders in this country. Now the Benedictine and the Franciscan, the Carmelite, the Capuchin and the Passionist are in the land; and of the religious Congregations, besides the Redemptorists and the Lazarists, who were here, there are many others—all building churches and schools, preaching Christ crucified, and converting and sanctifying souls. Nor should I forget those whose prototypes stood most numerous at the foot of Calvary's Cross and were the first to visit the sepulchre of their resuscitated Saviour—the female religious, who fifty years ago were as numerous as the males; and much less will I forget that the female Orders first in this country were introduced by the Jesuit Archbishops of Baltimore, and that to them is due the existence of Mother Seton's Congregation of the Sisters of Charity, which has done more than any other to conciliate the mind and win the praise of Protestants, who appreciate what is done to alleviate the miseries of the body.

Equal, even greater, has been the progress of the Church in general. Thousands of other strong and active laborers have entered into the fields "white already with the harvest, which was great, but the laborers were few," and from my heart I cry out with Moses, who, when Josue appealed to him to forbid others to prophecy, exclaimed: "Why hast thou emulation for me? O, that all the people might prophecy and that the Lord would give them His spirit." (Num. xi, 29.) Yet, more, I cry, O Lord! yet more laborers for Thy vineyard. So that, in the language of St. Paul to the Philippians, "by all means, whether by occasion or by truth, Christ he preached: in this also I rejoice, yea, and I will rejoice." (i, 18.) Let no one, brethren, say, "I, indeed, am of Paul; and, another, I am of Apollo. What then is Apollo, and what is Paul? The ministers of Him in whom you have believed. I have planted, Apollo watered, but God gave the increase. Therefore, neither he that planteth is any thing, nor he that watereth, but God that giveth the increase. We are God's coadjutors; you are God's husbandry, you are God's building. I have laid the foundation, and another buildeth thereon. Let no man, therefore, glory in men. For all things are yours, whether it be Paul, or Apollo, or Cephas, or the world, or life, or death, or things present, or things to come, for all are yours, and you are Christ's, and Christ is God's." (1 Cor. iii.) So that God be served, honored, loved, it matters not by whom, rejoice and be exceedingly glad. Rejoice, then, brethren, that, whereas in 1833 there were but ten dioceses in the United States—but one of these dioceses comprised all the New England States, another all the country west of the Mississippi—there are now 63 dioceses and eight Vicariates Apostolic. Then there were 19 Bishops, two of them being coadjutors; now there are a Cardinal, 13 Archbishops and 59 Bishops. Then there were scarce 250 priests, and a Catholic population of half a million; now there are more than 6.500 priests, 7,400 churches and chapels, 31 ecclesiastical seminaries, 81 colleges, 580 academies, 275 asylums, 185 hospitals, and a Catholic population of nearly 7,000,000.

Of all the Prelates and priests who attended the first Council of Baltimore, only one is now living, the Archbishop of Cincinnati; and of all who were members of the Jesuit Mission of Maryland when it became a Province, July 8, 1833, only four are living, three who were priests—Fathers Finnigan, Havermann and Curley—and one who was a novice, Father Ward, now of Loyola College. All the others have passed in funeral procession through the gate-way of death into the regions of eternity; and with them have passed, almost without an exception, the people whom they sought to enlighten, sanctify and save.

The Church in America.—That long before the ninth century, Catholicity was transplanted from the shores of Europe, Asia or Africa to those of America, by bold navigators and hardy adventurers is highly probable. But, interesting as the examination of such a question might prove, we cannot attempt it now, but must be satisfied with the statement that, according to the records which have thus far come to light, the first Christians who visited this country came from Greenland and Iceland, known to geographers as Danish America.

In 829 Catholic missionaries visited Danish America—more than a thousand years ago. In 834 Pope Gregory IV. placed Iceland and Greenland under the jurisdiction of Anagar, Archbishop of Hamburg, whom he appointed his Apostolic Legate for the North. Iceland and Greenland being entirely Catholic as early as 1004, the interest of religion in those countries required the erection of Episcopal Sees, and in the year 1055 Adalbert, Archbishop of Bremen-Hamburg—these two cities then formed one Archiepiscopal See—consecrated Jon Bishop of Skalholt in Iceland, and Albert Bishop of Gardar in Greenland.

Bishop Jon, who was a Scot, after a four years' residence in Iceland, came to this country in the year 1059, to convert the natives and administer to the spiritual wants of the Catholic Scandinavian population—colonists from Denmark, Norway, Sweden, Iceland, and Greenland—who from time to time had formed settlements in what they called Vineland, a tract of country described in old maps as extending over the entire portion of Massachusetts and a part of Rhode Island, commencing at Cape Ann and terminating with Narragansett Bay. More, then, than eight hundred years ago, and consequently nearly six hundred years before the Puritan pilgrims set foot upon Plymouth Rock, the Catholic Church had a Bishop there; yes, and a martyr too, for the saintly prelate fell a victim of zeal and charity beneath the deadly arrows of those for whom he was endeavoring to open the gates of heaven. More than fifty years before this time, in the year 1008, one of the headlands of Massachusetts, near the present city of Boston, was called the Promontory of the Cross, from the grave of Thorwald, a Catholic explorer, whose dying request, when he had been mortally wounded by the Esquimaux, was that his companions should bury him there and place a cross at his head and another at his feet. The first birth from Catholic parents, and therefore the first baptism in America, was that of Snorre, who was born in 1009, of Thorfinn and Gudrida, on the western shore of Mt. Hope Bay, in Bristol county, Rhode Island. This family returned to Iceland, and thence, after the death of her husband and the marriage of her son, Gudrida went on a pilgrimage to Rome and gladdened the heart of the Holy Father with news from his children in the New World. Thus you perceive that the first Catholic mother of America was the first pilgrim from the Western World to the shrine of St. Peter and the Court of the Vatican—and this more than eight hundred years ago! A historian, who records this fact, writes: "Rome lent a ready ear to accounts of geographical discoveries and carefully collected maps and narratives. Every discovery seemed an extension of Papal dominion and a new field for the preaching of the gospel." I might disappoint your laudable curiosity, were I not to add that this pious woman returned to Iceland and ended her days as a nun in a Benedictine convent built by her son; and that son had among his grandchildren three who were Bishops of Iceland.

The martyr Jon was not the only Bishop who visited what is now Rhode Island. In the year 1121 Erick, Bishop of Gardar, in Greenland, went to Vineland, and, like Bishop Jon, ended his life in this country. What, more than two centuries ago, people called "the old stone mill," at Newport, admitted by all to be a work of the Norsemen, antiquarians say was erected about the time of Erick, and was a baptistery, built after the style of many of the baptisteries of the middle ages. As the Catholic colonists of America were for centuries dependent on the Bishops of Greenland and Iceland, it may be well to remark that these Bishops were, by order of Pope Gregory IV., in 834, suffragans of the Archbishop of Hamburg; that in 1099 they became suffragans of the Archbishop of Lund, by order of Pope Urban II.; and finally, in 1154, they became suffragans of the Archbishop of Drontheim, in Norway, by order of Pope Anastasius IV.; and history testifies that from time to time they crossed the ocean to attend the Provincial Councils held in those metropolitan cities. In 1276 the Crusades were preached in America, and Peter-pence were collected here and sent to Rome by order of Pope John XXI., and subsequently by order of his successors, Nicholas III. and Martin V. Catholicity, in a word, was in a flourishing condition in Iceland and Greenland, and consequently we may infer in Vineland, till the middle of the sixteenth century; when, the northern nations of Europe having to a great degree apostatized from the faith, King Christian, of Denmark, in 1540, sent preachers to Danish America to substitute Lutheranism for the old faith, a substitution which was inaugurated by dragging off one of the Bishops of Iceland, Augmund of Skalnoit, to a prison in Denmark, and beheading the other, Jon Arieson, of Horlum, in 1551; the people meanwhile protesting against the change of religion, with the declaration that it belonged not to the King of Denmark, but to the Roman Pontiff to teach them what they were to believe.

This adhesion to the teaching of the Roman See characterized the Greenlanders also, as Pope Nicholas V. testifies in a letter written in 1448, in which he also states that they had then been Catholics for nearly six hundred years. The last Bishop of Gardar was Vincent, who was consecrated in 1537—forty-five years, as you perceive, after the discovery of America by Columbus, and nearly one hundred years after the erection of that See. We may reasonably conclude that for several years the Divine Sacrifice of the Mass, with its inseparable thanksgiving, was simultaneously offered in Vineland by the descendants of the Norsemen, and on the shores of Florida and in the islands off our southern coast by the missionaries who followed in the track of Columbus. Finally, deprived of their pastors, the scattered flock gradually lost their faith; and now nothing remains to tell of the Christianity of Vineland but the ancient documents from which I have quoted, the remains of the stone baptistery at Newport, R. I., which some of you no doubt have seen, and some tombs of those early adventurers which are occasionally discovered, one of which, found in Virginia, some fifteen miles southwest of Washington, besides its Catholic inscription, "May the Lord have mercy on her," bears the date of 1051.

If I have dwelt long upon the Catholic history of the Norsemen in what are now the New England States, it was because I supposed the subject would be equally novel and interesting. Nor can I leave it without stating that the form of government in Iceland, Greenland and Vineland was republican from the foundation of the respective colonies till the year 1691 when they became dependencies of the crown of Norway. There was, therefore, a little Catholic republic on this continent seven hundred, perhaps eight hundred years ago. Referring to these early republics, Malte-Brun remarks: "The genius of liberty and of poetry brought into action the brightest powers of the human mind at the ends of the habitable earth."—*From Rev. F. W. Clarke's Centennial Discourse.*

From a Lecture of Rev. E. A. McGurk, of Loyola College, Baltimore.—From this very place we can almost touch the soil on which the Jesuit Fathers stepped from the Ark and Dove. They came in the company of honorable men, weary of the struggles for conscience sake. Governmental intolerance of their peculiar tenets drove the Quakers to Pennsylvania, the Episcopalians to Virginia, the Puritans to Plymouth and the Catholics to Maryland. The circle of freedom which all of them but one drew around them was only large enough to inclose themselves. The banner of but one ship proclaimed universal tolerance, and that was the ship which brought the Catholics to Maryland.

To Sir George Calvert were our Catholic ancestors indebted for this. Until 1624 he was a Protestant. His conversion involved great personal sacrifices. He held the high and lucrative office of secretary of state under James I. To continue to hold office was to share in the iniquitous laws which persecuted his Catholic fellow-citizens, and that he could not do. He led in person a colony to Newfoundland, but its soil was too sterile. He sailed southward, but failed in his attempt to associate with the Episcopalians of Virginia. They wanted freedom, but it was only freedom for themselves, not for Catholics, and they would have exacted an oath from him which would have degraded him below the slaves on their plantations. He returned to England and obtained a liberal grant under which his son Leonard planted the colony of freemen in Maryland. The gallant little ship left England November 22, 1633. The colony was numerically Protestant, but politically, socially and religiously Roman Catholic. The expedition consisted of Leonard Calvert as Governor, Jerome Hawley and Capt. Thos. Cornwallys, assistants, with 20 gentlemen, and 200 mechanics, laboring men, servants and others. The superior of the three Jesuit priests of the party was Father Andrew White, the apostle of Maryland. At the outset they placed their ships under the protection of God, committing their success to the keeping of the blessed St. Ignatius and the guardian Angel of Maryland. All denominations respect the influence of their ministers, but a Catholic's need of a priest is founded on a deeper faith in his holier usefulness. He has power to say thy sins are forgiven thee. He leaves the land of stately temples, but bears authority to offer the victim of mercy on altars rude as the unchiseled rocks. The two most notable personages who gazed on the new land were Leonard Calvert and Andrew White. There the missionary felt his prayer and chants might mingle with the songs of birds and his words flow free as the rivers that poured their waters into the ocean. None knew better than Father White what havoc of faith tyranny had made. A site for a city was chosen, and St. Mary's the name given to it. But in days when traveling through a county was like a journey across a continent, it had to be abandoned for a place more accessible as a capital to the interior of the colony. Annapolis, its successor, though it has never grown to be a giant, is not without its title to fame.

CATHOLIC LOCAL HISTORY. 213

The author of old Maryland Manors says "it was at Annapolis that soft crabs, terrapin and canvas-back ducks obtained their renown as the greatest delicacies of the world." He quotes from a French traveler of the last century: "In that inconsiderable town at the mouth of the Severn at least three-fourths of the houses may be styled elegant and grand. The State House is a very beautiful building—I think the most—of any I have seen in America. Female luxury exceeds what is known in France. A French hair-dresser is a man of importance among them, and it is said a certain dame here hires one of that craft at one thousand crowns a year."

In 1638 Father White wrote to his superior in Rome: "By the spiritual exercises of St. Ignatius we have formed most of the inhabitants to the practice of piety, and the sick and dying have all been attended in spite of the distances of their dwellings." His labors were equally fruitful among the Indians. It is an honor of Maryland not shown by the other colonies, that from the beginning friendly relations existed between the white man and the Indians. Need it be repeated that Father White and his missionaries were Jesuits? At that time the order was in the zenith of its glory. The superiors of the order, true to their sagacity of sending the best men to China, Japan and Paraguay, appointed for Maryland men of great learning and ability. The history of the Jesuits shows that the most gifted men were the best for this humble work. Xavier, Ricois, Ortega, Father White, were all men of distinction in the great schools of Europe. The first history of Maryland is from his pen in Latin. Will any one wonder that the Jesuit loves Maryland? He has lived here two centuries and a-half, and is not likely soon to move. St. Ignatius, founder of the Jesuits, was the patron of the Ark and Dove, and the State is still under his patronage. The provincial of the order gave up to the proprietary the manors of Mattapony, Immaculate Conception and St. Gregory.

The act of religious toleration of 1648 is a cherished memory. It was passed in the Assembly sitting in St. Mary's City. But what is religious toleration? The question is pertinent, because it is said the church's teachings are inconsistent with toleration. There is a right kind of toleration and a wrong kind. The wrong kind advocates the license of believing just what a man chooses. Revelation has fixed beyond the right of man to change it to just what we shall believe. He must submit to slavery and death rather than yield up that truth. But there is a kind of toleration consistent with Catholic principles. While we hold in the abstract that unity of religion would conduce best to the best interests of man, there may be conditions of society when freedom of differing in religion is altogether necessary for the happiness and prosperity of the State. In such conditions of society the Catholic says, I will not force you to believe as I do. I will not debar you from any position of honor or gain because you are not a Catholic. This was the character of religious toleration in Maryland; this kind of toleration is necessary for the well being of our republic. Other colonies were colonies of persecuted men for their religious opinions; Maryland was a colony of persecuted Roman Catholics. It is not to the purpose to say there were Protestants on the Ark and Dove. It was emancipation of Roman Catholics that inspired the emigration from the mother country. Maryland alone—a Catholic colony—granted freedom to every man. The charter granted to the first Lord Baltimore secured religious freedom long before the act of toleration was passed. The second Lord Baltimore (Cecilius) was most earnest in carrying out that charter. Not one case of intolerance can be cited against Leonard Calvert. "Peace to all, persecution of none," was his favorite motto. He convicted John Lewis, an ardent Catholic, for forbidding his Protestant servants reading the Protestant Bible. The same chapel was used at one hour for Catholic sacrifice, at another hour for Protestant prayers. In the memorable Assembly of 1649, while the Catholics were in the majority, the Protestants acknowledged the act of toleration was adhered to, and passed a resolution to that effect, which was sent to England. These were glad tidings to every nation of Europe and where religious dissensions prevailed.

The lecturer argued that to attribute the toleration in Maryland to motives of self-interest in Lord Baltimore and the Catholics was to give him no nobler views and motives than a Yankee peddler might claim. But Lord Baltimore is safe in Protestant as in Catholic hands from such an imputation. He quoted the recent historical review of the circumstances of those times by Gen. Bradley T. Johnson in proof of the nobler claims of Lord Baltimore on the admiration of posterity, Marylanders, and all friends of liberty.

A Missionary's Death.—Rev. Judocus Francis Van Assche, S. J., departed this life Tuesday, June 26, at 12 o'clock noon, in his seventy-eighth year. On the 26th of last May he started on horseback to visit the sick, carrying with him the Blessed Sacrament. When two miles from Florissant, Mo., out on the Cross Keys Roads, he was suddenly attacked with paralysis, falling from his horse. The faithful animal stood still, seemingly waiting for him to rise and remount. He lay helpless on the ground, till a gentleman, happening to pass that way, assisted him upon his horse. He wished to go on to the house of the sick person, but after riding a short distance he felt that he could proceed no further, and he turned about and returned to his home at Florissant, which he reached with much difficulty. Dr. Hereford being called, found the attack to be a serious one, and to offer little hope of recovery. The patient was removed to the St. Stanislaus Novitiate, where, despite all that the medical art and the kindness of friends could do for him, he gradually sank until he breathed his last.

The word rapidly travelled to the village and through the surrounding country to this city that "good Father Van Assche is dead;" and perhaps none that knew him personally, ever knew another person to whom the epithet 'good' in all its meaning, could be so appropriately given—for Father Van Assche was a man of remarkable goodness, both by nature and from every available virtue. He

NEVER HAD AN ENEMY

and an unkind word was never spoken against him. He had the simplicity of a child; he was so cheerful, so kindly in his manners, so ready to serve others, and to give the peference to any one over himself, that no man knew him that did not love him, and no one could meet him without desiring again to see him and converse with him. Every member of his congregation looked on him as a special friend, and all revered him as a wise and saintly man. He was a father to the poor and those in sorrow; and he never turned away a beggar from his door without giving something, even when having little for himself: "for," he would say to his friends, "even if the beggar be an undeserving drunkard, he must be in great need if he will come to ask a small pittance of me." Father Van Assche realized in his whole life and conduct the ideal of a Christian pastor, made perfect beyond all ordinary men, by a charity that was unfeigned, because it knew no exception, it refused no work, and it feared no sacrifice. His zeal was not like that of the Pharisees, fiery and intolerant; it was persuasive and gentle, making duty a pleasure, not an insupportable burden. He was distinguished for his practical good sense and the solidity of his judgment concerning all the affairs of human life; he was observant and thoughtful; his opinions showed so much wisdom and prudence on all matters falling under his notice that his advice was sought for and most highly valued even by most learned acquaintances. It was instruction to hear him express his thoughts on public and social questions. Having spent in the United States fifty-six years of his long life, he had become attached to the country and its institutions as if he had known no other. He often said pleasantly to his young friends who were born here: "I am more of an American than you for two reasons; one is, I am here longer than you have been; and the other is, that I am an American by choice, while you are one by accident." He lamented the rapid growth of avarice among our citizens during late years, saying "Now the people no longer work for a living, but all are now working to become rich." He

FIRST BEGAN TO MINISTER

at the altar in 1837, now fifty years ago; he baptized in their infancy the grand-parents of many now living in St. Louis and in St. Louis County. "Good Father Van Assche," as he was for many years styled by every one, was buried on the spot—a little mound—where repose the remains of Father De Smet, the illustrious Indian missionary, and those of Father Meurin, who died at Kaskaskia in 1777. Fifty long years ago Father Van Assche heard the whip-poor-will's nightly song from its perch on the tall trees covering the ground beneath whose sod he will now sleep his last long sleep.

When this good and much-loved old missionary first reached St. Louis, May 30, 1823, it was then but a struggling frontier town.

Father Judocus F. Van Assche was born at St. Amand, which is on the banks of the Scheld, and is five leagues above Antwerp. His father, Judocus Van Assche, dealt in spun cotton and flax. Young Van Assche wished to be a sailor, and his father applied to a captain, known to be a good man, to receive him, but the captain whom he applied to declined to accept any more boys. The youth was sent to school at Mechlin. His playfulness caused his teacher, by not rightly estimating the innocent vivacity of a boyish nature, to request his father to recall him from school. His father declined to do so till his son was given further trial The youth soon became distinguished for his diligence in study, obedience to rules, success in his classes, and all virtues becoming his age.

In 1816, the illustrious Kentucky missionary, Father Chas. Nerinckx, went to his native country, Belgium, in the interest of his various missions in the diocese of Bardstown, Ky. On his return to the United States, in 1817, he was accompanied by James Oliver Van de Velde, who joined the Jesuit Society at Georgetown College, D. C In Belgium the latter was tutor of French to young Judocus F. Van Assche, who would have accompanied him had not his youth and the lack of means rendered such a step impracticable at that time. His desire to join his friend at Georgetown he however kept, and he only waited for an opportunity to go to America. In 1820, Father Nerinckx again visited Belgium, and passing by way of Georgetown, he was made the bearer of a letter from Mr. Van de Velde to young Van Assche, which was delivered to the parents of the youth. Young Van Assche resolved to accompany the Rev. Mr. Nerinckx on his return to America, and revealing his intention to his schoolmate, John B. Elet, he too determined to go with the missionary to America. A little after, John B. Smedts joined them in their proposed journey, and then P. J. De Smet, Felix Verreydt, and P. J. Verhaegen also determined to join the party. In order to raise the funds necessary for the trip they disposed of their books, furniture, pawning their pianos and watches for redemption by their parents. After overcoming many difficulties they collected together on the Texal, a small island off the coast of North Holland. Near the island the ship "Columbus," on which they were to sail, rode at anchor waiting for them. They boarded and went quietly out upon the main sea. They seemed to have cast no lingering, longing looks back upon the shores which most of them were never to see again; for their purpose was to give up all in order to devote their lives to the Indian missions of America.

THEY REACHED PHILADELPHIA

on Sunday, September 23, 1821, whence they proceeded at once by way of Baltimore to Georgetown.

They were received as novices and sent at once to the house of probation, at Whitemarsh; the place was so named in commemoration of the illustrious Father White, S. J., who accompanied the first colony of English Catholics, who, leaving their country for conscience sake, settled in Maryland.

In the year 1823, Bishop Dubourg, who was bishop of Upper and Lower Louisiana, went to Georgetown to request a colony of Jesuits to be furnished him by the provincial of the Maryland province, for the evangelization of the Indians in the State of Missouri. Father Van Quickenborne, with Messrs. Van Assche, De Smet, Verhaegen, Verreydt, Smedts, Elet and Brother de Meyer, who still survives at the good old age of eighty-four, offered themselves for the missions in the far West. They left Whitemarsh about the middle of April, 1823, went to Baltimore, where they procured wagons for their luggage and started on their journey to Wheeling, W. Va. They went by way of Frederick, Md., Conewago, Pa., Cumberland, Md., thence across the Alleghaney Mountains, reaching Wheeling after a journey of about two weeks. They were here entertained for a few days by a kind gentleman, Mr. Thompson, whose daughter subsequently became a distinguished member of the Sacred Heart order. They procured two flat boats, which they lashed together, placing upon one of them a wagon, some negroes that accompanied them, their stock of provisions for the journey, etc.,—the Reverend gentlemen, with their library and various articles of Church furniture, being in the other boat. After a trip down the river of some twelve days, without striking incidents, they reached Louisville, where they met the Rev. Charles Nerinckx, who was there awaiting their arrival, he having a few days previous gone to Louisville to start for the "Barrens" in Perry Co., Mo.—a colony of his sisterhood, the Loretto Nuns—there to establish a school. A "Falls pilot" was engaged to get their boats safely over the falls, and in his trip down the rapids, Mr. Van Assche accompanied him. They went down the Ohio to Shawneetown, where they disembarked, and sending their baggage around to St. Louis by steamboat, they journeyed across the land to the same destination.

THEY REACHED ST. LOUIS

May 30, and on the evening of the same day Father Van Quickenborne rode on horseback out to Florissant. The present novitiate farm, or at least that part of it on which the houses stand, had been donated by Bishop Dubourg to Father Van Q. and companions. They took possession of the place, and began at once to clear land around the dwelling in order to make a garden; and on July 31 they began to dig the cellar for a dwelling which, in the style of that day, was a log cabin. Mr. Van Assche was ordained priest in 1827, and assumed two years later the regular charge of the congregation at the village of Florissant. The congregation had been for a year in charge of the Trappists, who gave it up in 1810, removing to Monks' Mound, on Cahokia Creek, Ill. When the monks left Illinois in 1813, to return to Europe, Rev M. Durand, a member of their order, remained in Missouri and had charge of the congregation at Florissant for some seven years, residing a part of that time in the village. His congregation was afterwards under the care of Rev. Mr. De Lacroix, from 1820 to 1823, during which time he built the present brick church of that place. In 1823 Mr. De Lacroix made over the church to the Jesuit Fathers, under whose charge it has remained till the present time. In 1832 Father Van Assche began to reside at Florissant. He lived a couple of years at Portage des Sioux, but in 1840 he was required by his physicians to leave the place, which was subject to malarious influences, on account of the low, wet lands surrounding it. He returned to Florissant, and with the exception of three years' residence at St. Charles, Father Van Assche made Florrissant his home till his death. He lived 54 years of his long life in Missouri; and, except for two short visits one to Cincinnati, and one to Chicago, he never in that time went beyond St Louis and St Charles' Counties He has now gone to the reward of a long and useful life, followed by the praises and the benisons of all that knew him. He was a man of God, who gave up native country, a home among loved ones—and all that is near and dear to the human heart, in order to make himself useful as a missionary in a strange land.

HE SET THE EXAMPLE
of a pious and blameless life; and full of days, and full of merit, he expired calmly at about noon, on Friday, June 26, at St Stanislaus' Novitiate, Florissant, Missouri. He bore his last illness without one murmur or complaint, and seemingly without any pain. No one, knowing him personally, will fail giving assent to the prayer, May he rest in peace ! and may my last end be like to that of good Father Van Assche !—*St. Louis Times, July,* 1877.

Miss Sally Lilly remembers having heard Father Van Quickenborne preach a very eloquent sermon at Littlestown, when passing Conewago for the West. They came from Baltimore in wagons, having servants with them. They collected blankets and other things at Conewago.

Old St. Inigo's Manor.—ST. INIGO'S, MD., JANUARY 18 —There is but one spot in Maryland which can be said to have remained in the hands of its original occupants and their legitimate successors since the planting of Lord Baltimore's colony. This spot is St. Inigo's Manor, still the property of the religious community that settled it—the Society of Jesus. Two rusty old cannon, insecurely mounted on loose piles of bricks, look out on the blue waters of the St. Mary's river as they did two centuries and a half ago; and, with the sweet-toned bell which has rung the Angelus three times a day since 1682, are the sole relics visible at the site of the manor-house of the old colonial days.

For many years there was exhibited at St. Mary's an elliptical table of English oak capable of dining thirty persons, which was brought over in the Ark, and used by the first Governor of the Province, Leonard Calvert, both as his dining and council table. Rev. Father Joseph E. Keller, late Superior of the Maryland Province of the Society of Jesus, in a letter to a friend in England some years ago said: "We have got at St. Inigo's, Maryland, the original round-table at which the first Governor and his wise men sat in council, and on which were written the laws of the Colony and the famous statute of liberty of conscience." After passing through a number of hands, the table became the property of a Mr. Campbell, at whose death it was purchased Jan. 7, 1832, by Rev. Joseph Carbery, S. J., for ten dollars, and placed at St. Inigo's, where it remained until a year or so ago, when it was removed to Georgetown College. Here it is exhibited to all who care to see it, and is an object of much curiosity and interest on the part of visitors.

The cannon were fished out of the St. Mary's river, into which they had tumbled owing to the gradual washing away of St. Inigo's Fort, (built by Leonard Calvert on a point jutting out into the river from the manor lands,) by Captain Thomas Carbery, of Washington, brother of Father Carbery, in 1824. In 1841, at the suggestion of William Coad, member of the House of Delegates from St. Mary's, one of them was presented by Father Carbery to the State of Maryland and placed in the State-house yard at Annapolis. Of the remaining three, (four in all were stated by Father Carbery to have been taken up,) one was used as a boundary mark on the manor line, and the other two were placed on the lawn at St. Inigo's, where they have since remained. It is the intention of the present superior of the mission to have them mounted on pedestals of masonry near the water side, and cleaned and renovated, so that they can be used for firing salutes. The metal has become rough and flaky from long immersion in mud and water, and their appearance is sufficient proof of their antiquity. The bell, which has graven on it the date 1682, is suspended from a pole in front of the mission house, and its silvery tones steal over the waters three times every day to the distant fisherman, who reverently doffs his cap and murmurs his prayers after the fashion of his forefathers generations back.

The founder of the Jesuit settlement at St. Inigo's was Rev. Thomas Copley, a father of the society, who on account of the penal laws against the Catholic clergy appears in the records, in common with many other Jesuit fathers, by the simple designation of "esquire" or "gentleman." Under the "Conditions of Plantation," published by Lord Baltimore in 1636, Thomas Copley, Esq., demanded grants of land in consideration of transporting Andrew White, John Althaui (Fathers White and Altham) and others, thirty in all, to Maryland in 1633, and Mr. John Knoles and others, to the number of nineteen, in 1637. He received in all twenty-eight thousand five hundred acres, of which he distributed the greater part to others, reserving 8,000 for the society. The first tract taken up was St. Inigo's, situated on St. Inigo's creek and St. Mary's river, including 2,000 acres on the mainland, St. George's Island 1,000 acres, and "town land" in and about St. Mary's city, 400 acres. The "town land," after remaining in the hands of the Jesuits for some time, was finally lost to them through an error in one of the numerous conveyances by which the property was transmitted. The second tract taken up was St. Thomas's and Cedar Point Neck, now in Charles county, near Port Tobacco. Like St. Inigo's, St. Thomas's manor is still the property of the Jesuits, as is also Newtown manor, formerly an estate of the lord proprietary, situated on the peninsula formed by Bretton's and St. Clement's bays, not far from Leonardtown.

Mattapany, afterwards the home of Charles, Lord Baltimore, was given to the Jesuits by King Pathuen, a chief of the Patuxent Indians, but was relinquished by them a few years later in pursuance of a contract entered into by them with Lord Baltimore, in which they agreed not to receive gifts of land in Maryland directly from the Indians. The present condition and appearance of Mattapany have already been described in a recent letter to THE SUN. At Newtown there is an ancient church, supplied by Father Jenkins and the other priests of the Leonardtown mission, and a manor-house almost if not quite as venerable. The bell, which bears the date of 1692, and the library, one of the oldest in Maryland, were removed to Leonardtown some years ago, and are now at the parochial residence there. The house at St. Thomas was burned in 1866, and a number of valuable old records and documents destroyed. Six years later the manor-house at St. Inigo's, erected in 1705, together with the library and records, met with a similar fate. The present building, a small brick structure, occupies the original site. and is composed in part of material from the ancient edifice, which was built of bricks from the old Catholic church at St. Mary's, erected about 1644.

About two thousand acres of land are comprised in the Jesuit estate at St. Inigo's, divided into farms, which are leased on liberal terms to tenants, who are selected with great care and usually remain on the property for long periods. The manor lands are owned by the Maryland-New York province of the Society of Jesus, and the revenue is applied to the support of Woodstock College and the Novitiate at Frederick. The ground allotted for the support of the priests stationed at St. Inigo's is only about forty acres, and the impression which generally prevails that they have the resources of the entire estate at their command is therefore erroneous. The present superior of the mission, Father David B. Walker, who succeeded Father Livius Vigilante a few months ago, was formerly treasurer of Mt. St. Mary's College, Emmittsburg, and more recently of the Archdiocese of Cincinnati. He is a gentleman of great energy and business tact, and has addressed himself resolutely to the task of restoring the dilapidated buildings and surroundings of old St. Inigo's. The house has been repaired and repainted, and the work of improving the garden, grounds and farm land attached to the residence will be commenced as soon as practicable. His assistant, Father J. P. Neale, has been stationed at the mission about ten years, and is well known to the people of the entire county for his tireless activity and enthusiastic devotion to his work. Father Neale is descended from the old colonial families of Neale and Pye, and cherishes a deep reverence for the local associations and traditions. Three thousand persons are included in the cure of the two priests of St. Inigo's, whose churches are scattered many miles apart, thus necessitating almost ceaseless activity. The parish church, which was built some sixty years ago, is situated about half a mile from the residence, and is a plain and unpretentious structure of brick. About six years ago a large frame structure was erected on the river bank for the accommodation in summer of the scholastics from the Frederick Novitiate, and here for about three weeks every year the young men enjoy a delightful holiday, inhaling the fresh, pure breezes from the St. Mary's, and spending much of their time in boating, bathing and kindred diversions.

The Jesuits in This Country.—There are in North America twenty-two Jesuit establishments, and twenty-one of the Jesuit colleges are in the United States. Until a few weeks ago the Jesuits in North America were divided among five provinces, but this number has been reduced to four by the consolidation of the provinces of New York and Maryland The district which was called New York province includes New York State and British America, and at the latest count had 86 priests, 132 scholastics and 121 lay brothers. The oldest province, Maryland, which, in addition to the territory acquired by the late consolidation, embraces New England, Pennsylvania, Delaware, Maryland, Virginia and the District of Columbia, had 201 fathers, 217 scholastics and 203 lay brothers. The province next in importance to Maryland is that of Missouri, which includes almost the entire Mississippi valley north of Louisiana. The fathers in these two provinces are all English-speaking. The third province is that of Lyons, with its headquarters at New Orleans and Mobile. The fathers there speak French. The fourth and last province, called Taurin, whose clergymen are Italian, is in California. There are also some German fathers at Buffalo, which is now in the province of Maryland. The head of the Maryland province is Father Brady ; of the Missouri, Father O'Neill ; of the Lyons, Father Jourdan ; and of the Taurin, Father Varsi.

THEIR SUPPRESSION HERE.

In the oldest province, Maryland, the Jesuits were established early in Colonial history, but in 1773 were practically suppressed, together with all the remainder of the order except that part of it which existed in Russia, by a brief of Pope Clement XV., who was forced to take that step by the hostile stand made against the followers of Loyola by France, Spain, Portugal, Parma, Naples and Austria. Prussia remained friendly to the order, and so did Russia, whose sovereign, Catharine, although a member of the Greek Church, manifested the warmest admiration for the Jesuits and kept them within her dominions because she believed that such a course was the best she could take for the cause of education. Her son, Paul, grandfather of the present Czar, was also a strong friend of the Jesuits, and some notable writers express the belief that but for his early death the Greek Church would have been reconciled with Rome.

Under the papal brief, the property of the order was confiscated, although in most countries the members received annuities and were allowed to live privately. It has been a mooted question whether the utterance of Pope Clement was a real suppression of the Jesuits, in accordance with the laws of the Church, the argument having been advanced that a bull would be required to suppress the order and that its abolition could not have been effected by a simple brief. In 1801, however, Pope Pius VII., after confirming the Russian branch of the order, under the head of a Vicar General, granted permission for the Jesuits in the Province of Maryland to resume their establishments upon condition of being considered as joined to the Russian branch, and in 1814, immediately after the fall of Napoleon, the same Pope re-established the order under its old form.

THE HEAD OF THE PREACHERS.

Father Maguire, who is to lead the mission that begins to-day at St. Edward's, is one of the ablest priests in his order. He was born in Ireland, and came to this country when very young. His mother died in Frederick, Maryland, leaving him apparently friendless and without resources. Father McElroy, of St. John's College, Frederick, took a fancy to the bright lad, however, adopted him, and put him to study. While a scholastic at that institution he proved an

CATHOLIC LOCAL HISTORY. 217

unusually excellent teacher of the junior students, and he had not been ordained priest a year when he was taken from the pastorate of Gonzaga Church, Washington, and made president of Georgetown College. His success in that position was remarkable, but his oratorical powers proved the cause of his removal from the presidency in order that he might be made head of the missionaries. In person he is tall and slim, with iron-gray hair, and, although having an ascetic expression of countenance, possesses a magnetic geniality. He would seem to be seventy years of age, but is not more than sixty-one. The ceaseless labor that has proved so effective has made its mark upon him, and yet he was never more eloquent than now and never undertook a task with greater energy. Whenever he preaches the building is densely thronged with people, and the crowd is by no means made up entirely of those professing the faith he teaches.

St. Edward's Church, of which the Rev. Edward Sullivan is pastor and the Rev. John Mellon assistant priest, was formerly an Episcopalian place of worship. It stands close to the place which was the headquarters of Washington at the time of the battle of Germantown. Upon the conclusion of the mission at St. Edward's the three Fathers, reinforced by two or three others of their order, will begin a mission at the Cathedral of St. Peter and St. Paul.—*From a sketch published when the Jesuits gave a Mission in Philadelphia, about eight or ten years ago.*

Toleration in Maryland.—At a meeting of the Maryland Historical Society, several years ago, Gen. Bradley T. Johnson read a paper on the foundation of Maryland. The paper recited the three theories of the origin of religious toleration in Maryland: First, that it was adopted by Lord Baltimore to attract settlers. This is the theory of Lodge and Doyle, the latest writers on the subject. Second, that he founded a Catholic colony as a refuge for Catholics, and declared freedom of conscience, moved by the teachings of the church. This is the theory of Cardinal Manning and Catholic writers generally. Third, that the Protestants were in the majority, and thus adopted and enforced it because it was the principle of their religion. This is the position of Mr. Gladstone and Protestant authors. Gen. Johnson contended that none of these is correct.

Lord Baltimore, satisfied that free institutions were about to perish in England in the reign of Charles I, formed the deliberate purpose of founding a State in which all the rights, liberties and franchises of Englishmen should be enjoyed, secured by all the guarantees of magna charta.— Many facts made known in 1878 by the publication of the "Records of the English Province of the Society of Jesus," preserved at Stonyhurst, prove this purpose of Lord Baltimore.

The original colony was organised by the appointment of Leonard Calvert governor and Jerome Hawley counsellor, Catholics, and Capt. Thomas Cornwallys, Protestant. The colony was largely Protestant, and was undertaken under the advice of Mutius Vitelleschi, general of the Society of Jesus at Rome, and of its provincial, Father Richard Blount, of England, who sent out two Jesuit priests with the expedition. The emigration of all Christians was encouraged by the promise of freedom of conscience by his proclamation in 1634.

Gen. Johnson referred to the code of laws prepared by Lord Baltimore and the early history of the proprietary government in support of his proposition. After the battle of Naseby had decided the fate of the English monarchy, in 1645, Lord Baltimore was obliged to reconcile the condition of affairs in his colony with that in England. In July, August and September, 1648, he counseled with Father Henry More, provincial of Jesuits in England, as to the proper measures to be adopted to reconcile Puritans and Roman Catholics—the Jesuits and his government in Maryland.

Father More was a great grandson of Sir Thomas More, Lord High Chancellor of England, who was a martyr for his religion. He was historian of the Jesuits, able, pious and learned. He prepared and proposed to Lord Baltimore the scheme which he adopted, to wit: That he should appoint Protestants to govern the province; that he should bind them by official oaths to disturb no one on account of his religion, especially no Roman Catholic; that he should forbid the Governor assenting to any law concerning religion; that he should issue new conditions of plantation, enforcing the statutes of Mortmain, and he prepared a code of sixteen laws, which the proprietary assented to beforehand, and which he stipulated must be adopted within twelve months without amendment or alteration. The first one of these sixteen laws was the act concerning religion— the Maryland act for religious toleration.

The terms of the settlement were sent to Maryland. The Assembly in 1649 adopted seven of the sixteen laws, first among them the toleration act, and in 1650 adopted the other nine of the proposed acts. That it is shown that the act concerning religion was but a part of the mature purpose of Lord Baltimore to found the State on the institutions of magna charta, and it was drawn up and proposed to him as part of a general scheme of compromise and settlement for Puritan and Catholic in the colony by Father Henry More, the provincial of the English province of the Society of Jesus.

Among the Jesuits.—Yesterday was the feast of St. Ignatius, the apostle of the Jesuits, and was fittingly observed at the church of that name in Baltimore. To-morrow the celebration will be continued by a grand high mass at eleven o'clock and a sermon by one of the most distinguished members of the order in this country. In the evening there will be solemn vespers, followed by benediction of the sacrament and another sermon. As usual on St. Ignatius' Day, the appointments and changes for the year were announced. Rev. Edward A. McGurk, who has been president of Loyola College, adjoining the church, for eight years, was transferred to the rectorship of Gonzaga College, Washington. This change was not unexpected, since it rarely happens that any Jesuit ever remains longer than three years at one college. Yet, Father McGurk had so endeared himself to all his parishioners that not a few of them hoped he would be continued here at least another year. No priest in the history of the order in this city has done so much for Loyola College and St. Ignatius' Church as Father McGurk. It was mainly through his indefatigable work that the interior of the church was recently made one of the handsomest in the city, and the college one of the leading institutions of learning. Besides this, he labored hard to reduce the debt on the property, and succeeded in doing so by many thousands of dollars. His successor will not be named for a few days, but he will probably be Rev. Francis A. Smith, S. J., at present stationed at Loyola, now in New York on a visit. In the meantime, Rev. Fater Dougherty, who last year taught the poetry and rhetoric classes here, is acting president. Afterward he goes to Washington to assist Father McGurk.

Prof. E. Spillam has likewise been transferred to Washington. Prof. M. Cunningham, who had charge of the preparatory department of Loyola, has gone to Jersey City to replace Prof. J.

Hann, who comes to Baltimore. Professors Morrison, Quigley and Van Rensslaer will go to Woodstock, the theological seminary of the order. Professor Woods, of Fordham University, and two members of the Woodstock scholasticate, will be stationed in Baltimore during the coming school year. Rev. D. Daly will be minister of Loyola next year. Changes at Woodstock and Frederick will be announced to-day. Loyola, as well as Woodstock, Frederick, Gonzaga and Georgetown Colleges are within the precincts of the New York-Maryland province, in charge of Very Rev. Robert Fulton, S. J., provincial, although he has no power to make changes or appointments. These are regulated by Father General Becks, through his vicar, the Very Rev. Anthony Anderledy, who, since the banishment of the Jesuits from France, has resided at Fresole, near Florence, Italy. New York, recently consolidated with the Maryland province, was formerly annexed to the Canadian province, which in turn has been consolidated with the province of England. The New York-Maryland and Canadian provinces are the only provinces in America. The former embraces, besides those two states, the territory of Pennsylvania and Massachusetts. Missions have been established in New Orleans, Buffalo, California, New Mexico, and in the Rocky Mountains.

The most important college in the province is at Woodstock where theological studies are pursued. The number of candidates is always large notwithstanding the very rigid course of studies and discipline. Great discrimination, however, is used in the choice of candidates for membership. Some circumstances or qualities form absolute impediments to admission; such as membership even for a day in another order, or notable weakness of intellect. Less serious impediments like ill-temper, obstinacy, injudicious enthusiasm or visionary devotion, etc., may be compensated for by other redeeming qualities and circumstances. The first probation consists of a period of some weeks spent in a house of the society where certain questions as to habits are asked and answered. The second probation consists of two years given up to spiritual exercises. At the end of this time the novice pronounces the simple vows of poverty, chastity and obedience, with a formal promise to enter the society at a future day. Then two more years are spent in the study of the Latin and Greek languages, after which three years are devoted to mental and moral philosophy and the sciences. Every six months the scholastic undergoes a searching examination before four sworn examiners. After this he is sent to teach in a college both for the purpose of enabling him to apply his acquired knowledge and to train him to the science of governing men. Three years later he is elevated to the priesthood. But few Jesuits rise to a position above the priesthood, as the order provides against all honors.—*Baltimore paper of August 1st, 1885.*

Keenan.—The late Father Keenan, of Lancaster, Pa., whose death occurred on Monday, the 19th ult., was born in County Tyrone, Ireland, and came to Philadelphia in 1820 with Bishop Conwell, second Bishop of Philadelphia. He was ordained in 1821 and went to St. Mary's College, Emmittsburg, Md., where he remained until the death of Father Holland, the pastor of St. Mary's, Lancaster, which occurred in 1823. He was then appointed to his first and only parish—St. Mary's, whose congregation then worshipped in a small stone edifice which still stands next the present church. Father Schenfelder, who was then assistant at Lancaster died shortly afterwards; and from that time until 1852 Father Keenan labored at Lancaster alone Priests were then few and far between, and Father Keenan had to attend at Columbia, Harrisburg, Lebanon, Elizabethtown, Coldbrooke, and other places. During the progress of State works he was frequently called to attend the sick thirty and forty miles The construction of canals and railroads was begun and large numbers of poor Irish laborers were employed on them. His life runs parallel with that of the celebrated Rev Father John McElroy, S. J., who was ordained in 1817 and who took charge of the little church in Frederick City in 1822, a year before Father Keenan settled in Lancaster, whom he yet survives.

Close by St Mary's new church, a handsome brick church, built by Father Keenan in 1852, stands the old church in which the Catholics of Lancaster and many miles around heard Mass for many long years· It is of stone, and well built, and has stood since 1769 The first church was a log structure, built in 1745, located on Vine street, near Prince. In 1760 it was destroyed by fire, and was replaced by this building, which was then reputed "a very commodious structure." An incident of its erection recalls the days of the primitive Christians, for the women mixed the mortar, and the men, after gathering stones in the fields, helped the masons to lay them.

Only think ! Thirty years before Independence Bell rang out the glad tidings of freedom to the land, when Catholics were few and poor, scattered and unpopular, when the Penal Laws were still unrepealed, a Molineaux, a Farmer, a Schneider, Pellentz, Ailing, Brosius Heliron, Rosseller, Stafford, Geisaler, Hamm, Montgrand, Fitzsimmons, Lewermond, Janin, Entzen, Coleman, Egan (afterwards Bishop of Philadelphia), De Barth, Becher, Stoecker, O'Connor, Byron, and Holland—all true priests ; some Jesuits, others seculars ; some Irish, some German—successively labored and toiled in the spiritual vineyard, and kept alive the faith in Lancaster and a wide circle of country.

In the graveyard near rest many of the faithful ; in the church—the old, dilapidated, plain edifice, now abandoned—once ministered the Most Rev. John Carroll, D. D., first Archbishop of Baltimore, and first Bishop consecrated for the United States.

In the old graveyard are monuments to the Flynns, (a very large handsome one near the road) Hoovers, McGranns, Donnellys, Thomsons, Stockslegers, Hooks, McConomys, Lachlers, Dalys, &c.—*Standard, March 10th, 1877.*

Frederick, Md., Sept. 19, 1877.—The venerable Father John McElroy, of the Society of Jesus, died this morning at the Novitiate in this city, aged 95 years, having been born in the town of Innis Killin, province of Ulster, and county of Fermannaugh, Ireland, in the year 1782. At the time of his death he was in the sixtieth year of his priesthood, and was the oldest living member of the Society of Jesus. Till within one year he had remained at his priestly duties, his practical retirement being enforced by blindness. For a short while in his early life he engaged in commercial pursuits, but soon entered the Georgetown College, where he was treasurer of all the temporalities of the institution for eight or nine years, studying during his leisure hours for the ministry. He was ordained in Georgetown College Chapel by Most Rev. Leonard Neal, Archbishop of Baltimore, on the 3d of May, 1817. at 35 years of age. During his ministration here he built the large and elegant church of Saint John, and also a large portion of the building now known as the Academy of the Visitation.

The Mexican war having broken out, President Polk called upon the Bishops for a chaplain for the army, and Father McElroy had the honor of being selected by them, with Father Ray, to accompany the troops. These were the only two chaplains in the army. Father McElroy took a very active part in the campaign, and had charge of the sick and wounded at Metamoras. After the war he was stationed at Boston, Mass., where he built the Church and College of the Immaculate Conception. As an evidence of his influence and the estimation in which he was held by his people, a single instance need be referred to. While the Washington branch of the Baltimore and Ohio railroad was being built a riot broke out among the laborers, and the military had to be called on to suppress it. Father McElroy hastened to the scene, and it was wholly due to his influence over the rioters that bloodshed was prevented.

Father McElroy lost the use of his eyes about the year 1868; still he remained active enough to attend to his essential duties as a priest, and these he continued to perform with all the fidelity that marked his earlier years. On the 2d of January, 1876, he preached his last public sermon in Saint John's Church. An immense congregation assembled to hear him, among whom were many Protestants. The scene as this man of God was led into the church by two attendants was deeply impressive, and many eyes were suffused with tears as they gazed upon his sightless orbs, trembling steps and long flowing hair, whitened by the frosts of more than four score winters. He was still a man of splendid physique, and as he sat uttering words of wisdom to his attentive auditors he reminded one of the patriarchs of old. In Frederick, where he lived more than twenty years as pastor, he was much beloved by all denominations, and his name is held in benediction. His funeral will take place Saturday. The sermon on the occasion will be preached by Father McGuire, of Pittsburg, and a number of prominent priests will be present.

Rev. Angelo M. Paresce, S. J., one of the most learned and distinguished member of the Jesuit Order in Maryland, died at Woodstock College, Howard County, on Wednesday, the 9th inst., in the 62d year of his age.

Deceased was a Neapolitan by birth, but his long residence in this country Americanised him to such a degree that the closest observer could scarcely tell he was of foreign birth.

In 1845, when the late Dr. Ryder was seeking recruits of young Jesuits in Italy for the province of Maryland, Father Paresce was Professor of Chemistry and Natural Sciences in the College of his Order at Benavento. He agreed to accompany Dr. Ryder to America. Arriving here in 1846, he prosecuted his studies in theology, and was ordained priest in 1848. Immediately on his ordination, he was appointed minister of Georgetown College under Dr. Ryder, where he continued in charge of the internal economy of the institution until 1851.

His zealousness and executive ability won the appreciation of his superiors, and he was appointed to the government and direction of the younger members of the Order in the Novitiate at Frederick. Here, as at Georgetown College, he was eminently successful in the discharge of the duties assigned him, and in 1861 he was appointed provincial superior.

His government in that capacity, though in troublesome times, was marked by the completion of Woodstock House of Studies. He was the first rector of the institution, and by his admirable tact and prudence, as displayed in former charges. Woodstock became famous even among the most famous of the colleges of which Europe boasts.

Declining health compelled him of late years to give up all active employment, but he remained still at Woodstock to help with the counsel those who succeeded him in its government. A man of the most broadened views and commanding talent, he could direct and supervise at the same time the highest and lowest studies, while his urbanity could smooth every difficulty and attract to himself the love and respect and veneration of all who dwelt in the same house, or were subject to him in the various houses of his jurisdiction.

His death, from paralysis of the brain, was very sudden, and his remains were interred among those of his brethren who had gone before, in the beautiful cemetery adjoining the college.—*April 19th, 1879.*

Death of an Eminent Theologian.—Many priests in this and other countries will regret to learn that their erudite and amiable professor, Rev. Joseph M. Duverney, S. J., is no more. He died in the midst of his religious brethren of the Society of Jesus at the Novitiate, Frederick, Md., at three minutes before nine on the evening of the 14th inst., having been carried away by an attack of pleuro-pneumonia, that just manifested itself on the previous Saturday. During his last illness, even during his last moments, he was, as he had always been during his long life, gentle and cheerful, with his life's great object as near to his heart and full in his mind as ever. Almost his last words were a commendation to those whom it concerned, to teach thoroughly and at any sacrifice the young religious, themselves destined to be professors, that had of late been the special objects of his love and labor. Three years ago he celebrated the golden jubilee of his fiftieth year as a Jesuit, during which period he had filled chairs of theology, Hebrew, canon law, philosophy, and modern languages at various times, but with unvaried success at the Universities of Friburg, in Switzerland, of Georgetown, D. C., at the Colleges of Fordham, N. Y., Boston, Mass., and Woodstock, Md., and finally, for the last few years, at the Novitiate. During a short interval he was engaged in parochial ministrations at St. Joseph's Church, Philadelphia. Truly, his seventy-two years of life were given wholly to God and his fellow-man; and he felt the sweetness of it at last, for he died with a smile on his lips, and his eyes looking wistfully to futurity for his reward exceeding great. R. I. P.—*Nov. 23d, 1878.*

Virginia Catholic.—"Let it suffice to say that as a part of the Spanish province of Florida, Virginia was Catholic before she was Protestant; that she was the colony of a Catholic power before the first Englishman trod her soil; that her first governor was Don Pedro Mendes, a devout Catholic; that in company with a Catholic priest, this Catholic governor visited her shores eight years before Captain John Smith was born; that the beautiful bay which washes her eastern shore was first named by Catholic discoverers in honor of the Blessed Virgin, Santa Maria Bay; and that there was a log chapel dedicated under the protection of the Immaculate Mother of God on the banks of the Rappahannock more than three centuries ago; a dozen years before the first voyage by Englishmen to the New World was undertaken by Sir Humphrey Gilbert, more than a third of a century before the first successful landing was made by the English at Jamestown, and fifty years before the Mayflower touched at Plymouth Rock.

"The Virginia Catholic of 1874 may, with some pride, reflect that the only civilised feet that trod Virginia's soil in 1574 were Catholic feet—chiefly the feet of members of that wonderful Society of Jesus, to whose zeal, devotion and heroism the discovery and christianization of the New World owe more than to all other human agencies combined."—MEMORANDA *of the History of the Catholic Church* in Richmond, Va., by A. M. KEILEY.

Philadelphia, June 27, 1885.—Rev. Domenic P. Coppens, S. J., died last evening of heart disease at the pastoral residence of the Church of the Gesu. His brother, Rev. Alphonse Coppens, is one of the assistant priests at the Gesu. The deceased was thirty-seven years of age. He came to this city from Washington, D. C., where he was assistant priest at the Church of St. Ignatius. He was born in Belgium, and was erdained a priest about seven years ago. His longest mission was at Frederick, Md.

Brute.—One of our exchanges in its report of the burial of the late Bishop de St. Palais, of Vincennes, says that the corpse of Bishop Brute was found in the vault in a state of perfect preservation, so that those who were familiar with his features could not fail to recognise him. "Corpora sanctorum in pace sepulta sunt et vivunt nomina eorum in perpetuum."—*July* 21, 1877.

When, in 1866, Bishop Shanahan took charge of the Diocese of Harrisburg, he had but twenty priests—he has now forty-one.—*Freeman's Journal, Dec.* 18, 1875.

RIGHT REV. JOHN TIMON, D. D.

Humble Missionary Priest and Holy Bishop. Born at Conewago, Feb. 12th, 1797. Died April 6th, 1867.

From an Engraving in Catholic Family Annual, 1896.

The edition of this Collection of Catholic History is very limited. As it is a history of the growth of the Catholic Church in the East, from missionary times, we hope the clergy, the religious, and those of the laity who appreciate our expense and labor, will encourage its sale. It is put up in cloth binding, and will be sent to any address, postage prepaid, on receipt of $2.
Address,   JOHN T. REILY.
    MARTINSBURG, WEST VA.

CONTENTS.

Photograph Pictures of Fathers Enders, Denockere, Villiger and Emig; View of Conewago Church with old Cupola; View of Interior, showing Marble Altar. Dedicatory, Introduction.

	PAGE
The Church and Its Heroes; The Discoverers of America; Labors of the Jesuits,	1
Penn and Calvert, Settlement of Maryland and Pennsylvania, Laws against Catholics	10
Boundary Difficulties, Troubles between Proprietaries and Settlers,	17
"Digges' Choice," Takes in the Conewago Valley, Early Settlers, Fatal Difficulty between Digges and Kitzmiller,	21
The Conewago Valley, Location, Settled by Catholics,	26
Early history of Conewago, Claims of the Carrolls, The Indians, Stage Roads, Hanover Settlement,	30
The Conewago of the Indians, Its Origin,	34
The First Place of Worship, Lands Taken Up, First Missionaries, Introduction of Catholicity into the Province, Father Greaton,	37
The Log Church Built, Theodore Schneider, S. J., Wm. Wapeler, S. J.,	45
First Resident Priest, Matthias Manners, S. J., Number of Catholics,	47
The Log Church Enlarged, The Md. Jesuits, Arrival of Revs. Pellentz, Frambach, Williams and Andrews,	50
The Sacred Heart Built, Bishop Carroll's Visit, Growth of the Church, Father Pellentz,	53
Father Pellentz to Father DeBarth, Fathers Brosius Erntzen, Sewall, Boarman, Manly, Mertz, Zocchi, Gallitzin,	57
Father DeBarth to Father Lekeu, Fathers Carr, Roloff, Marshall, Lekeu, Rantzau, Mayerhoffer, Cummiskey, Stogan, Beschter, O'Connor, DeBarth, Britt, Byrne, Larhue, Dween or Divin,	61
Father Lekeu to Fr. Enders, Improvements at Conewago, Fathers Kohlman, Dougherty, Dween, Beschter, Barber, Kendeler, Steinbacher, Sacchi, Tuffer, Gibbons, Villiger, Cotting, &c.	66
The Work of Father Enders, Church Enlarged, Fathers Deneckere, Manns, Villiger, Dougherty, Kreighton, Dietz, Reiter, Haller, Cattani, Dom Pierl, Tuffer, Bellwalder, &c.	70
Father Enders Returns, New Steeple Built, Marble Altar Erected; Fathers Deneckere, Manns, Emig, Villiger, Flannigan, Archambault, Richards, Jamieson, Casey, Dufour; Father Enders' Golden Jubilee; His Death, Father Forhan succeeds,	74

Education at Conewago, Schools Established, The Sisters of McSherrystown,..79
The "Seminary Farm," Fathers Heront, Tessier, Griffin, Myers, Dubois, Dillet, Deluol, Marshall, Trappist Monks at the Pigeon Hills,...84
 The Paradise Church..88
 The Littlestown Church..95
 The Hanover Church,..97
 The New Oxford Church,..101
 The Bonneauville Church,...102
 The Gettysburg Church,..104
 The Mountain Church,..106
 The Taneytown Church,..108
 The Westminster Church,..112
 The Frederick Church,..118
 The Hagerstown Church,..116
The York, Harrisburg, Carlisle and Chambersburg Churches,..123
 The Keyser Church,..129
 The Church in West Virginia,..132
 The Martinsburg Church,..188
 The Cumberland Church,..144
Biographical Sketches, Engravings of Fathers Gallitzin and Pellentz and Conewago Chapel; Sketches of Fathers Gallitzin, Pellentz, Frambach, Bishop Timon, Frs. Villiger, Manns, Deneckere, Emig, Cotting, Enders, DeBarth, Barber, Heront, Baron De Beelen,..145
 The Winchester Church,..159
 The Gettysburg Church,..161
A Collection of Scraps About Conewago and the Priests,...166
 Death of Father Deneckere,..175
 A Diary of One of the Conewago Priests, 1844 to 1846,.........178
 Outline Drawing of the Old Conewago Church,................188
 Enlargement of Conewago Church, 1850,.............................184
 Conewago Notes by Mrs. Jane Jenkins,..................................192
Sketch and Picture of Cardinal McCloskey and Old St. Peter's Church, New York,...197
 Corrections and Additions,..198
List of Jesuit Superiors of Maryland, Presidents of Colleges, &c.,...204
 List of Catholic Archbishops and Bishops of U. S.,..............206
 Addenda, Early Priests and Old Families,..............................208
Newspaper Clippings,—Jesuits' Golden Jubilee, Old St. Inigoes, Missionary's Death, Church at Lancaster, Deaths of Fathers Parasce, Duverney, McElroy; Lecture by Father McGurk, Church in America, Jesuit Matters, Toleration in Maryland, The Church in Virginia, Engraving of Bishop John Timon,..209

www.ingramcontent.com/pod-product-compliance
Lightning Source LLC
Chambersburg PA
CBHW020813230426
43666CB00007B/997